160 Chinese Wok & Stir-fry Recipes

160 Chinese Wok & Stir-fry Recipes

Authentic stove-top cooking shown step-by-step with over 200 colour photographs

Contributing Editor: Jenni Fleetwood

southwater

This edition is published by Southwater

Southwater Books is an imprint of Anness Publishing Ltd
Hermes House, 88–89 Blackfriars Road, London SE1 8HA
tel. 020 7401 2077; fax 020 7633 9499
www.southwaterbooks.com; www.annesspublishing.com

If you like the images in this book and would like to investigate using them for publishing, promotions or advertising, please visit our website www.practicalpictures.com for more information.

UK agent: The Manning Partnership Ltd,
tel. 01225 478444; fax 01225 478440; sales@manning-partnership.co.uk
UK distributor: Grantham Book Services Ltd,
tel. 01476 541080; fax 01476 541061; orders@gbs.tbs-ltd.co.uk
North American agent/distributor: National Book Network,
tel. 301 459 3366; fax 301 429 5746; www.nbnbooks.com
Australian agent/distributor: Pan Macmillan Australia, tel. 1300 135 113;
fax 1300 135 103; customer.service@macmillan.com.au
New Zealand agent/distributor: David Bateman Ltd,
tel. (09) 415 7664; fax (09) 415 8892

A CIP catalogue record for this book is available from the British Library.

Publisher: Joanna Lorenz
Editorial Director: Helen Sudell
Editors: Catherine Stuart and Elizabeth Woodland
Copy-editor: Jenni Fleetwood
Design: SMI and Diane Pullen
Cover Design: Nigel Partridge
Production Controller: Wendy Lawson

Previously published as part of a larger volume, *500 Chinese Recipes*

Main cover image shows Chilli Beef & Butternut - for recipe, see page 63

Ethical Trading Policy
Because of our ongoing ecological investment programme, you, as our customer, can have the pleasure and reassurance of knowing that a tree is being cultivated on your behalf to naturally replace the materials used to make the book you are holding. For further information about this scheme, go to www.annesspublishing.com/trees

Notes

Bracketed terms are intended for American readers.

For all recipes, quantities are given in both metric and imperial measures and, where appropriate, in standard cups and spoons. Follow one set, but not a mixture, because they are not interchangeable. Standard spoon and cup measures are level. 1 tsp = 5ml, 1 tbsp = 15ml, 1 cup = 250ml/8fl oz. Australian standard tablespoons are 20ml. Australian readers should use 3 tsp in place of 1 tbsp for measuring small quantities of gelatine, flour, salt etc. American pints are 16fl oz/2 cups. American readers should use 20fl oz/2.5 cups in place of 1 pint when measuring liquids.

Electric oven temperatures in this book are for conventional ovens. When using a fan oven, the temperature will probably need to be reduced by about 10–20°C/20–40°F. Since ovens vary, you should check your manufacturer's instruction book for guidance.

The nutritional analysis given for each recipe is calculated per portion (i.e. serving or item), unless otherwise stated. If the recipe gives a range, such as Serves 4–6, then the nutritional analysis will be for the smaller portion size, i.e. 6 servings. Measurements for sodium do not include salt added to taste. Medium (US large) eggs are used unless otherwise stated.

Important: pregnant women, the elderly, the ill and very young children should avoid recipes using raw or lightly cooked eggs.

Contents

Introduction

If you've ever been impressed by the range of dishes on offer at a Chinese restaurant, you'll be overwhelmed by what this book has to offer – over 150 quick and easy wok recipes for every occasion, from appetizers and light bites to a variety of main courses. Many of the dishes will be familiar, including classics like Prawn Toasts with Sesame Seeds, Crispy Shanghai Spring Rolls, Chow Mein, Stir-Fried Crispy Duck and Chicken with Lemon Sauce. Others are less well known, but the superb full colour photographs of the finished dishes will tempt you to try such specialities as Red Snapper in Banana Leaves and Squid in Hot Yellow Sauce.

China is a vast country with several distinctly different cuisines. From the south comes Cantonese cooking, characterized by subtle, yet sophisticated sauces and restrained use of spices. Sweet and sour dishes come from this region, and snack foods, including dim sum pastries and dumplings, are a speciality. You can create your own dim sum party with a number of dishes from the Appetizer and Light Bites chapter of this book, including treats such as Five-Spice Steamed Rolls, Crab and Tofu Dumplings, Crispy Salt and Pepper Squid and Steamed Pork Balls.

In the east, dishes tend to be sweeter. This applies to meat and poultry as well as the grain-based foods for which the area is well known. In western China, Sichuan cooking is hot and spicy. Liberal use of chillies, Sichuan peppercorns, garlic and onions make for dishes like Bang Bang Chicken, which pack a pleasurable punch.

Chinese cooks enjoy experimenting with new flavours and textures, and will happily adapt, and adopt, recipes from neighbouring lands like Thailand, Vietnam, India, Korea, and even Japan. These countries, in turn, have embraced traditional Chinese dishes, and it is sometimes difficult to determine the origin of some dishes.

In all its many guises, Chinese food remains immensely popular throughout the world, with the result that once-scarce ingredients are now commonplace. Fresh root ginger is to be found in every supermarket and even lemon grass and galangal are widely available. You can obtain fresh shiitake, oyster and even enokitake mushrooms – or grow them yourself, using kits that produce a fine crop on garden logs or even recycled books. Sauces are a staple of Chinese cooking, and many supermarkets stock several kinds of soy sauce, including shoyu and kecap manis, as well as black and yellow bean sauces, oyster and mushroom, hoi-sin and plum. Noodles and spring roll wrappers are also on sale everywhere, so finding what you need to make the dishes in this exciting collection should never prove a problem. If you do lack a key ingredient, however, don't instantly reach for your car keys. You may well have a suitable substitute in your refrigerator or pantry. Many recipes include suggestions for variations, and you will doubtless come up with even more, some of which may prove to be successful surprises.

The biggest challenge could be in choosing just what to make first. It might be a popular treat such as Lettuce Parcels, or a sticky bowl of Spicy Pork Spareribs. Perhaps you fancy a light snack, like some Crab Spring Rolls or Scented Chicken Wraps. Vegetarians are exceptionally well catered for, with such delights as Tofu and Broccoli with Fried Shallots, Aubergine and Sweet Potato Stew and Stir-fried Water Spinach providing a welcome change from more prosaic choices. If seafood is what is fancied, try Trout with Tamarind, Steamed Sea Bass with Chilli Sauce or Spiced Scallops and Sugar Snaps. With more than 150 superb recipes, you will never be short of delicious exotic and tantalizing meals to treat your friends and family to.

Preparation Techniques

Successful wok cooking is all about preparation, especially when you are stir-frying, which is so fast it is essential to have everything ready before you begin. That means slicing vegetables, meat or fish to the size required, having sauces handy and making sure that implements needed are within reach.

CUTTING AND SLICING VEGETABLES

Asian cooks take great care over the preparation of ingredients. There's an aesthetic reason for this – food must look as well as taste good – but careful cutting also serves a practical purpose. Cutting all the pieces to a similar size means they cook quickly and evenly.

Root Vegetables

Firm root vegetables, such as carrots, parsnips and mooli (daikon), can be diced, sliced or cut into matchsticks. Use a cook's knife or a cleaver. Trim the vegetable, then take a thin slice off each side to square it up. Slice lengthways. Pile the slices on top of each other and cut them into sticks.

Onions

Valued for their flavour, all members of the onion family are used in stir-fries and other dishes. Shallots have a mild flavour but are fiddly to prepare. Spring onions (scallions) are often used cooked, raw and as a garnish in many Asian and Eastern cooking traditions. They make a perfect stir-fry ingredient, as their flavour is retained. If shreds are called for, cut off the dark green top, then slice the portions of stem lengthways in half, then into strips.

Above: Use a mixture of peppers for maximum colour impact.

Above: Cut meat into small pieces or strips so that it cooks quickly.

Other Vegetables

Aubergines (eggplants), courgettes (zucchini), sweet (bell) peppers, green beans, mushrooms and corn are common stir-fry ingredients.

Less robust than root vegetables, courgettes shouldn't be cut too small. Ovals, sliced at an angle, work best. Aubergines are thinly sliced for tempura, cubed for slow-cooked dishes, or cut into strips for frying. If peppers are called for in a dish, cut them in thin slices, as they can take longer to cook than other ingredients.

Mushrooms of all kinds are favourite ingredients. Shitake mushrooms are a particular favourite of Chinese and Thai cooks, and are often used dried for a more intense flavour.

If fresh corn is in season, and a recipe calls for it as an ingredient, use this instead of canned or frozen. To free the corn from the cob, hold the top with one hand, and slice the kernels away.

Green beans for stir-fries should be the very freshest available; if they are slightly woody, trim the sides as well as the tops and bottoms, and slice thinly. Broccoli and cauliflower should be cut into small florets for stir-fries.

PREPARING MEAT, FISH AND POULTRY

How you prepare meat and fish depends on the type and dish, but for stir-fries you should always use the best and freshest cuts. The cheaper cuts, such as stewing beef or belly pork. are ideal for slow cooked dishes that have time to tenderize. When you are using chicken or pork in a stir-fry, you need to make sure it is cooked right through, and shows no sign of pinkness.

For stir-fries cut meat and fish across the grain. This not only helps the food to cook evenly, but also prevents it from disintegrating. Prawns (shrimp) and scallops can be left whole, and need only minutes to cook. They are usually the last ingredient to be added to a stir-fry, to prevent them going rubbery.

Below: Spring onions are used as a garnish.

Below: Prawns can be left in their shells or peeled.

Stir-Frying Techniques

Most of the cooking you are likely to do in your wok will be stir-frying, so it makes sense to get to grips with the technique from the start. Have all the ingredients close at hand, including measured items such as sauces.

PREHEATING THE WOK

The most important thing to remember is that the wok must be preheated. If the wok is hot when you add the oil, it will coat the surface with a thin film, preventing food from sticking. The best way to do this is to add a trickle of oil, necklace-fashion, around the inner rim so that it runs down evenly. You don't need much – 15–30ml/1–2 tbsp will be ample. Tilt the pan, if necessary, to spread the oil evenly.

Have the heat as high as possible if you are stir-frying meat, so that it is seared the moment it touches the wok. For fish or vegetables, the heat can be slightly lower. A simple test to ensure the wok is hot enough for stir-frying is to flick a few drops of water on to the surface after oiling. If this results in a loud sizzling sound, and the water immediately boils off, add your meat. If the water sizzles but remains visible for a few seconds before vanishing, the heat is right for fish or vegetables. Use oil with a high smoking point, such as groundnut (peanut) or corn oil.

COOKING AROMATICS

Individual recipes vary, but it is usual to start a stir-fry by adding aromatics such as garlic, ginger, chillies and spring onion (scallions) to the oil, then to fry meat, if used, and finish with the vegetables. Cooking aromatics flavours the oil. If this is their only function, they are fished out before anything else is added to the wok.

Above: Sauces are added at the end of the cooking process.

STIR-FRYING MEAT

When stir-frying meat, don't overload the wok or you will bring down the temperature. Add a few pieces at a time, sear them for a few seconds, flip them over and sear the other side, then push them away from the centre, where the heat is concentrated, and add more meat to the well. When the meat has been sealed, either push the pieces on to the sloping sides of the wok, so they will stay warm without continuing to fry, or remove them to a dish.

STIR-FRYING VEGETABLES

Add the vegetables to the wok, starting with varieties that take the longest to cook, such as chopped carrots, broccoli and sweet (bell) peppers. Vegetables that need very little cooking, such as mooli (daikon), onions and mushrooms should be added next, with the soft, leafy green vegetables tossed in right at the end. Keep the food on the move all the time, flipping and turning it with a spatula. Although the technique is called stir-frying, use a tossing and turning action, rather than stirring.

ADDING A SAUCE

When the vegetables are lightly cooked but still crisp, mix in the meat or other ingredients and then add any suggested sauces. A cornflour (cornstarch) mixture will thicken as well as flavour the mixture. If you are using a cornflour-based sauce, make a well in the stir-fry so you can stir it on its own for a minute or so before mixing it in.

Below: Make sure the oil in the wok is hot before adding any ingredients.

Below: When cooking aromatics, be careful not to let them burn.

Below: The wok is ideal for frying meat because of its high and even heat.

Deep-Frying Techniques

Provided a few safety precautions are taken, a wok is a useful pan for shallow and deep-frying. The shape means that you need less oil than in a conventional deep-fryer, yet still have a large surface area for cooking the food.

HEATING THE OIL

Start by making sure that the wok is stable. A flat-based wok is safest for deep-frying. If you use a round-based wok, make sure it will not wobble. Use a stand if necessary. The wok must be cold when the oil is added. This is the opposite advice to that given for stir-frying, when oil is added to a hot wok. Use an oil with a low smoking point and never fill the wok more than one-third full. This is more than adequate for most foods, and there will be less risk of the cook being splashed with hot fat or, worse, of the fat catching fire.

THE RIGHT TEMPERATURE

For deep-frying, oil needs to be at just the right temperature, so that the outside of the food becomes beautifully crisp while the centre cooks through to tender perfection. The precise temperature required will depend upon the density of what is being cooked and whether it has a coating of some kind, but around 180–190°C/350–375°F is suitable for most foods. A deep-fat thermometer, which can be clipped safely to the side of the wok before the oil is heated, is the safest and surest way of checking the temperature, but you can also test it by adding a cube of bread to the hot oil. The bread should brown in 45 seconds, if it sinks or fries more slowly any food cooked in the wok would be greasy; if it burns, the same fate

Below: Make sure there is enough oil for the volume of food being fried.

Above: Wrappers create a delicious crispy coating and keep food moist.

lies in wait for the food; if it sizzles on contact and bobs up to float on the surface, the temperature is just right.

COATING

Food can be coated in batter or a simple egg-and-breadcrumb mixture before being deep-fried. This protects, adds a contrasting texture and locks in the flavour. Dip the item to be coated in to the batter and gently shake off any excess before adding it to the hot oil. Flour or cornflour (cornstarch), egg and breadcrumbs can also be used for coating. Another method of protecting delicate food is to enclose it in a dough wrapper before deep-frying. This method is used for wontons and spring rolls, and the crispy result is delicious.

DEEP-FRYING TIPS

Don't overcrowd the wok. Add a few pieces at a time, lowering them gently into the oil to avoid splashing. Lift out carefully and either drain on a rack that has been clipped on to the side of the wok, or drain on kitchen paper and keep hot. Wait a minute or two before cooking successive batches, so that the oil gets the chance to return to its optimum temperature.

Above: Coating food before frying helps retain its moisture and flavour.

Hot Tips for Safe Deep-frying

- Don't fill the wok more than one-third full.
- Make sure it is stable.
- Be extra careful when adding food to the oil or retrieving it.
- Never leave a hot wok unattended.
- If the oil does catch fire, turn off the heat if you can and cover the wok with a heavy cloth or mat to exclude the air. This will put out the fire. Never throw water on an oil fire and don't try to move the wok.

Below: Lift deep-fried food in and out of the hot wok with a long-handled tool.

Steaming Techniques

This is a supremely healthy method, since the food is cooked without added fat and most of the nutrients are preserved. It is also simple, fast and efficient, whether you use a steamer specifically made for the wok or improvise with a trivet and a plate.

SUITABLE FOR STEAMING

All sorts of foods can be steamed, from fish to vegetables, poultry and even pancakes, custards and breads. Tender cuts of chicken cook well in the steamer but this is not the ideal cooking method for red meat. Check your chosen recipe for any advance preparation required. If you are cooking fish, is it whole or in portions? If whole, you may be advised to slit the skin and insert flavourings, such as fresh herbs, chopped ginger, citrus slices or even a spicy rub. Delicate foods may need to be wrapped before being steamed. Banana leaves and lettuce leaves are popular for this purpose, as wraps or to line the steamer.

SELECTING A STEAMER

A steamer is simply a device for cooking foods by means of moist heat. The food should never touch the water that generates the steam, and the moisture must be trapped. You can steam food by simply placing it on a raised plate inside your wok, but steaming is simpler in a utensil designed for the purpose. Bamboo steamers are good to use, as they are cheap to buy, and efficient and easy to use. So are stainless-steel steamers, but they tend to be much more expensive. It is also possible to steam foods on the metal rack supplied with your wok, but this will only accommodate small amounts of food.

Above: A bamboo steamer is best when steaming in a wok, as it fits perfectly.

ASSEMBLING THE STEAMER

Food can be placed directly in the steamer basket, but this method tends to be reserved for dim sum or breads. It is more usual for a recipe to recommend lining the steamer with baking parchment or leaves before adding the food. This stops the food sticking and prevents small pieces from slipping through the slats. If you use this technique, make sure steam can still circulate. Using leaves for lining won't pose problems as steam will find its way around them, but parchment should be pierced. Alternatively, the food can be put on a plate or bowl inside the steamer so long as the steam holes are not blocked. Custards and some fish dishes are cooked this way.

Before you use a steamer in your wok for the first time, check the fit. You may have to use a trivet or upturned cup to keep the base of the steamer above the water. If a steamer is large, the sloping sides of the wok may prevent it from descending to the water level.

Steamer baskets are stackable, so you can cook several items at once, with the most delicate foods on top. The steamer will probably have its own cover, but if it doesn't, you will need to cover the wok itself, preferably with a domed lid so that condensed water runs down the sides and drips back into the water, rather than on to the food.

GETTING UP STEAM

The liquid to generate the steam can be water or stock. Aromatic flavourings like lemon grass, ginger or seaweed can be used to scent the steam. Fill the wok to a depth of around 5cm/2in, bring the liquid to the boil, carefully insert the steamer and cover with the lid. During steaming, keep checking the water level and top up if necessary. Slope the lid away from you to avoid being scalded.

Below: The metal rack supplied with the wok can be used to steam food.

Below: Whole chickens, when steamed, have a special flavour and tenderness.

Below: These five-spice rolls are steamed to retain flavour and texture.

Simmering & Smoking

Although the wok is most closely associated with stir-fries and steamed food, it is also great for soups and sauced dishes such as Thai curries, braised pork belly or Beef Rendang. The frying stage that is the starting point for many of these dishes is easily accomplished in a wok, and after more ingredients are added, simmering is a cinch.

RAPID REDUCTION

The shape of the wok, with a wide surface area tapering to a narrow heat base, makes for rapid reduction of sauces. Where the aim is to concentrate the liquid, this is ideal, but you need to keep an eye on what's cooking, and top up the stock or sauce if necessary. For this reason, a wok isn't the best pan for a stew or similar dish that needs to be cooked for a very long time. A heavy pan is better for that purpose, but if you do use a wok, make it a stainless steel or non-stick one. Extended slow cooking in a carbon steel wok may erode the seasoned surface.

BLANCHING AND BOILING

For stir-frying, vegetables are usually cooked in relays, as some are much denser than others. Blanching toughies such as carrots and broccoli in boiling water gives them a head start so they can be stir-fried alongside more tender vegetables. Bring a wok of water to the boil, add the vegetables and cook for the required length of time (usually about 2–3 minutes). Lift the vegetables out of the wok with a skimmer or spider, plunge them into cold water so that they stop cooking, then drain and pat dry.

A wok can also be used for poaching fruit and cooking rice or noodles.

Above: Fast boiling reduces a sauce, and gives a more intense flavour.

Above: Slow, gentle simmering produces a rich creamy taste and texture.

Below: The wok is ideal for boiling or blanching green leafy vegetables.

Wok Smoking

You don't need elaborate equipment to smoke poultry or seafood. A carbon steel wok works well, especially if you follow the Chinese tradition and use a tea leaf mixture as the smoking medium. The only drawback is the obvious one – use an extractor fan or be prepared for your smoke alarm to go off.

1 Line a carbon steel wok (not any other type) with foil, allowing a generous overlap. Sprinkle in 30ml/2 tbsp each of raw long grain rice, sugar and tea leaves.

2 Fit a wire rack on top of the wok and place the food to be smoked in a single layer on top. Mackerel fillets, salmon and duck or chicken breast portions work well. Cover the wok with a lid or inverted pan and cook over a very high heat until you see smoke.

3 Lower the heat so that the smoke reduces to wisps that seep from under the lid, and cook until the food is done. A mackerel fillet takes around 8–10 minutes; large fresh prawns (shrimp) 5–7 minutes, duck or chicken breast portions 18–20 minutes.

Cooking Rice & Noodles

Many of the Chinese and Thai recipes in this book are based on rice or noodles, which may be used as an accompaniment rather than part of the main dish. If you are using your wok for the meat or vegetable accompaniment, you will probably be cooking your rice or noodles in a pan.

COOKING RICE

There are several ways of cooking rice, but the absorption method is best for jasmine rice, basmati, short grain rice and glutinous rice. The proportion of water to rice will depend on the type of rice used, but as a guide, you will need about 600ml/1 pint/2½ cups water for every 225g/8oz/generous 1 cup rice.

1 Rinse the rice thoroughly and put it in a pan. Pour in the water. Do not add salt. Bring to the boil, then reduce the heat to the lowest possible setting.

2 Cover tightly and cook for 20–25 minutes, or until the liquid is absorbed.

3 Without lifting the lid, remove the pan from the heat. Leave it to stand in a warm place for 5 minutes to rest, and complete the cooking process. If cooked rice is required for a fried rice dish, cool it quickly, then chill it before frying.

Steamed Sticky Rice

Thais like their accompanying rice to be sticky. To get the authentic texture steam it in a bamboo steamer. Make sure you buy the right rice, usually called sticky or glutinous rice.

Rinse the rice in several changes of water, then leave to soak overnight in a bowl of cold water. Line a large bamboo steamer with muslin (cheesecloth). Drain the rice and spread out evenly on the muslin. Cover the rice and steam for 25–30 minutes, until the rice is tender. (Check the water level and add more if necessary.)

Making a Risotto in the Wok

The wok is not only suitable for Asian dishes, it also makes great risotto. Have the hot stock ready in a pan.

Melt butter, oil or a mixture of both in a wok and fry an onion. Add the risotto rice and stir until the grains are all coated in the butter or oil.. Add a dash of white wine, then when that is absorbed begin adding hot stock, just a ladleful at a time. Stir constantly until the stock is absorbed, then add more. It will take about 20 minutes for the rice to become tender. Add a little butter and stir in. Remove the pan from the heat and cover. Leave for 2 minutes, then serve.

COOKING NOODLES

If you are cooking noodles, either to serve solo or as part of a composite dish, do not rely entirely on the recipe – check the packet, too. Par-cooked noodles only need to be soaked in hot water; others must be boiled. Ready-to-use noodles need no attention at all, and can simply be added to a stir-fry and tossed over the heat until hot.

Preparing Rice Noodles

Rice noodles have been par-cooked when you buy them, so they only need to be soaked in hot water before use.

Add the noodles to a large bowl of just-boiled water and leave for 5–10 minutes or until softened, stirring occasionally to separate.

Preparing Wheat Noodles

Wheat noodles have to be cooked in boiling water. They take very little time, however.

Bring a large pan of water to the boil, add the fresh egg noodles and cook for 2–4 minutes or until tender. Drain well. If the noodles are going to be mixed into a stir-fry and cooked further, give them just 2 minutes initially.

Stuffed Omelettes

A chilli filling makes an interesting contrast to the delicate flavour of the egg.

Ingredients
30ml/2 tbsp groundnut (peanut) oil
2 garlic cloves, finely chopped
1 small onion, finely chopped
225g/8oz minced (ground) pork
30ml/2 tbsp fish sauce
5ml/1 tsp sugar
2 tomatoes, peeled and chopped
15ml/1 tbsp chopped fresh coriander (cilantro)
ground black pepper
fresh coriander (cilantro) sprigs and sliced fresh red chillies, to garnish

For the omelettes
5 eggs
15ml/1 tbsp fish sauce
30ml/2 tbsp groundnut (peanut) oil

Serves 4

1 Heat the oil in a wok and fry the garlic and onion for 3–4 minutes, until soft. Add the pork and cook for about 8 minutes, stirring frequently, until lightly browned.

2 Stir in the fish sauce, sugar and tomatoes, season to taste with pepper and simmer until slightly thickened. Mix in the fresh coriander. Remove from the heat and cover to keep warm while you make the omelettes.

3 Beat the eggs and fish sauce together lightly with a fork. Heat 15ml/1 tbsp of the oil in an omelette pan over a medium heat. When the oil is hot, but not smoking, add half the egg mixture and immediately tilt the pan to spread the egg into a thin, even layer. Cook over a medium heat until the omelette is just set and the underside is golden.

4 Spoon half the filling into the centre of the omelette. Fold into a neat square parcel by bringing the opposite sides of the omelette towards each other. Slide the parcel on to a serving dish, folded side down. Make another omelette parcel in the same way. Garnish with the coriander sprigs and chillies. Cut each omelette in half to serve.

Popiah

This tasty creation is a great do-it-yourself dish.

Ingredients
45ml/3 tbsp vegetable oil
225g/8oz firm tofu, rinsed, drained and diced
4 garlic cloves, finely chopped
4 rashers (strips) streaky (fatty) bacon, finely sliced
45ml/3 tbsp fermented soya beans, mashed
450g/1lb fresh prawns (shrimp), peeled and deveined
225g/8oz jicama (sweet turnip), peeled and shredded
450g/1lb bamboo shoots, rinsed and grated
15ml/1 tbsp dark soy sauce
10ml/2 tsp sugar
4–6 fresh red chillies, seeded and pounded
6–8 garlic cloves, crushed
kecap manis
12 cos or romaine lettuce leaves
1 small cucumber, peeled, seeded and finely shredded
225g/8oz/1 cup beansprouts
2 Chinese sausages, fried and sliced
225g/8oz cooked prawns (shrimp), peeled
225g/8oz cooked crab meat
1 omelette, sliced into thin ribbons
fresh coriander (cilantro) leaves, roughly chopped
12 popiah wraps or Mexican corn tortillas

Serves 4–6

1 Heat the oil in a wok or heavy pan. Fry the tofu until golden brown. Remove from the oil and pat dry on kitchen paper.

2 Fry the garlic and bacon in the oil until they begin to colour. Stir in the fermented soya beans and fresh prawns. Add the jicama, bamboo shoots, soy sauce and sugar. Fry over a high heat to reduce the liquid. Toss in the fried tofu and cook the mixture gently until almost dry. Transfer to a serving dish.

3 Put the remaining ingredients in separate bowls on the table. Place the wraps on a serving plate. To serve, let everyone help themselves to a wrap. Smear the wrap with the chilli and garlic pastes, followed by the kecap manis, a lettuce leaf, a layer of cucumber and beansprouts, and a spoonful of the cooked filling. Add Chinese sausage, prawns and crab meat. Place a few strips of omelette on top with a sprinkling of coriander, then fold the edge of the wrap over the filling, tuck in the ends and roll it up.

stuffed omelettes Energy 305kcal/1267kJ; Protein 19.2g; Carbohydrate 4.8g, of which sugars 4.5g; Fat 23.6g, of which saturates 5.7g; Cholesterol 275mg; Calcium 48mg; Fibre 0.7g; Sodium 130mg.
popiah Energy 457kcal/1916kJ; Protein 32.3g; Carbohydrate 39.3g, of which sugars 5.8g; Fat 20.1g, of which saturates 4.9g; Cholesterol 213mg; Calcium 396mg; Fibre 4.5g; Sodium 989mg.

Hard-boiled Eggs in Red Sauce

A perennially popular snack, this spicy egg dish originally came from Indonesia. Served wrapped in a banana leaf, the Malays often eat it with plain steamed rice, sliced chillies, onion and coriander – ideal for a quick, tasty snack or light lunch.

Ingredients

vegetable oil, for deep-frying
8 eggs, hard-boiled and shelled
1 lemon grass stalk, trimmed, quartered and crushed
2 large tomatoes, skinned, seeded and chopped to a pulp
5–10ml/1–2 tsp sugar
30ml/2 tbsp dark soy sauce
juice of 1 lime
fresh coriander (cilantro) and mint leaves, coarsely chopped, to garnish

For the rempah

4–6 fresh red chillies, seeded and chopped
4 shallots, chopped
2 garlic cloves, chopped
2.5ml/½ tsp shrimp paste

Serves 4

1 Using a mortar and pestle or food processor, grind the ingredients for the rempah to form a smooth puree. Set aside.

2 Heat enough oil for deep-frying in a wok or heavy pan and deep-fry the whole boiled eggs until golden brown. Lift them out and drain.

3 Reserve 15ml/1 tbsp of the oil and discard the rest. Heat the oil in the wok or heavy pan and stir in the rempah until it becomes fragrant. Add the lemon grass, followed by the tomatoes and sugar. Cook for 2–3 minutes, until it forms a thick paste. Reduce the heat and stir in the soy sauce and lime juice.

4 Add 30ml/2 tbsp water to thin the sauce. Toss in the eggs, making sure they are thoroughly coated, and serve hot, garnished with chopped coriander and mint leaves.

Variation

For a fusion twist, serve these with a cucumber raita.

Tempeh Cakes with Dipping Sauce

These tasty little rissoles go very well with the light dipping sauce that accompanies them.

Ingredients

1 lemon grass stalk, outer leaves removed and inside finely chopped
2 garlic cloves, chopped
2 spring onions (scallions), finely chopped
2 shallots, finely chopped
2 fresh red chillies, seeded and finely chopped
2.5cm/1in piece fresh root ginger, finely chopped
60ml/4 tbsp chopped fresh coriander (cilantro), plus extra to garnish
250g/9oz/2¼ cups tempeh, thawed if frozen, sliced
15ml/1 tbsp fresh lime juice
5ml/1 tsp sugar
45ml/3 tbsp plain (all-purpose) flour
1 large (US extra large) egg, lightly beaten
salt and ground black pepper
vegetable oil, for frying

For the dipping sauce

45ml/3 tbsp mirin
45ml/3 tbsp white wine vinegar
2 spring onions (scallions), thinly sliced
15ml/1 tbsp sugar
2 fresh red chillies, seeded and finely chopped
30ml/2 tbsp chopped fresh coriander (cilantro)
large pinch of salt

Makes 8

1 Make the dipping sauce. Mix together the mirin, vinegar, spring onions, sugar, chillies, coriander and salt in a small bowl. Cover with clear film (plastic wrap) and set aside.

2 Place the lemon grass, garlic, spring onions, shallots, chillies, ginger and coriander in a food processor or blender, then process to a coarse paste. Add the tempeh, lime juice and sugar and process until combined. Add the flour and egg, with salt and pepper to taste. Process to a coarse, sticky paste.

3 Scrape the paste into a bowl. Take one-eighth of the mixture at a time and form it into rounds with your hands.

4 Fry the tempeh cakes in a wok for 5–6 minutes, turning once, until golden. Drain, then serve with the sauce.

eggs in red sauce Energy 266kcal/1104kJ; Protein 15.6g; Carbohydrate 7.1g, of which sugars 6.7g; Fat 19.9g, of which saturates 4.2g; Cholesterol 387mg; Calcium 99mg; Fibre 1g; Sodium 739mg.
tempeh cakes w. sauce Energy 79kcal/332kJ; Protein 4.5g; Carbohydrate 9.1g, of which sugars 4.3g; Fat 2.3g, of which saturates 0.4g; Cholesterol 26mg; Calcium 192mg; Fibre 0.8g; Sodium 15mg.

Crispy Salt & Pepper Squid

These delicious morsels of squid look stunning and are perfect served with drinks, or as an appetizer. The crisp, golden coating contrasts beautifully with the succulent squid inside. Serve them piping hot straight from the wok.

Ingredients

750g/1lb 10oz fresh squid, cleaned
juice of 4–5 lemons
15ml/1 tbsp ground black pepper
15ml/1 tbsp sea salt
10ml/2 tsp caster (superfine) sugar
115g/4oz/1 cup cornflour (cornstarch)
3 egg whites, lightly beaten
vegetable oil, for deep-frying
chilli sauce or sweet-and-sour sauce, for dipping
skewers or toothpicks, to serve

Serves 4

1 Cut the squid into large bitesize pieces and score a diamond pattern on each piece, using a sharp knife or a cleaver.

2 Trim the tentacles. Place in a large mixing bowl and pour over the lemon juice. Cover and marinate for 10–15 minutes. Drain well and pat dry.

3 In a separate bowl mix together the pepper, salt, sugar and cornflour. Dip the squid pieces in the egg whites and then toss lightly in the seasoned flour, shaking off any excess.

4 Fill a wok one-third full of oil and heat to 180°C/350°F or until a cube of bread, dropped into the oil, browns in 40 seconds. Working in batches, deep-fry the squid for 1 minute. Drain the crispy pieces on kitchen paper and serve immediately, threaded on to skewers, with chilli or sweet-and-sour sauce for dipping.

Cook's Tip
Keep egg whites in a sealed plastic tub in the freezer, ready to thaw for use in dishes such as this.

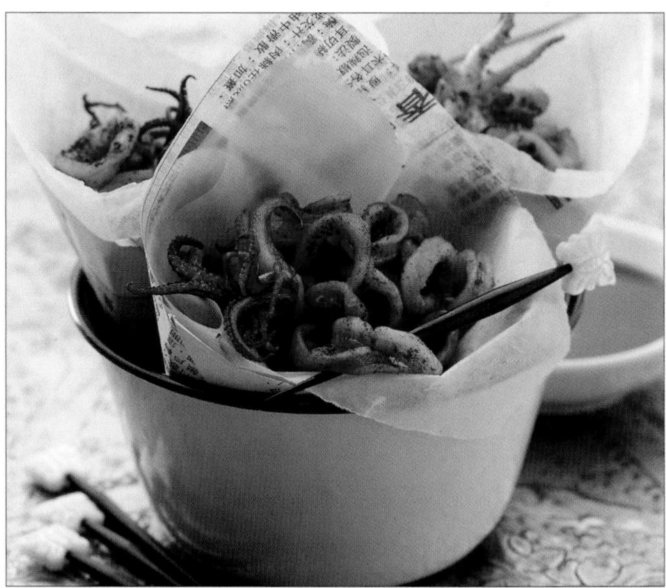

Sweet & Sour Deep-fried Squid

This is an example of a dish where the Western influence comes into play – with tomato ketchup and Worcestershire sauce used alongside more traditional ingredients.

Ingredients

900g/2lb fresh young, tender squid
vegetable oil, for deep-frying

For the marinade

60ml/4 tbsp light soy sauce
15ml/1 tbsp sugar

For the dipping sauce

30ml/2 tbsp tomato ketchup
15ml/1 tbsp Worcestershire sauce
15ml/1 tbsp light soy sauce
15ml/1 tbsp vegetable/sesame oil
sugar or honey, to sweeten
chilli oil, to taste

Serves 4

1 First prepare the squid. Hold the body in one hand and pull off the head with the other. Sever the tentacles and discard the rest. Remove the backbone and clean the body sac inside and out. Pat dry using kitchen paper and cut into rings.

2 In a bowl, mix the soy sauce with the sugar until it dissolves. Toss in the squid rings and tentacles and marinate for 1 hour.

3 Meanwhile prepare the sauce. Mix together the tomato ketchup, Worcestershire sauce, soy sauce and oil. Sweeten with sugar or honey to taste and a little chilli oil to give the sauce a bit of bite. Set aside.

4 Heat enough oil for deep-frying in a wok or heavy pan. Thoroughly drain the squid of any marinade, pat with kitchen paper to avoid spitting, and fry until golden and crispy. Pat dry on kitchen paper and serve immediately with the dipping sauce.

Cook's Tip
To avoid the spitting fat, lightly coat the squid in flour before deep-frying. Alternatively, fry in a deep-fat fryer with a lid or use a spatterproof cover on the wok or pan.

salt & pepper squid Energy 346kcal/1462kJ; Protein 31.2g; Carbohydrate 31.3g, of which sugars 2.6g; Fat 11.6g, of which saturates 1.8g; Cholesterol 422mg; Calcium 32mg; Fibre 0g; Sodium 1741mg.
sweet & sour squid Energy 315kcal/1320kJ; Protein 35.2g; Carbohydrate 4.5g, of which sugars 1.7g; Fat 17.6g, of which saturates 2.5g; Cholesterol 506mg; Calcium 39mg; Fibre 0g; Sodium 1361mg.

Stir-fried Clams with Orange

Zesty orange juice combined with pungent garlic and shallots make surprisingly good partners for the sweet-tasting shellfish. Fresh, plump clams will release plenty of juices while they are cooking, so serve this tangy dish with a spoon, or with some crusty bread so you can mop up all the delicious sauce. You could also serve this with rice or noodles.

Ingredients

1kg/2¼lb fresh clams
15ml/1 tbsp sunflower oil
30ml/2 tbsp finely chopped garlic
4 shallots, finely chopped
105ml/7 tbsp vegetable or fish stock
finely grated rind and juice of 1 orange
a large handful of roughly chopped flat leaf parsley
salt and ground black pepper

Serves 4

1 Wash and scrub the clams under cold running water. Check carefully and discard any that are open and do not close when tapped lightly with a knife or on the worktop.

2 Heat a wok over a high heat and add the sunflower oil. When hot, add the garlic, shallots and clams and stir-fry the mixture for 4–5 minutes.

3 Add the stock and orange rind and juice to the wok and season well. Cover and cook for 3–4 minutes, or until all the clams have opened. (Discard any unopened clams.)

4 Stir the chopped flat leaf parsley into the clams, then remove from the heat and serve immediately.

Cook's Tip

To avoid the risk of food poisoning, it is essential that the clams are live before cooking. Tap any open clams with the back of a knife. Any that do not close are dead and so must be discarded; and any that remain closed after cooking should also be thrown away immediately.

Fried Prawn Balls

When the moon waxes in September, the Japanese celebrate the arrival of autumn by making an offering to the moon. The dishes offered, such as tiny rice dumplings, sweet chestnuts and these balls, should all be round in shape.

Ingredients

150g/5oz raw prawns (shrimp), peeled
75ml/5 tbsp freshly made dashi (kombu and bonito stock) or instant dashi
1 large (US extra large) egg white, well beaten
30ml/2 tbsp sake
15ml/1 tbsp cornflour (cornstarch)
1.5ml/¼ tsp salt
vegetable oil, for deep-frying

To serve

25ml/1½ tbsp ground sea salt
2.5ml/½ tsp sansho
½ lemon, cut into 4 wedges

Makes about 14

1 Mix the prawns, dashi stock, beaten egg white, sake, cornflour and salt in a food processor or blender, and process until smooth. Scrape from the mixture into a small mixing bowl.

2 In a wok or small pan, heat the vegetable oil to 175°C/347°F.

3 Take two dessertspoons and wet them with a little vegetable oil. Scoop about 30ml/2 tbsp prawn-ball paste into the spoons and form a small ball. Carefully plunge the ball into the hot oil and deep-fry until lightly browned. Drain on a wire rack. Repeat this process, one at a time, until all the prawn-ball paste is used.

4 Mix the salt and sansho on a small plate. Serve the fried prawn balls on a large serving platter or on four serving plates. Garnish with lemon wedges and serve hot with the sansho salt.

Cook's Tip

Sansho is ground spice made from the dried pod of the prickly ash. Serve the sansho and salt in separate mounds if you like.

clams w. orange Energy 142kcal/596kJ; Protein 21.4g; Carbohydrate 5.9g, of which sugars 1.6g; Fat 3.8g, of which saturates 0.6g; Cholesterol 84mg; Calcium 121mg; Fibre 1.2g; Sodium 1506mg.
fried prawn balls Energy 41kcal/170kJ; Protein 2.1g; Carbohydrate 1g, of which sugars 0g; Fat 3.2g, of which saturates 0.4g; Cholesterol 21mg; Calcium 9mg; Fibre 0g; Sodium 446mg.

Prawn Toasts with Sesame Seeds

This healthy version of the ever-popular appetizer has lost none of its classic crunch and taste. Serve it as a snack, too. It is great for getting a party off to a good start.

Ingredients

6 slices medium-cut white bread, crusts removed
225g/8oz raw tiger prawns (jumbo shrimp), peeled and deveined
50g/2oz/⅓ cup drained, canned water chestnuts
1 egg white
5ml/1 tsp sesame oil
2.5ml/½ tsp salt
2 spring onions (scallions), finely chopped
10ml/2 tsp dry sherry
15ml/1 tbsp sesame seeds, toasted (see Cook's Tip)
shredded spring onion (scallion), to garnish

Serves 4–6

1 Preheat the oven to 120°C/250°F/Gas ½. Cut each slice of bread into four triangles. Spread out on a baking sheet and bake for 25 minutes or until crisp.

2 Meanwhile, put the prawns in a food processor with the water chestnuts, egg white, sesame oil and salt. Process the mixture, using the pulse facility, until a coarse purée is formed.

3 Scrape the mixture into a bowl, stir in the chopped spring onions and sherry and set aside for 10 minutes at room temperature to allow the flavours to blend.

4 Remove the toast from the oven and raise the temperature to 200°C/400°F/Gas 6.

5 To toast sesame seeds, put them in a wok and place over a medium heat until the seeds change colour. Shake the wok constantly so the seeds brown evenly and do not burn.

6 Spread the prawn mixture on the toast, sprinkle with the toasted sesame seeds and bake for 12 minutes.

7 Garnish the prawn toasts with spring onion and serve hot.

Firecrackers

It's easy to see how these snacks got their name. They whiz round the wok like rockets, and when you take a bite, they explode with flavour.

Ingredients

16 large, raw king prawns (jumbo shrimp), heads and shells removed but tails left on
5ml/1 tsp red curry paste
15ml/1 tbsp fish sauce
16 small wonton wrappers, about 8cm/3¼in square, thawed if frozen
16 fine egg noodles, soaked in water until soft
oil, for deep-frying

Makes 16

1 Place the prawns on their sides and cut two slits through the underbelly of each, one about 1cm/½in from the head end and the other about 1cm/½in from the first cut, cutting across the prawn. This will prevent the prawns from curling when cooked.

2 Mix the curry paste with the fish sauce in a shallow dish. Add the prawns and turn them in the mixture until they are well coated. Cover and leave to marinate for 10 minutes.

3 Place a wonton wrapper on the work surface at an angle so that it forms a diamond shape, then fold the top corner over so that the point is in the centre. Place a prawn, slits down, on the wrapper, with the tail projecting from the folded end, then fold the bottom corner over the other end of the prawn.

4 Fold each side of the wrapper over in turn to make a tightly folded roll. Tie a noodle in a bow around the roll and set it aside. Repeat with the remaining prawns and wrappers.

5 Heat the oil in a wok to 190°C/375°F or until a cube of bread, added to the oil, browns in 40 seconds.

6 Fry the prawns, a few at a time, for 5–8 minutes, until golden brown and cooked through. Drain well on kitchen paper and keep hot while you cook the remaining batches.

toasts w. seeds Energy 392kcal/1635kJ; Protein 19.1g; Carbohydrate 21.1g, of which sugars 1.2g; Fat 25.9g, of which saturates 3.4g; Cholesterol 110mg; Calcium 270mg; Fibre 2.7g; Sodium 558mg.
firecrackers Energy 71kcal/298kJ; Protein 3.2g; Carbohydrate 7.1g, of which sugars 0.2g; Fat 3.5g, of which saturates 0.5g; Cholesterol 25mg; Calcium 20mg; Fibre 0.3g; Sodium 30mg.

Crisp-fried Crab Claws

Crab claws are readily available from the freezer cabinet of many Asian stores and supermarkets. Thaw them thoroughly and dry on kitchen paper before coating them.

Ingredients

50g/2oz/⅓ cup rice flour
15ml/1 tbsp cornflour (cornstarch)
2.5ml/½ tsp sugar
1 egg
60ml/4 tbsp cold water
1 lemon grass stalk
2 garlic cloves, finely chopped
15ml/1 tbsp chopped fresh coriander (cilantro)
1–2 fresh red chillies, seeded and finely chopped
5ml/1 tsp fish sauce
vegetable oil, for deep-frying
12 half-shelled crab claws, thawed if frozen
ground black pepper

For the chilli vinegar dip

45ml/3 tbsp sugar
120ml/4fl oz/½ cup water
120ml/4fl oz/½ cup red wine vinegar
15ml/1 tbsp fish sauce
2–4 fresh red chillies, seeded and chopped

Serves 4

1 First make the chilli vinegar dip. Mix the sugar and water in a pan. Heat gently, stirring until the sugar has dissolved, then bring to the boil. Lower the heat and simmer for 5–7 minutes. Stir in the red wine vinegar, fish sauce and chopped chillies, pour into a serving bowl and set aside.

2 Combine the rice flour, cornflour and sugar in a bowl. Beat the egg with the cold water, then stir the egg and water mixture into the flour mixture and beat well until it forms a light batter without any lumps.

3 Cut off the lower 5cm/2in of the lemon grass stalk and chop it finely. Add the lemon grass to the batter, with the garlic, coriander, red chillies and fish sauce. Stir in pepper to taste.

4 Heat the oil in a wok or deep-fryer to 190°C/375°F or until a cube of bread browns in 40 seconds. Dip the crab claws into the batter, then fry, in batches, until golden. Serve with the dip.

Crab & Tofu Dumplings

These little crab and ginger-flavoured dumplings are usually served as a side dish.

Ingredients

115g/4oz frozen white crab meat, thawed
115g/4oz tofu
1 egg yolk
30ml/2 tbsp rice flour or wheat flour
30ml/2 tbsp finely chopped spring onion (scallion), green part only
2cm/¾in fresh root ginger, grated
10ml/2 tsp light soy sauce
salt
vegetable oil, for deep-frying
50g/2oz mooli (daikon), very finely grated, to serve

For the dipping sauce

120ml/4fl oz/½ cup vegetable stock
15ml/1 tbsp sugar
45ml/3 tbsp dark soy sauce

Serves 4–6

1 Squeeze as much moisture out of the crab meat as you can. Press the tofu through a fine strainer with the back of a tablespoon. Combine the tofu and crab meat in a bowl.

2 Add the egg yolk, rice or wheat flour, spring onion, ginger and soy sauce and season to taste with salt. Mix thoroughly with a metal spoon to form a light paste.

3 To make the dipping sauce, combine the vegetable stock, sugar and soy sauce in a serving bowl.

4 Line a baking sheet with kitchen paper. Heat the vegetable oil in a wok or frying pan to 190°C/375°F. Meanwhile, shape the crab and tofu mixture into thumb-sized pieces. Fry in batches of three at a time for 1–2 minutes. Drain on the kitchen paper and serve with the sauce and mooli.

Cook's Tip

Grate the mooli before serving and press it in a sieve or strainer to remove excess liquid.

crips-fried crab claws Energy 224kcal/933kJ; Protein 10.1g; Carbohydrate 16.9g, of which sugars 0g; Fat 12.9g, of which saturates 1.7g; Cholesterol 78mg; Calcium 62mg; Fibre 0.3g; Sodium 256mg.
crab & tofu dumplings Energy 74kcal/310kJ; Protein 6.3g; Carbohydrate 7.8g, of which sugars 3.6g; Fat 2g, of which saturates 0.4g; Cholesterol 47mg; Calcium 132mg; Fibre 0.3g; Sodium 762mg.

Crab Spring Rolls

Chilli and grated ginger add heat to these little treats.

Ingredients

15ml/1 tbsp groundnut (peanut) oil
5ml/1 tsp sesame oil
1 garlic clove, crushed
1 fresh red chilli, seeded and finely sliced
450g/1lb fresh stir-fry vegetables, such as beansprouts and shredded carrots, peppers and mangetouts (snow peas)
30ml/2 tbsp chopped coriander (cilantro)
2.5cm/1in piece of fresh root ginger, grated
15ml/1 tbsp dry sherry
15ml/1 tbsp soy sauce
350g/12oz fresh dressed crab meat (brown and white meat)
12 spring roll wrappers
1 small egg, beaten
oil, for deep-frying
salt and ground black pepper
lime wedges and fresh coriander, to garnish
sweet-sour dipping sauce, to serve

Serves 4–6

1 Heat the groundnut and sesame oils in a clean, preheated wok. When hot, stir-fry the crushed garlic and chilli for 1 minute. Add the vegetables, coriander and ginger and stir-fry for 1 minute more. Drizzle over the rice wine or dry sherry and soy sauce. Allow the mixture to bubble up for 1 minute.

2 Using a slotted spoon, transfer the vegetables to a bowl. Set aside until cool, then stir in the crab meat and season with salt and pepper.

3 Soften the spring roll wrappers, following the directions on the packet. Place some of the filling on a wrapper, fold over the front edge and the sides and roll up neatly, sealing the edges with a little beaten egg. Repeat with the remaining wrappers and filling.

4 Heat the oil for deep-frying in the wok and fry the spring rolls in batches, turning several times, until brown and crisp. Remove with a slotted spoon, drain on kitchen paper and keep hot while frying the remainder. Garnished with lime wedges and coriander and serve with a dipping sauce.

Crackling Rice Paper Fish Rolls

The wrappers hold their shape during cooking, yet dissolve in your mouth when eaten.

Ingredients

12 rice paper sheets, each about 20 x 10cm/8 x 4in
45ml/3 tbsp flour mixed to a paste with 45ml/3 tbsp water
vegetable oil, for deep-frying
fresh herbs, to garnish

For the filling

24 young asparagus spears, trimmed
225g/8oz raw prawns (shrimp), peeled and deveined
25ml/1½ tbsp olive oil
6 spring onions (scallions), finely chopped
1 garlic clove, crushed
2cm/¾in piece of fresh root ginger, grated
30ml/2 tbsp chopped fresh coriander (cilantro)
5ml/1 tsp five-spice powder
5ml/1 tsp finely grated lime or lemon rind
salt and ground black pepper

Makes 12

1 Make the filling. Bring a pan of lightly salted water to the boil; cook the asparagus for 3–4 minutes until tender. Drain, refresh under cold water and drain again. Cut the prawns into thirds.

2 Heat half of the oil in a small frying pan or wok and stir-fry the spring onions and garlic over a low heat for 2–3 minutes until soft. Transfer to a bowl and set aside.

3 Heat the remaining oil in the pan and stir-fry the prawns until they start to go pink. Add to the spring onion mixture with the remaining ingredients. Stir to mix.

4 To make each roll, brush a sheet of rice paper liberally with water and lay it on a clean surface.

5 Place two asparagus spears and a spoonful of the prawn mixture just off centre. Fold in the sides and roll up to make a fat cigar. Seal the ends with a little of the flour paste.

6 Heat the oil in a deep-fryer and fry the rolls in batches until pale golden. Drain well, garnish with herbs and serve.

crab spring rolls Energy 203kcal/844kJ; Protein 15g; Carbohydrate 13.9g, of which sugars 1.9g; Fat 9.3g, of which saturates 1.3g; Cholesterol 74mg; Calcium 94mg; Fibre 1.6g; Sodium 515mg.
crackling rice paper fish rolls Energy 105kcal/438kJ; Protein 5g; Carbohydrate 8.8g, of which sugars 0.7g; Fat 5.6g, of which saturates 0.7g; Cholesterol 37mg; Calcium 36mg; Fibre 0.8g; Sodium 38mg.

Fiery Tuna Spring Rolls

This modern take on the classic spring roll is substantial enough to serve as a main meal.

Ingredients

1 large chunk of very fresh thick tuna steak
45ml/3 tbsp light soy sauce
30ml/2 tbsp wasabi
16 mangetouts (snow peas), trimmed
8 spring roll wrappers
sunflower oil, for deep-frying
soft noodles and stir-fried Asian greens, to serve
soy sauce and sweet chilli sauce, for dipping

Serves 4

1 Place the tuna on a board. Using a sharp knife cut it into eight slices, each measuring about 12 x 2.5cm/4½ x 1in.

2 Place the tuna in a large, non-metallic dish in a single layer. Mix together the soy sauce and the wasabi and spoon evenly over the fish. Cover and marinate for 10–15 minutes.

3 Meanwhile, blanch the mangetouts in boiling water for about 1 minute, drain and refresh under cold water. Drain and pat dry with kitchen paper.

4 Place a spring roll wrapper on a clean work surface and place a piece of tuna on top, in the centre.

5 Top the tuna with two mangetouts and fold over the sides and roll up. Brush the edges of the wrappers to seal.

6 Repeat with the remaining tuna, mangetouts and wrappers.

7 Fill a large wok one-third full with oil and heat to 180°C/350°F or until a cube of bread browns in 45 seconds. Working in batches, deep-fry the rolls for 1–2 minutes, until crisp and golden.

8 Drain the rolls on kitchen paper and serve immediately with soft noodles and Asian greens. Serve the spring rolls with side dishes of soy sauce and sweet chilli sauce for dipping.

Crispy Shanghai Spring Rolls

Crunchy on the outside, succulent in the centre, these are irresistible.

Ingredients

12 spring roll wrappers
30ml/2 tbsp plain (all-purpose) flour mixed to a paste with water
sunflower oil, for deep-frying

For the filling

6 Chinese dried mushrooms, soaked for 30 minutes in warm water
150g/5oz fresh firm tofu
30ml/2 tbsp sunflower oil
225g/8oz minced (ground) pork
225g/8oz peeled cooked prawns (shrimp), roughly chopped
2.5ml/½ tsp cornflour (cornstarch), mixed to a paste with 15ml/1 tbsp soy sauce
75g/3oz each shredded bamboo shoot or grated carrot, sliced water chestnuts and beansprouts
6 spring onions (scallions) or 1 young leek, finely chopped
a little sesame oil

Makes 12

1 Make the filling. Drain the mushrooms. Cut off and discard the stems and slice the caps finely. Slice the tofu.

2 Heat the oil in a wok and stir-fry the pork for 2–3 minutes or until the colour changes. Add the prawns, cornflour paste and bamboo shoot or carrot. Stir in the water chestnuts.

3 Increase the heat, add the beansprouts and spring onions or leek and toss for 1 minute. Stir in the mushrooms and tofu. Season, then stir in the sesame oil. Cool quickly on a platter.

4 Separate the spring roll wrappers. Place a wrapper on the work surface with one corner nearest you. Spoon some of the filling near the centre of the wrapper and fold the nearest corner over the filling. Smear a little of the flour paste on the free sides, turn the sides to the middle and roll up. Repeat this procedure with the remaining wrappers and filling.

5 Deep-fry the spring rolls in batches until they are crisp and golden. Drain and serve at once with a dipping sauce.

fiery tuna spring rolls Energy 171kcal/717kJ; Protein 14.1g; Carbohydrate 11.4g, of which sugars 1.7g; Fat 8g, of which saturates 1.3g; Cholesterol 14mg; Calcium 36mg; Fibre 0.8g; Sodium 825mg.
crispy shaghai spring rolls Energy 38kcal/161kJ; Protein 1.1g; Carbohydrate 6.6g, of which sugars 0.6g; Fat 1g, of which saturates 0.1g; Cholesterol 0mg; Calcium 15mg; Fibre 0.5g; Sodium 88mg.

Five-spice Steamed Rolls

A great favourite at the hawker stalls in South-east Asia, these deep-fried steamed rolls are delicious with a dipping sauce.

Ingredients

225g/8oz minced (ground) pork
150g/5oz fresh prawns (shrimp), peeled and finely chopped
115g/4oz water chestnuts, finely chopped
15ml/1 tbsp light soy sauce
15ml/1 tbsp dark soy sauce
15ml/1 tbsp sour plum sauce
7.5ml/1½ tsp sesame oil
10ml/2 tsp Chinese five-spice powder
5ml/1 tsp glutinous rice flour or cornflour (cornstarch)
1 egg, lightly beaten
4 fresh tofu sheets or rice-paper roll wrappers, 18–20cm/7–8in square, soaked in warm water
vegetable oil, for deep-frying
chilli oil, for drizzling
soy sauce mixed with chopped chillies, to serve

Serves 4

1 Put the minced pork, chopped prawns and water chestnuts in a bowl. Add the soy sauces, sour plum sauce and sesame oil and mix well. Stir in the five-spice powder, glutinous rice flour or cornflour, and egg. Mix well.

2 Lay the tofu sheets on a flat surface and divide the minced pork mixture between them, placing spoonfuls towards the edge nearest you. Pull the nearest edge up over the filling, tuck in the sides and roll into a log, just like a spring roll. Moisten the last edge with a little water to seal the roll.

3 Fill a wok one-third of the way up with water and place a bamboo steamer into it. Heat the water and place the tofu rolls in the steamer. Cover and steam for 15 minutes. Remove the steamed rolls with tongs and place them on a clean dishtowel.

4 Heat enough oil for deep-frying in a wok. Fry the steamed rolls in batches until crisp and golden. Drain them on kitchen paper and serve whole or sliced into portions. Drizzle with chilli oil and serve with a bowl of soy sauce mixed with chopped chillies for dipping.

Salmon & Ginger Fish Cakes

These light fish cakes are scented with the exotic flavours of sesame, lime and ginger. They make a tempting appetizer served simply with a wedge of lime for squeezing over, but are also perfect for a light lunch or supper, served with a crunchy, refreshing salad.

Ingredients

500g/1¼lb salmon fillet, skinned and boned
45ml/3 tbsp dried breadcrumbs
30ml/2 tbsp mayonnaise
30ml/2 tbsp sesame seeds
30ml/2 tbsp light soy sauce
finely grated rind of 2 limes
10ml/2 tsp finely grated fresh root ginger
4 spring onions (scallions), finely sliced
vegetable oil, for frying
salt and ground black pepper
spring onions (scallions), to garnish
lime wedges, to serve

Makes 25

1 Finely chop the salmon and place in a bowl. Add the breadcrumbs, mayonnaise, sesame seeds, soy sauce, lime rind, ginger and spring onions and use your fingers to mix well.

2 With wet hands, divide the mixture into 25 portions and shape each into a small round cake. Place the cakes on a baking sheet lined with baking parchment, cover and chill for at least two hours. They can be left overnight.

3 When you are ready to cook the fish cakes, heat about 5cm/2in vegetable oil in a wok and fry the fish cakes in batches, over a medium heat, for 2–3 minutes on each side.

4 Drain the fish cakes well on kitchen paper and serve warm or at room temperature, garnished with spring onion slivers and plenty of lime wedges for squeezing over.

Cook's Tip

When chopping the salmon, look out for stray bones and pick these out with tweezers.

five-spiced rolls Energy 278kcal/1157kJ; Protein 20.4g; Carbohydrate 10.8g, of which sugars 1.8g; Fat 17g, of which saturates 3.7g; Cholesterol 158mg; Calcium 61mg; Fibre 0.6g; Sodium 740mg.
salmon/ginger fish cakes Energy 83kcal/343kJ; Protein 4.6g; Carbohydrate 1.6g, of which sugars 0.2g; Fat 6.5g, of which saturates 0.9g; Cholesterol 11mg; Calcium 16mg; Fibre 0.2g; Sodium 117mg.

Scallops with Ginger Relish

Buy scallops in their shells to ensure their freshness; your fishmonger will open them for you if you find this difficult. The shells make excellent serving dishes.

Ingredients

8 king or queen scallops
4 whole star anise
30ml/2 tbsp vegetable oil
salt and ground white pepper
fresh coriander (cilantro) sprigs and whole star anise, to garnish

For the relish

½ cucumber, peeled
salt, for sprinkling
5cm/2in piece fresh root ginger, peeled and sliced into strips
10ml/2 tsp caster (superfine) sugar
45ml/3 tbsp rice wine vinegar
10ml/2 tsp syrup from a jar of preserved stem ginger
5ml/1 tsp sesame seeds, for sprinkling

Serves 4

1 To make the relish, halve the cucumber lengthways, remove the seeds, then slice the cucumber into a colander and sprinkle liberally with salt. Set aside to drain for 30 minutes.

2 To prepare the scallops, cut each into 2–3 slices and place the scallop with the corals in a bowl.

3 Coarsely grind the star anise using a mortar and pestle and add it with the seasoning. Cover the bowl and marinate the scallops in the refrigerator for about 1 hour.

4 Rinse the cucumber under cold water, then drain and pat dry with kitchen paper. Place in a bowl with the ginger, sugar, rice wine vinegar and syrup. Mix well, then cover with clear film (plastic wrap) and chill until the relish is needed.

5 Heat a wok and add the oil. When the oil is very hot, add the scallop slices and stir-fry them for 2–3 minutes. Place the cooked scallops on kitchen paper to drain off any excess oil.

6 Garnish the scallops with sprigs of coriander and whole star anise, and serve with the cucumber relish, sprinkled lightly with sesame seeds.

Steamed Pork Balls

Bitesize balls of steamed pork and mushrooms rolled in jasmine rice make a fabulous snack.

Ingredients

30ml/2 tbsp vegetable oil
200g/7oz/scant 3 cups finely chopped shiitake mushrooms
400g/14oz lean minced (ground) pork
4 spring onions (scallions), chopped
2 garlic cloves, crushed
15ml/1 tbsp fish sauce
15ml/1 tbsp soy sauce
15ml/1 tsp grated root ginger
60ml/4 tbsp finely chopped coriander (cilantro)
1 egg, lightly beaten
salt and ground black pepper
200g/7oz/1 cup cooked jasmine rice

For the dipping sauce

120ml/4fl oz/½ cup sweet chilli sauce
105ml/7 tbsp soy sauce
15ml/1 tbsp Chinese rice wine
5–10ml/1–2 tsp chilli oil

Serves 4

1 Heat the oil in a wok, then stir-fry the mushrooms for 2–3 minutes. Transfer to a food processor with the pork, spring onions, garlic, fish sauce, soy sauce, ginger, coriander and beaten egg. Process for 30–40 seconds. Scrape the mixture into a bowl, cover and chill for 3–4 hours or overnight.

2 Place the jasmine rice in a bowl. With wet hands, divide the mushroom mixture into 20 portions and roll each one into a firm ball. Roll each ball in the rice then arrange the balls, spaced apart, in two baking parchment-lined tiers of a bamboo steamer.

3 Cover the steamer and place over a wok of simmering water. Steam for 1 hour 15 minutes.

4 Meanwhile, combine all the dipping sauce ingredients in a small bowl.

5 When the pork balls are fully cooked, remove them from the steamer and serve them warm with the spicy dipping sauce.

scallops w. ginger relish Energy 130kcal/542kJ; Protein 12.1g; Carbohydrate 4.9g, of which sugars 3.2g; Fat 7g, of which saturates 1g; Cholesterol 24mg; Calcium 31mg; Fibre 0.3g; Sodium 92mg.
pork balls Energy 322kcal/1353kJ; Protein 25.8g; Carbohydrate 29.9g, of which sugars 14.3g; Fat 11.8g, of which saturates 2.7g; Cholesterol 111mg; Calcium 39mg; Fibre 0.8g; Sodium 893mg.

Spicy Pork Spareribs

These make a great appetizer – if slightly messy – to an informal meal.

Ingredients

675–900g/1 ½–2lb meaty pork spareribs
5ml/1 tsp Sichuan peppercorns
30ml/2 tbsp coarse sea salt
2.5ml/½ tsp Chinese five-spice powder
25ml/1 ½ tbsp cornflour (cornstarch)
groundnut (peanut) oil, for deep-frying
coriander (cilantro) sprigs, to garnish

For the marinade

30ml/2 tbsp light soy sauce
5ml/1 tsp caster (superfine) sugar
15ml/1 tbsp dry sherry
ground black pepper

Serves 4

1 Using a sharp, heavy cleaver, chop the spareribs into pieces about 5cm/2in long. Place them in a shallow dish and set aside.

2 Heat a wok to medium heat. Add the Sichuan peppercorns and salt and dry-fry for about 3 minutes, stirring until the mixture colours slightly. Remove from the heat and stir in the five-spice powder. Cool, then grind to a fine powder.

3 Sprinkle 5ml/1 tsp of the spice powder over the spareribs and rub in well with your hands. Add all the marinade ingredients and toss the ribs to coat thoroughly. Cover and leave in the refrigerator to marinate for about 2 hours.

4 Pour off any excess marinade from the spareribs. Sprinkle the ribs with the cornflour and mix to coat evenly.

5 Deep fry the spareribs in batches for 3 minutes until golden. Remove and set aside. When all the batches have been cooked, reheat the oil and deep-fry the ribs for a second time for 1–2 minutes, until crisp and thoroughly cooked. Drain on kitchen paper. Transfer the ribs to a warm serving platter and sprinkle over 5–7.5ml/1–1 ½ tsp of the remaining spice powder.

6 Garnish with coriander sprigs and serve immediately.

Chicken Teriyaki

A simple bowl of boiled rice is the ideal accompaniment to this subtle-flavoured chicken dish.

Ingredients

450g/1lb boneless chicken breast portions, skinned
orange segments and mustard and cress (fine curled cress), to garnish

For the marinade

5ml/1 tsp sugar
15ml/1 tbsp sake
15 ml/1 tbsp dry sherry
30ml/2 tbsp dark soy sauce
grated rind of 1 orange

Serves 4

1 Place the chicken on a board and slice into long, thin strips using a cleaver or sharp knife.

2 Mix together the sugar, sake, dry sherry, soy sauce and grated orange rind in a bowl.

3 Place the chicken in a separate bowl, pour over the marinade and set aside to marinate for 15 minutes.

4 Add the chicken and the marinade to a preheated wok and stir-fry for 4–5 minutes, until the chicken is fully cooked. Serve garnished with orange segments and mustard and cress.

Cook's Tip

Chicken Teriyaki makes a good sandwich filling. Let it cool in the marinade so that it remains moist and succulent. Watercress goes well with the chicken, as would a little pickled ginger.

Variation

This Japanese classic has gained exceptional popularity in the United States, where it is served at food outlets nationwide. Some recipes add fresh ginger, and a tablespoon or honey or maple syrup instead of the sugar to sweeten the marinade.

spicy pork spareribs Energy 424kcal/1763kJ; Protein 32.2g; Carbohydrate 2.6g, of which sugars 1.3g; Fat 31.4g, of which saturates 9.8g; Cholesterol 111mg; Calcium 33mg; Fibre 0g; Sodium 345mg.
chicken teriyaki Energy 149kcal/630kJ; Protein 27.4g; Carbohydrate 3.8g, of which sugars 3.8g; Fat 1.3g, of which saturates 0.3g; Cholesterol 79mg; Calcium 21mg; Fibre 0.5g; Sodium 70mg.

Lettuce Parcels

Known as Sang Choy in Hong Kong, this is a popular "assemble-it-yourself" treat.

Ingredients

2 chicken breast fillets
4 Chinese dried mushrooms, soaked for 30 minutes in warm water to cover
30ml/2 tbsp vegetable oil
2 garlic cloves, crushed
6 drained canned water chestnuts, thinly sliced
30ml/2 tbsp light soy sauce
5ml/1 tsp Sichuan peppercorns, dry fried and crushed
4 spring onions (scallions), finely chopped
5ml/1 tsp sesame oil
vegetable oil, for deep-frying
50g/2oz cellophane noodles
salt and ground black pepper
1 crisp lettuce and 60ml/4 tbsp hoisin sauce, to serve

Serves 6

1 Remove the skin from the chicken fillets, pat dry and set aside. Chop the chicken into thin strips. Drain the soaked mushrooms. Cut off and discard the mushroom stems; slice the caps finely and set aside.

2 Heat the oil in a wok or large frying pan. Add the garlic, then add the chicken. Stir-fry until the pieces are cooked through.

3 Add the sliced mushrooms, water chestnuts, soy sauce and peppercorns. Toss for 2–3 minutes, then season, if needed. Stir in half of the spring onions, then the sesame oil. Remove from the heat and set aside.

4 Cut the chicken skin into strips, deep fry in hot oil until very crisp and drain on kitchen paper. Deep fry the noodles until crisp. Drain on kitchen paper.

5 Crush the noodles and put in a serving dish. Top with the chicken skin, chicken mixture and the remaining spring onions. Arrange the lettuce leaves on a platter. Toss the chicken and noodles to mix. Invite guests to take a lettuce leaf, spread the inside with hoisin sauce and add a spoonful of filling, turning in the sides of the leaf and rolling it into a parcel before eating it.

Scented Chicken Wraps

For sheer sophistication, these leaf-wrapped chicken bites take a lot of beating. They are surprisingly easy to make and can be deep-fried in minutes in the wok.

Ingredients

400g/14oz skinless chicken thighs, boned
45ml/3 tbsp soy sauce
30ml/2 tbsp finely grated garlic
15ml/1 tbsp cumin
15ml/1 tbsp ground coriander
15ml/1 tbsp golden caster (superfine) sugar
5ml/1 tsp finely grated fresh root ginger
1 fresh bird's eye chilli
30ml/2 tbsp oyster sauce
15ml/1 tbsp fish sauce
1 bunch of pandanus leaves, to wrap
vegetable oil, for deep-frying
sweet chilli sauce or chilli sambal, to serve

Serves 4

1 Using a cleaver or sharp knife, cut the chicken into bitesize pieces and place in a large mixing bowl.

2 Place the soy sauce, garlic, cumin, coriander, sugar, ginger, chilli, oyster sauce and fish sauce in a blender and process until smooth. Pour over the chicken, cover and leave to marinate in the refrigerator for 6-8 hours.

3 When ready to cook, drain the chicken from the marinade and wrap each piece in a pandanus leaf (you will need to cut the leaves to size) and secure with a cocktail stick (toothpick).

4 Fill a wok one-third full of oil and heat to 180°C/350°F or until a cube of bread, dropped into the oil, browns in 45 seconds. Carefully add the chicken parcels, 3–4 at a time, and deep-fry for 3–4 minutes, or until cooked through. Drain on kitchen paper and serve with the chilli sauce or sambal. (Do not eat the leaves!)

Cook's Tip

Pandanus leaves are usually available from Asian supermarkets.

lettuce parcels Energy 237kcal/984kJ; Protein 15.3g; Carbohydrate 7.6g, of which sugars 1.1g; Fat 16.1g, of which saturates 2g; Cholesterol 41mg; Calcium 24mg; Fibre 0.6g; Sodium 41mg.
chicken wraps Energy 159kcal/669kJ; Protein 24.5g; Carbohydrate 6.8g, of which sugars 6.6g; Fat 3.9g, of which saturates 0.6g; Cholesterol 70mg; Calcium 10mg; Fibre 0.1g; Sodium 1055mg.

Yellow Vegetable Curry

This hot and spicy curry made with coconut milk has a creamy richness that contrasts wonderfully with the heat of chilli and the bite of lightly cooked vegetables.

Ingredients

30ml/2 tbsp sunflower oil
30–45ml/2–3 tbsp yellow curry paste (see Cook's Tip)
200ml/7fl oz/scant 1 cup coconut cream
300ml/½ pint/1¼ cups coconut milk
150ml/¼ pint/⅔ cup vegetable stock
200g/7oz snake beans, cut into 2cm/¾in lengths
200g/7oz baby corn
4 baby courgettes (zucchini), sliced
1 small aubergine (eggplant), cubed or sliced
10ml/2 tsp palm sugar (jaggery)
fresh coriander (cilantro) leaves, to garnish
noodles or rice, to serve

Serves 4

1 Heat a large wok over a medium heat and add the oil. When hot add the curry paste and stir-fry for 1–2 minutes. Add the coconut cream and cook gently for 8–10 minutes, or until the mixture starts to separate.

2 Add the coconut milk, stock and vegetables and cook gently for 8–10 minutes, until the vegetables are just tender. Stir in the palm sugar, garnish with coriander leaves and serve with noodles or rice.

Cook's Tip

To make the curry paste, mix 10ml/2 tsp each hot chilli powder, ground coriander and ground cumin in a sturdy food processor, preferably one with an attachment for processing smaller quantities. Add 5ml/1 tsp ground turmeric, 15ml/1 tbsp chopped fresh galangal, 10ml/2 tsp crushed garlic, 30ml/2 tbsp finely chopped lemon grass, 4 finely chopped red shallots and 5ml/1 tsp chopped lime rind. Add 30ml/2 tbsp cold water and blend to a smooth paste. Add a little more water is necessary.

Aubergine & Sweet Potato Stew

This is a particularly good combination of flavours.

Ingredients

60ml/4 tbsp vegetable oil
400g/14oz baby aubergines (eggplants), halved
225g/8oz Thai red shallots or other small shallots or pickling onions
5ml/1 tsp fennel seeds, lightly crushed
4–5 garlic cloves, thinly sliced
25ml/1½ tbsp finely chopped fresh root ginger
475ml/16fl oz/2 cups vegetable stock
2 lemon grass stalks, outer layers discarded, finely chopped
15g/½oz/⅔ cup fresh coriander (cilantro), stalks and leaves chopped separately
3 kaffir lime leaves, lightly bruised
2–3 small fresh red chillies
60ml/4 tbsp green curry paste
675g/1½lb sweet potatoes, cut in chunks
400ml/14fl oz/1⅔ cups coconut milk
2.5–5ml/½–1 tsp light brown sugar
250g/9oz/3½ cups mushrooms, thickly sliced
juice of 1 lime, to taste
salt and ground black pepper
basil leaves, to garnish

Serves 6

1 Heat half the oil in a wok and cook the aubergines until lightly browned on all sides. Remove from the pan; set aside.

2 Slice four shallots. Cook the whole shallots in the oil remaining in the wok, until lightly browned. Add to the aubergines. Add more oil to the wok and cook the sliced shallots, fennel seeds, garlic and ginger over a low heat for 5 minutes.

3 Add the stock, lemon grass, chopped coriander stalks, lime leaves and chillies. Simmer for 5 minutes, the stir in half the curry paste and the sweet potatoes. Simmer for 10 minutes, add the aubergines and shallots and cook for 5 minutes more.

4 Stir in the coconut milk and sugar. Season, then stir in the mushrooms and simmer until the vegetables are cooked. Stir in more curry paste and lime juice to taste, followed by the chopped coriander leaves. Sprinkle basil leaves over the stew and serve with rice in warm bowls.

yellow vegetable curry Energy 126kcal/528kJ; Protein 4.7g; Carbohydrate 12.7g, of which sugars 11.9g; Fat 6.7g, of which saturates 1.1g; Cholesterol 5mg; Calcium 90mg; Fibre 2.5g; Sodium 752mg.
aubergine/sweet potato Energy 228kcal/960kJ; Protein 4.3g; Carbohydrate 34g, of which sugars 13.4g; Fat 9.3g, of which saturates 1.2g; Cholesterol 0mg; Calcium 130mg; Fibre 7.2g; Sodium 159mg.

Stir-fried Water Spinach

In the countryside, this dish is a favourite with roadside vendors. Water spinach is an excellent source of Vitamin A, which helps to promote healthy bones, skin, hair and also aids vision. Serve this aromatic dish as part of a vegetarian meal, or as a side dish to accompany main meat or fish courses.

Ingredients

30ml/2 tbsp groundnut (peanut) oil
2 garlic cloves, finely chopped
2 fresh red or green chillies, seeded and finely chopped
500g/1 1/4lb fresh water spinach
45ml/3 tbsp chilli sauce
salt and ground black pepper

Serves 3–4

1 Heat a wok or large pan and add the oil. Stir in the garlic and chillies and stir-fry for 1 minute, then add the water spinach and toss around the pan.

2 Once the water spinach leaves begin to wilt, add the chilli sauce, making sure it coats the spinach. Season to taste with salt and pepper and serve immediately.

Variations

• Although water spinach is traditionally favoured in this recipe, you coud substitute it for any type of green, leafy vegetable, particularly ordinary spinach. The latter – a relative in common name only – has a slightly tougher texture, however, and leaves should be blanched in boiling water prior to stir-frying with the other ingredients. Thoroughly wash the spinach and trim off the stems, then immerse the leaves in boiling water for about 15 seconds until softened slightly.

• Some non-leafy vegetables also work well as the principal component. Cauliflower and, when in season, asparagus, can be stir-fried in the same way. With the cauliflower, simply cut off the heads, divide into florets and add directly to the pan with the garlic and chillies. The asparagus will require blanching. Trim off the woody tips and stand the heads in a small jug (pitcher) of boiling water for 3–4 minutes. Slice and add to the pan.

Fried Rice with Mushrooms

A tasty rice and mushroom dish that is very low in saturated fat, yet sufficiently filling to be almost a meal in itself.

Ingredients

225g/8oz/1 1/4 cups long grain rice
15ml/1 tbsp vegetable oil
1 egg, lightly beaten
2 garlic cloves, crushed
175g/6oz/2 1/4 cups button (white) mushrooms or mixed wild and cultivated mushrooms, sliced
15ml/1 tbsp light soy sauce
1.5ml/1/4 tsp salt
2.5ml/1/2 tsp sesame oil
cucumber matchsticks, to garnish

Serves 4

1 Rinse the rice until the water runs clear, then drain well. Place in a pan. Measure the depth of the rice against your index finger, then cover with cold water to the same depth.

2 Bring the water to the boil. Stir the rice, boil for a few minutes, then cover the pan. Lower the heat to a simmer and cook for 5–8 minutes until all of the water has been absorbed.

3 Remove the pan from the heat and, without lifting the lid, leave for another 10 minutes before forking up the rice.

4 Heat 5ml/1 tsp of the vegetable oil in a non-stick frying pan or wok. Add the egg and cook, stirring with a chopstick or wooden spoon until scrambled. Immediately remove the egg and set aside in a bowl.

5 Add the remaining vegetable oil in the pan or wok. When it is hot, stir-fry the garlic for a few seconds, then add the mushrooms and stir-fry for 2 minutes, adding a little water, if needed, to prevent burning. Stir in the cooked rice and cook for 4 minutes more.

6 Add the scrambled egg, soy sauce, salt and sesame oil. Mix together and cook for 1 minute to heat through. Serve the rice immediately, garnished with cucumber matchsticks.

stir-fried water spinach Energy 92kcal/379kJ; Protein 3.8g; Carbohydrate 4.6g, of which sugars 4g; Fat 6.5g, of which saturates 0.8g; Cholesterol 0mg; Calcium 214mg; Fibre 2.8g; Sodium 297mg.
rice w. mushrooms Energy 245kcal/1023kJ; Protein 6.6g; Carbohydrate 45.4g, of which sugars 0.4g; Fat 3.8g, of which saturates 0.7g; Cholesterol 48mg; Calcium 21mg; Fibre 0.5g; Sodium 287mg.

Stir-fried Vegetables & Rice

The ginger gives this mixed rice and vegetable dish a wonderful flavour.

Ingredients

115g/4oz/generous ½ cup brown basmati rice, rinsed and drained
350ml/12fl oz/1½ cups vegetable stock
2.5cm/1in piece fresh root ginger
1 garlic clove, halved
5cm/2in piece pared lemon rind
115g/4oz/1½ cups shiitake mushrooms
15ml/1 tbsp vegetable oil
175g/6oz baby carrots, trimmed
225g/8oz baby courgettes (zucchini), halved
175–225g/6–8oz/about 1½ cups broccoli, broken into florets
6 spring onions (scallions), diagonally sliced
15ml/1 tbsp light soy sauce
10ml/2 tsp toasted sesame oil

Serves 2–4

1 Put the rice in a pan and pour in the vegetable stock. Thinly slice the ginger and add it to the pan with the garlic and lemon rind. Slowly bring to the boil, then cover and simmer for 20–25 minutes until the rice is tender. Discard the flavourings and keep the rice hot.

2 Slice the mushrooms, discarding the stems. Heat the oil in a wok and stir-fry the carrots for 4–5 minutes, the add the mushrooms and courgettes and stir-fry for 2–3 minutes. Add the broccoli and spring onions and cook for 3 minutes more, by which time all the vegetables should be tender but should still retain a bit of "bite".

3 Add the cooked rice to the vegetables, and toss briefly over the heat to mix and heat through. Toss with the soy sauce and sesame oil. Spoon into a bowl and serve immediately.

Cook's Tip

Keep fresh root ginger in the freezer. It can be sliced or grated and thaws very quickly.

Coconut Noodles & Vegetables

When everyday vegetables are livened up with Thai spices and flavours, the result is a delectable dish that everyone will enjoy.

Ingredients

30ml/2 tbsp sunflower oil
1 lemon grass stalk, finely chopped
15ml/1 tbsp red curry paste
1 onion, thickly sliced
3 courgettes (zucchini), thickly sliced
115g/4oz Savoy cabbage, thickly sliced
2 carrots, thickly sliced
150g/5oz broccoli, stem thickly sliced and florets separated
2 x 400ml/14fl oz cans coconut milk
475ml/16fl oz/2 cups vegetable stock
150g/5oz dried egg noodles
30ml/2 tbsp soy sauce
60ml/4 tbsp chopped fresh coriander (cilantro)

For the garnish

2 lemon grass stalks, split
1 bunch fresh coriander (cilantro)
8–10 small fresh red chillies

Serves 4–6

1 Heat the oil in a wok. Add the lemon grass and red curry paste and stir-fry for 2–3 seconds. Add the onion and cook over medium heat, stirring occasionally, until softened.

2 Add the courgettes, cabbage, carrots and slices of broccoli stem. Toss the vegetables with the onion mixture.

3 Cook over low heat for a further 5 minutes.

4 Increase the heat, stir in the coconut milk and vegetable stock and bring to the boil. Add the broccoli florets and the noodles, lower the heat and simmer gently for 20 minutes.

5 To make the garnish, gather the coriander into a small bouquet and lay it on a platter. Tuck the lemon grass halves into the coriander bouquet and add the chillies to resemble flowers.

6 Stir the soy sauce and chopped coriander into the noodle mixture. Spoon on to the platter, taking care not to disturb the herb bouquet, and serve immediately.

vegetables & rice Energy 430kcal/1788kJ; Protein 12.5g; Carbohydrate 58.2g, of which sugars 11.2g; Fat 16.2g, of which saturates 2.2g; Cholesterol 0mg; Calcium 127mg; Fibre 6.5g; Sodium 569mg.
coconut noodles & veg. Energy 192kcal/808kJ; Protein 5.6g; Carbohydrate 29.4g, of which sugars 11.5g; Fat 6.6g, of which saturates 1.4g; Cholesterol 8mg; Calcium 83mg; Fibre 2.4g; Sodium 554mg.

Tung Tong

Popularly called "gold bags", these crisp pastry purses have a coriander-flavoured filling based on water chestnuts and corn. They are the perfect vegetarian snack and look very impressive.

Ingredients

18 spring roll wrappers, about 8cm/3¼in square, thawed if frozen
oil, for deep-frying
plum sauce, to serve

For the filling

4 baby corn cobs
130g/4½oz can water chestnuts, drained and chopped
1 shallot, coarsely chopped
1 egg, separated
30ml/2 tbsp cornflour (cornstarch)
60ml/4 tbsp water
small bunch fresh coriander (cilantro), chopped
salt and ground black pepper

Makes 18

1 Make the filling. Place the baby corn, water chestnuts, shallot and egg yolk in a food processor or blender. Process to a coarse paste. Place the egg white in a cup and whisk it lightly with a fork.

2 Put the cornflour in a small pan and stir in the water until smooth. Add the corn mixture and chopped coriander and season with salt and pepper to taste. Cook over a low heat, stirring constantly, until thickened.

3 Leave the filling to cool slightly, then place 5ml/1 tsp in the centre of a spring roll wrapper. Brush the edges with the beaten egg white, then gather up the points and press them firmly together to make a pouch or bag.

4 Repeat with remaining wrappers and filling, keeping the finished bags and the wrappers covered until needed so they do not dry out.

5 Heat the oil in a deep-fryer or wok until a cube of bread, added to the oil, browns in about 45 seconds. Fry the bags, in batches, for about 5 minutes, until golden brown. Drain on kitchen paper and serve hot, with the plum sauce.

Vegetable Tempura

These deep-fried fritters are perfect for parties.

Ingredients

2 medium courgettes (zucchini)
½ medium aubergine (eggplant)
1 large carrot
½ small Spanish onion
1 egg
120ml/4fl oz/½ cup iced water
115g/4oz/1 cup plain (all-purpose) flour
salt and ground black pepper
vegetable oil, for deep-frying
sea salt flakes, lemon slices and Japanese soy sauce (shoyu), to serve

Serves 4

1 Using a potato peeler, pare strips of peel from the courgettes and aubergine to give a striped effect.

2 Cut the courgettes, aubergine and carrot into strips about 7.5–10cm/3–4in long and 3mm/⅛in wide.

3 Put the courgettes, aubergine and carrot into a colander and sprinkle liberally with salt. Leave for about 30 minutes, then rinse thoroughly under cold running water. Drain well.

4 Thinly slice the onion from top to base, discarding the plump pieces in the middle. Separate the layers so that there are lots of fine, long strips. Mix all the vegetables together and season with salt and pepper.

5 Make the batter immediately before frying. Mix the egg and iced water in a bowl, then sift in the flour. Mix briefly with a fork or chopsticks. Do not overmix; the batter should remain lumpy. Add the vegetables to the batter and mix to combine.

6 Half-fill a wok with oil and heat to 180°C/350°F. Scoop up one heaped tablespoon of the mixture at a time and carefully lower it into the oil. Deep-fry in batches for approximately 3 minutes, until golden brown and crisp.

7 Drain on kitchen paper. Serve each portion with salt, slices of lemon and a tiny bowl of Japanese soy sauce for dipping.

tung tong Energy 55kcal/229kJ; Protein 1.2g; Carbohydrate 6.3g, of which sugars 0.4g; Fat 2.9g, of which saturates 0.4g; Cholesterol 12mg; Calcium 19mg; Fibre 0.5g; Sodium 42mg.
vegetable tempura Energy 313kcal/1305kJ; Protein 7.1g; Carbohydrate 30.6g, of which sugars 7.3g; Fat 18.9g, of which saturates 2.5g; Cholesterol 48mg; Calcium 94mg; Fibre 3.6g; Sodium 28mg.

Mooli, Beetroot & Carrot Stir-fry

This is a dazzlingly colourful dish with a crunchy texture and fragrant taste. It is low in saturated fat and is cholesterol-free and would be ideal for a summer lunch.

Ingredients
25g/1oz/1/3 cup pine nuts
115g/4oz mooli (daikon), peeled
115g/4oz raw beetroot (beet), peeled
115g/4oz carrots, peeled
15ml/1 tbsp vegetable oil
1 orange
30ml/2 tbsp chopped fresh coriander (cilantro)
salt and ground black pepper

Serves 4

1 Heat a non-stick wok or frying pan. Add the pine nuts and toss over medium heat until golden brown.

2 Remove the nuts and spread them on a plate. Set aside.

3 Using a sharp knife, cut the mooli, beetroot and carrots into long, thin strips. Keep them separate on a chopping board.

4 Reheat the wok or frying pan, then add the oil. When the oil is hot, add the mooli, beetroot and carrots and stir-fry for 2–3 minutes over medium to high heat. Remove the vegetables from the wok, put them in a bowl and keep hot.

5 Cut the orange in half. Squeeze the juice, using a citrus juicer or a reamer, and pour the juice into a bowl.

6 Arrange the vegetables on a warmed platter, sprinkle over the coriander and season twith salt and pepper.

7 Reheat the wok or frying pan, then pour in the orange juice and simmer for 2 minutes.

8 Drizzle the reduced orange juice over the top of the stir-fried vegetables, sprinkle the top with the pine nuts, and serve immediately.

Mixed Stir-fry with Peanut Sauce

Wherever you go in Asia, stir-fried vegetables will be on the menu.

Ingredients
6 Chinese black mushrooms (dried shiitake), soaked in lukewarm water for 20 minutes
20 tiger lily buds, soaked in lukewarm water for 20 minutes
60ml/4 tbsp sesame oil
225g/8oz tofu, sliced
1 large onion, finely sliced
1 large carrot, finely sliced
300g/11oz pak choi (bok choy), leaves separated from stems
225g/8oz can bamboo shoots, drained and rinsed
50ml/2fl oz/1/4 cup soy sauce
10ml/2 tsp sugar

For the peanut sauce
15ml/1 tbsp sesame oil
2 garlic cloves, finely chopped
2 fresh red chillies, seeded and finely chopped
90g/3 1/2oz/scant 1 cup unsalted roasted peanuts, finely chopped
150ml/5fl oz/2/3 cup coconut milk
30ml/2 tbsp hoisin sauce
15ml/1 tbsp soy sauce
15ml/1 tbsp sugar

Serves 4–6

1 To make the sauce, heat the oil in a wok and stir-fry the garlic and chillies until they begin to colour, then add almost all of the peanuts. Stir-fry for 2–3 minutes, then add the remaining ingredients. Boil, then simmer until thickened. Keep warm.

2 Drain the mushrooms and lily buds and squeeze out any excess water. Cut the mushroom caps into strips and discard the stalks. Trim off the hard ends of the lily buds and tie a knot in the centre of each one.

3 Heat 30ml/2 tbsp of the oil in a wok and brown the tofu on both sides. Drain and cut it into strips.

4 Heat the remaining oil in the wok and stir-fry the onion, carrot and pak choi stems for 2 minutes. Add the mushrooms, lily buds, tofu and bamboo shoots and stir-fry for 1 minute more. Toss in the pak choi leaves, soy sauce and sugar. Stir-fry until heated through. Garnish with the remaining peanuts and serve with the peanut sauce.

mooli, beetroot & carrot Energy 103kcal/427kJ; Protein 2.1g; Carbohydrate 7.8g, of which sugars 7.5g; Fat 7.2g, of which saturates 0.7g; Cholesterol 0mg; Calcium 33mg; Fibre 2.1g; Sodium 31mg.
stir-fry w. peanut sauce Energy 157kcal/656kJ; Protein 5.5g; Carbohydrate 13g, of which sugars 11.4g; Fat 9.6g, of which saturates 2.1g; Cholesterol 0mg; Calcium 110mg; Fibre 5.5g; Sodium 65mg.

Herb & Chilli Aubergines

Plump and juicy aubergines taste sensational steamed until tender and then tossed in a fragrant mint and coriander dressing with crunchy water chestnuts.

Ingredients

500g/1¼lb firm baby aubergines (eggplants)
30ml/2 tbsp vegetable oil
6 garlic cloves, very finely chopped
15ml/1 tbsp fresh root ginger, very finely chopped
8 spring onions (scallions), cut diagonally into 2.5cm/1in lengths
2 fresh red chillies, seeded and thinly sliced
45ml/3 tbsp light soy sauce
15ml/1 tbsp Chinese rice wine
15ml/1 tbsp golden caster (superfine) sugar
a large handful of mint leaves
30–45ml/2–3 tbsp roughly chopped coriander (cilantro) leaves
8 drained canned water chestnuts
50g/2oz/½ cup roasted peanuts, roughly chopped
steamed egg noodles or rice, to serve

Serves 4

1 Cut the aubergines in half lengthways and place them on a heatproof plate. Fit a steamer rack in a wok and add 5cm/2in of water. Bring the water to the boil, lower the plate on to the rack and reduce the heat to low.

2 Cover the plate and steam the aubergines for 25–30 minutes, until they are cooked through. Remove the plate from on top of the steamer and set the aubergines aside to cool.

3 Heat the oil in a clean, dry wok and place over medium heat. When hot, add the garlic, ginger, spring onions and chillies and stir-fry for 2–3 minutes. Remove from the heat and stir in the soy sauce, rice wine and sugar.

4 Add the mint leaves, chopped coriander, water chestnuts and peanuts to the cooled aubergine and toss.

5 Pour the garlic-ginger mixture evenly over the vegetables, toss gently and serve with steamed egg noodles or rice.

Braised Aubergine & Courgettes

Fresh vegetables and red chillies form the basis of a dish that is simple, spicy and looks quite sensational. Serve it as an impressive accompaniment, or with rice or noodles as a main vegetarian meal.

Ingredients

1 aubergine (eggplant), about 350g/12oz
2 small courgettes (zucchini)
15ml/1 tbsp vegetable oil
2 garlic cloves, finely chopped
2 fresh red chillies, seeded and finely chopped
1 small onion, diced
15ml/1 tbsp black bean sauce
15ml/1 tbsp soy sauce
45ml/3 tbsp cold water
salt
chilli flowers (optional), to garnish

Serves 4

1 Trim the aubergine and slice it in half lengthways, then across into 1cm/½in thick slices. Layer the slices in a colander, sprinkling each layer with salt. Leave the aubergine to stand for about 20 minutes.

2 Roll cut the courgettes by slicing off one end diagonally, then rolling the courgette through 180 degrees and taking off another diagonal slice, which will form a triangular wedge. Make more wedges of courgette in the same way.

3 Rinse the aubergine slices well, drain and dry thoroughly on kitchen paper.

4 Heat the oil in a wok or non-stick frying pan. Stir-fry the garlic, chillies and onion with the black bean sauce for a few seconds.

5 Add the aubergine slices and stir-fry for 2 minutes, sprinkling over a little water to prevent them from burning.

6 Stir in the courgettes, soy sauce and measured water. Cook, stirring occasionally, for 5 minutes. Serve hot, garnished with chilli flowers.

herb & chilli aubergines Energy 177kcal/739kJ; Protein 6.2g; Carbohydrate 12.1g, of which sugars 9g; Fat 12g, of which saturates 1.9g; Cholesterol 0mg; Calcium 46mg; Fibre 4.4g; Sodium 823mg.
braised aubergine Energy 66kcal/276kJ; Protein 3g; Carbohydrate 6.1g, of which sugars 4.2g; Fat 3.5g, of which saturates 0.5g; Cholesterol 0mg; Calcium 34mg; Fibre 2.9g; Sodium 270mg

Glazed Pumpkin

Pumpkins, butternut squash and winter melons can all be cooked in this way. Variations of this sweet, mellow dish are often served as an accompaniment to rice or a spicy curry.

Ingredients

200ml/7fl oz/scant 1 cup coconut milk
15ml/1 tbsp fish sauce
30ml/2 tbsp palm sugar (jaggery)
30ml/2 tbsp groundnut (peanut) oil
4 garlic cloves, finely chopped
25g/1oz fresh root ginger, peeled and finely shredded
675g/1½lb pumpkin flesh, cubed
ground black pepper
a handful of curry or basil leaves, to garnish
chilli oil, for drizzling
fried onion rings, to garnish
plain or coconut rice, to serve

Serves 4

1 In a bowl, beat the coconut milk and the fish sauce with the sugar, until it has dissolved. Set aside.

2 Heat the oil in a wok or heavy pan and stir in the garlic and ginger. Stir-fry until they begin to colour, then stir in the pumpkin cubes, mixing well.

3 Pour in the coconut milk and mix well. Reduce the heat, cover and simmer for about 20 minutes, until the pumpkin is tender and the sauce has reduced. Season with pepper and garnish with curry or basil leaves and fried onion rings. Serve hot with plain or coconut rice, drizzled with a little chilli oil.

Cook's Tip

For a quick coconut rice, rinse 350g/12oz/1¾ cups Thai fragrant rice and put in a pan with 400ml/14 fl oz/1¾ cups coconut milk, 2.5ml/½ tsp ground coriander, a cinnamon stick, a bruised lemon grass stalk and a bay leaf. Add salt to taste. Bring to the boil, cover and simmer for 8–10 minutes, or until the liquid has been absorbed. Fork through lightly, remove the solid spices and serve.

Sweet Pumpkin & Peanut Curry

A hearty, soothing curry perfect for autumn or winter evenings. Its cheerful colour alone will raise the spirits – and the combination of pumpkin and peanuts tastes great.

Ingredients

30ml/2 tbsp vegetable oil
4 garlic cloves, crushed
4 shallots, finely chopped
30ml/2 tbsp yellow curry paste
600ml/1 pint/2½ cups vegetable stock
2 kaffir lime leaves, torn
15ml/1 tbsp chopped fresh galangal
450g/1lb pumpkin, peeled, seeded and diced
225g/8oz sweet potatoes, diced
90g/3½oz/scant 1 cup unsalted, roasted peanuts, chopped
300ml/½ pint/1¼ cups coconut milk
90g/3 1/2oz/1½ cups chestnut mushrooms, sliced
30ml/2 tbsp soy sauce
50g/2oz/⅓ cup pumpkin seeds, toasted, and fresh green chilli flowers, to garnish

Serves 4

1 Heat the oil in a wok. Add the garlic and shallots and cook over a medium heat, stirring occasionally, for 10 minutes, until softened and golden. Do not let them burn.

2 Add the yellow curry paste and stir-fry over medium heat for 30 seconds, until fragrant, then add the stock, lime leaves, galangal, pumpkin and sweet potatoes. Bring to the boil, stirring frequently, then simmer gently for 15 minutes.

3 Add the peanuts, coconut milk and mushrooms. Stir in the soy sauce and simmer for 5 minutes more. Spoon into bowls, garnish with the pumpkin seeds and chillies and serve.

Cook's Tip

The well-drained vegetables from any of these curries would make a very tasty filling for a pastry or pie. This may not be a Thai tradition, but it is a good example of fusion food.

glazed pumpkin Energy 114kcal/477kJ; Protein 1.5g; Carbohydrate 14.3g, of which sugars 13.4g; Fat 6g, of which saturates 0.9g; Cholesterol 0mg; Calcium 68mg; Fibre 1.7g; Sodium 323mg.
pumpkin & peanut Energy 306kcal/1279kJ; Protein 9.6g; Carbohydrate 24.5g, of which sugars 11.4g; Fat 19.6g, of which saturates 3.3g; Cholesterol 0mg; Calcium 160mg; Fibre 6.4g; Sodium 409mg.

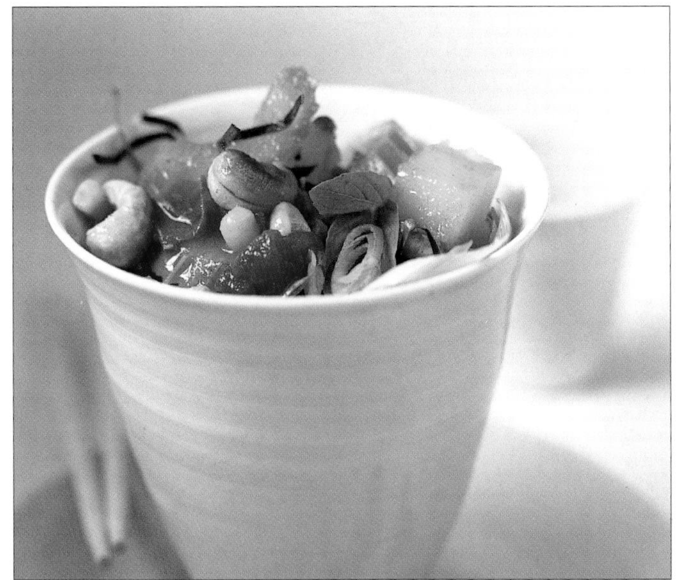

Corn & Cashew Nut Curry

This is a substantial curry, thanks largely to the potatoes and corn kernels, which makes it a great winter dish. It is deliciously aromatic, but, as the spices are added in relatively small amounts, the resulting flavour is fairly mild.

Ingredients

30ml/2 tbsp vegetable oil
4 shallots, chopped
90g/3½oz/scant 1 cup cashew nuts
5ml/1 tsp red curry paste
400g/14oz potatoes, peeled and cut into chunks
1 lemon grass stalk, finely chopped
200g/7oz can chopped tomatoes
600ml/1 pint/2½ cups boiling water
200g/7oz/generous 1 cup drained canned whole kernel corn
4 celery sticks, sliced
2 kaffir lime leaves, central rib removed, rolled into cylinders and thinly sliced
15ml/1 tbsp tomato ketchup
15ml/1 tbsp light soy sauce
5ml/1 tsp palm sugar (jaggery) or light muscovado (brown) sugar
4 spring onions (scallions), thinly sliced
small bunch fresh basil, chopped

Serves 4

1 Heat the oil in a wok. Add the shallots and stir-fry over a medium heat for 2–3 minutes, until softened. Add the cashew nuts and stir-fry for a few minutes until they are golden.

2 Stir in the red curry paste. Stir-fry for 1 minute, then add the potatoes, lemon grass, tomatoes and boiling water.

3 Bring back to the boil, then reduce the heat to low, cover and simmer gently for 15–20 minutes, or until the potatoes are tender when tested with the tip of a knife.

4 Stir the corn, celery, lime leaves, ketchup, soy sauce, sugar and spring onions into the wok. Simmer for a further 5 minutes, until heated through, then spoon into warmed serving bowls.

5 Sprinkle with the sliced spring onions and basil and serve.

Mushrooms with Loofah Squash

Winter gourds, such as pumpkins, bitter melons, loofah squash and a variety of other squash that come under the kabocha umbrella, are popular ingredients for soups and braised vegetable dishes. Any of these vegetables can be used for this side dish, but loofah squash – also known as ridged gourd – is easy to work with and is available in most Asian markets. It resembles a long courgette, usually lighter in colour and with ridges from one end to the other.

Ingredients

750g/1lb 10oz loofah squash, peeled
30ml/2 tbsp groundnut (peanut) or sesame oil
2 shallots, halved and sliced
2 garlic cloves, finely chopped
115g/4oz/1½ cups button (white) mushrooms, quartered
15ml/1 tbsp mushroom sauce
10ml/2 tsp soy sauce
4 spring onions (scallions), cut into 2cm/¾in pieces
fresh coriander (cilantro) leaves and thin strips of spring onion (scallion), to garnish

Serves 4

1 Using a sharp knife, cut the loofah squash diagonally into 2cm/¾in-thick pieces and set aside.

2 Heat the oil in a large wok or heavy pan. Stir in the halved shallots and garlic, stir-fry until they begin to colour and turn golden, then add the mushrooms.

3 Add the mushroom and soy sauces, and the squash. Reduce the heat, cover and cook gently for a few minutes until the squash is tender. Just before serving, stir in the spring onion pieces and allow to warm through. Spoon into warmed serving bowls and garnish with the coriander and spring onion strips.

Cook's Tip

Choose a mushroom sauce suitable for vegetarians. Some contain anchovies, so check the label. Mushroom seasoning is usually a safe bet.

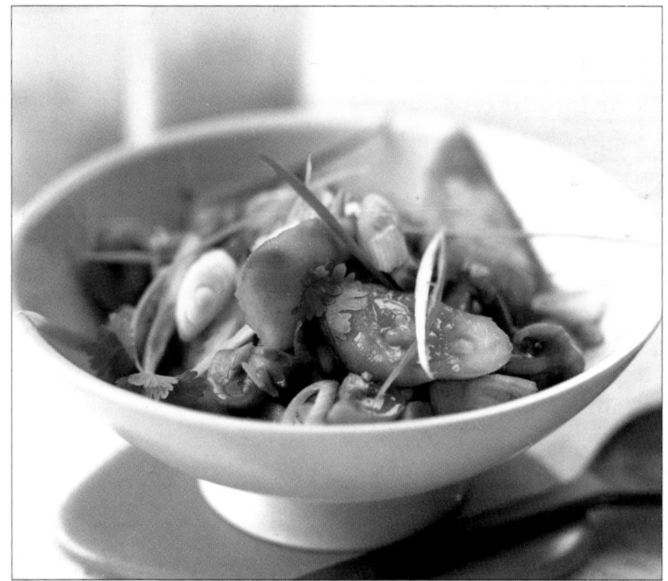

corn & cashew nut Energy 298kcal/1245kJ; Protein 8.8g; Carbohydrate 27.6g, of which sugars 8.9g; Fat 17.7g, of which saturates 3.1g; Cholesterol 0mg; Calcium 33mg; Fibre 3.5g; Sodium 981mg.
mushrooms w. luffa squash Energy 89kcal/371kJ; Protein 2.3g; Carbohydrate 6.7g, of which sugars 5.2g; Fat 6.1g, of which saturates 0.9g; Cholesterol 0mg; Calcium 65mg; Fibre 2.6g; Sodium 221mg.

Tofu with Four Mushrooms

Four different kinds of mushrooms combine beautifully with tofu in this sophisticated and substantial recipe.

Ingredients

350g/12oz firm tofu
2.5ml/½ tsp sesame oil
10ml/2 tsp light soy sauce
15ml/1 tbsp vegetable oil
2 garlic cloves, finely chopped
2.5ml/½ tsp grated fresh root ginger
115g/4oz/scant 2 cups fresh shiitake mushrooms, stalks removed
175g/6oz/scant 2 cups fresh oyster mushrooms
115g/4oz/scant 2 cups canned straw mushrooms, drained
115g/4oz/scant 2 cups button (white) mushrooms, halved
15ml/1 tbsp dry sherry
15ml/1 tbsp dark soy sauce
90ml/6 tbsp vegetable stock
5ml/1 tsp cornflour (cornstarch)
15ml/1 tbsp cold water
ground white pepper
salt
2 shredded spring onions (scallions), to garnish

Serves 4

1 Put the tofu in a dish. Sprinkle with the sesame oil, light soy sauce and a large pinch of pepper. Marinate for 10 minutes, then drain and cut into 2.5 x 1cm/1 x ½in pieces.

2 Heat the vegetable oil in a large non-stick frying pan or wok. Add the garlic and ginger and stir-fry for a few seconds. Add all the mushrooms and stir-fry for a further 2 minutes.

3 Stir in the dry sherry, dark soy sauce and stock. Season to taste. Lower the heat and simmer gently for 4 minutes.

4 Place the cornflour in a bowl with the water. Mix to make a smooth paste. Stir the cornflour mixture into the pan or wok and cook, stirring constantly to prevent lumps, until thickened.

5 Carefully add the pieces of tofu, toss gently to coat thoroughly in the sauce and simmer for 2 minutes.

6 Sprinkle the shredded spring onions over the top of the mixture to garnish and serve immediately.

Tofu with Lemon Grass & Basil

In parts of Asia, aromatic pepper leaves are used as the herb element in this dish but, because these can be difficult to track down, you can use basil leaves instead. For the best results, leave the tofu to marinate for the full hour. This very tasty dish is a wonderful way to cook tofu.

Ingredients

3 lemon grass stalks, finely chopped
45ml/3 tbsp soy sauce
2 fresh red Serrano chillies, seeded and finely chopped
2 garlic cloves, crushed
5ml/1 tsp ground turmeric
10ml/2 tsp sugar
300g/11oz tofu, rinsed, drained, patted dry and cut into bitesize cubes
30ml/2 tbsp groundnut (peanut) oil
45ml/3 tbsp roasted peanuts, chopped
1 bunch fresh basil, stalks removed
salt

Serves 3–4

1 In a bowl, mix together the lemon grass, soy sauce, chillies, garlic, turmeric and sugar until the sugar has dissolved. Add a little salt to taste and add the tofu, making sure it is well coated. Leave to marinate for 1 hour.

2 Heat a wok or heavy pan. Pour in the oil, add the marinated tofu, and cook, stirring frequently, until it is golden brown on all sides. Add the peanuts and most of the basil leaves and stir-fry quickly so that the basil becomes aromatic without wilting.

3 Divide the tofu among individual serving dishes, sprinkle the remaining basil leaves over the top and serve hot or at room temperature.

Variation
Lime, coriander (cilantro) or curry leaves would work well in this simple stir-fry.

tofu w. four mushrooms Energy 118kcal/491kJ; Protein 9.3g; Carbohydrate 2.9g, of which sugars 1.1g; Fat 7.4g, of which saturates 0.9g; Cholesterol 0mg; Calcium 456mg; Fibre 1.2g; Sodium 455mg.
tofu w. lemon grass Energy 115kcal/480kJ; Protein 7.4g; Carbohydrate 4.5g, of which sugars 3.9g; Fat 7.6g, of which saturates 1g; Cholesterol 0mg; Calcium 388mg; Fibre 0.2g; Sodium 804mg.

Crisp-fried Tofu in Tomato Sauce

This is a light, tasty tofu-based dish. Soy sauce is used here, but fish sauce can be substituted for those who eat fish. You can use a combination of vegetable and peanut oils if you want the nutty taste without fear of burning.

Ingredients

vegetable or groundnut (peanut) oil, for deep-frying
450g/1lb firm tofu, rinsed and cut into bitesize cubes
4 shallots, finely sliced
1 fresh red chilli, seeded and chopped
25g/1oz fresh root ginger, peeled and finely chopped
4 garlic cloves, finely chopped
6 large ripe tomatoes, peeled, seeded and finely chopped
15–30ml/1–2 tbsp light soy sauce
10ml/2 tsp sugar
mint leaves and strips of fresh red chilli, to garnish
ground black pepper

Serves 4

1 Heat enough oil for deep-frying in a wok or heavy pan. Fry the tofu, in batches, until crisp and golden. Remove with a slotted spoon and drain on kitchen paper.

2 Reserve 30ml/2 tbsp oil in the wok. Add the shallots, chilli, ginger and garlic and stir-fry until fragrant. Stir in the tomatoes, soy sauce and sugar. Reduce the heat and simmer the mixture for 10–15 minutes until it resembles a sauce. Stir in 105ml/7 tbsp water and bring to the boil.

3 Season with a little pepper and return the tofu to the pan. Mix well and simmer gently for 2–3 minutes to heat through. Spoon into heated bowls, garnish with mint leaves and chilli strips and serve immediately.

Cook's Tip

This recipe is delicious as a side dish or as a main dish with noodles or rice. It is nutritious too, thanks to the tofu, which is an excellent vegetable protein, free from cholesterol.

Tofu & Broccoli with Fried Shallots

This meltingly tender tofu flavoured with spices and served with broccoli makes a perfect lunch. To give the recipe that little bit extra, deep-fry some crispy shallots to serve on the side, if you like.

Ingredients

500g/1¼lb block of firm tofu, drained
45ml/3 tbsp kecap manis
30ml/2 tbsp sweet chilli sauce
45ml/3 tbsp soy sauce
5ml/1 tsp sesame oil
5ml/1 tsp finely grated fresh root ginger
400g/14oz tenderstem broccoli, halved lengthways
45ml/3 tbsp roughly chopped coriander (cilantro), and 30ml/2 tbsp toasted sesame seeds, to garnish

Serves 4

1 Make the crispy shallots. Add the shallot rings to a wok one-third full of hot oil, then lower the heat and stir constantly until crisp. Lift out and spread on kitchen paper to drain.

2 Cut the tofu into 4 triangular pieces: slice the block in half widthways, then diagonally. Place in a heatproof dish.

3 In a small bowl, combine the kecap manis, chilli sauce, soy sauce, sesame oil and ginger, then pour over the tofu. Leave the tofu to marinate for at least 30 minutes, turning occasionally.

4 Place the broccoli on a heatproof plate and place on a trivet or steamer rack in the wok. Cover and steam for 4–5 minutes, until just tender. Remove and keep warm.

5 Place the dish of tofu on the trivet or steamer rack in the wok, cover and steam for 4–5 minutes. Divide the broccoli among four warmed serving plates and top each one with a triangle of tofu.

6 Spoon the remaining juices over the tofu and broccoli, then sprinkle with the coriander and toasted sesame seeds. Serve immediately with steamed white rice or noodles.

tofu in tomato sauce Energy 234kcal/974kJ; Protein 11g; Carbohydrate 11.1g, of which sugars 10.1g; Fat 16.5g, of which saturates 2g; Cholesterol 0mg; Calcium 619mg; Fibre 2.7g; Sodium 25mg.
tofu/broccoli w. shallots Energy 202kcal/840kJ; Protein 16.5g; Carbohydrate 6.9g, of which sugars 5.6g; Fat 12.1g, of which saturates 1.7g; Cholesterol 0mg; Calcium 750mg; Fibre 3.5g; Sodium 938mg.

Stir-fried Crispy Tofu

The asparagus grown in the part of Asia where this recipe originated tends to have slender stalks. Look for it in Thai markets or substitute the thin asparagus popularly known as sprue.

Ingredients

250g/9oz fried tofu cubes
30ml/2 tbsp groundnut (peanut) oil
15ml/1 tbsp green curry paste
30ml/2 tbsp light soy sauce
2 kaffir lime leaves, rolled into cylinders and thinly sliced
30ml/2 tbsp sugar
150ml/¼ pint/⅔ cup vegetable stock
250g/9oz Asian asparagus, trimmed and sliced into 5cm/2in lengths
30ml/2 tbsp roasted peanuts, finely chopped

Serves 2

1 Preheat the grill (broiler) to medium. Place the tofu cubes in a grill pan and grill (broil) for 2–3 minutes, then turn them over and continue to cook until they are crisp and golden brown all over. Watch them carefully; they must not be allowed to burn.

2 Heat the oil in a wok or heavy frying pan. Add the green curry paste and cook over a medium heat, stirring constantly, for 1–2 minutes, until it gives off its aroma.

3 Stir the soy sauce, lime leaves, sugar and vegetable stock into the wok or pan and mix well. Bring to the boil, then reduce the heat to low so that the mixture is just simmering.

4 Add the asparagus and simmer gently for 5 minutes. Meanwhile, chop each piece of tofu into four, then add to the pan with the peanuts.

5 Toss to coat all the ingredients in the sauce, then spoon into a warmed dish and serve immediately.

Variation
Substitute slim carrot sticks or broccoli florets for the asparagus.

Sweet-and-Sour Vegetables with Tofu

Big, bold and beautiful, this is a hearty stir-fry that will satisfy the hungriest guests.

Ingredients

4 shallots
3 garlic cloves
30ml/2 tbsp groundnut (peanut) oil
250g/9oz Chinese leaves (Chinese cabbage), shredded
8 baby corn cobs, sliced diagonally
2 red (bell) peppers, seeded and thinly sliced
200g/7oz/1¾ cups mangetouts (snow peas), trimmed and sliced
250g/9oz firm tofu, rinsed, drained and cut in 1cm/½in cubes
60ml/4 tbsp vegetable stock
30ml/2 tbsp light soy sauce
15ml/1 tbsp sugar
30ml/2 tbsp rice vinegar
2.5ml/½ tsp dried chilli flakes
small bunch of fresh coriander (cilantro), chopped

Serves 4

1 Slice the shallots thinly using a sharp knife. Finely chop the garlic cloves.

2 Heat the oil in a wok or large frying pan and cook the shallots and garlic for 2–3 minutes over a medium heat, until golden. Do not let the garlic burn or it will taste bitter.

3 Add the shredded Chinese leaves, toss over the heat for 30 seconds, then add the sliced baby-corn cobs and repeat the process.

4 Add the red peppers, mangetouts and tofu in the same way as the leaves and baby-corn, each time adding a single ingredient and tossing it over the heat for about 30 seconds before adding the next ingredient.

5 Pour in the stock and soy sauce. Mix together the sugar and vinegar in a small bowl, stirring until the sugar has dissolved, then add to the wok or pan.

6 Tip the mixture into a warmed bowl, sprinkle over the chilli flakes and coriander, toss to mix well and serve.

crispy tofu Energy 287kcal/1195kJ; Protein 14.3g; Carbohydrate 20.3g, of which sugars 19.5g; Fat 17g, of which saturates 2.1g; Cholesterol 0mg; Calcium 682mg; Fibre 2.1g; Sodium 1075mg.
sweet-&-sour veg. Energy 144kcal/604kJ; Protein 5.2g; Carbohydrate 23.7g, of which sugars 18.2g; Fat 3.7g, of which saturates 0.5g; Cholesterol 0mg; Calcium 73mg; Fibre 4.7g; Sodium 611mg.

Spring Vegetable Stir-fry

Fast, fresh and packed with healthy vegetables, this stir-fry is delicious served with marinated tofu and rice or noodles. This recipe contains very little saturated fat, so scores highly with slimmers, but has sufficient bulk to ward off hunger. Ideal as a quick supper on the go.

Ingredients

2 spring onions (scallions)
175g/6oz spring greens or collard greens
15ml/1 tbsp vegetable oil
5ml/1 tsp toasted sesame oil
1 garlic clove, chopped
2.5cm/1in piece fresh root ginger, finely chopped
225g/8oz baby carrots
350g/12oz broccoli florets
175g/6oz asparagus tips
30ml/2 tbsp light soy sauce
15ml/1 tbsp apple juice
15ml/1 tbsp sesame seeds, toasted

Serves 4

1 Trim the spring onions and cut them diagonally into thin slices, using a sharp knife.

2 Wash the spring greens or collard greens and drain in a colander, then blot with kitchen paper and shred finely.

3 Heat a frying pan or wok over high heat. Add the vegetable oil and the sesame oil, and reduce the heat. Add the garlic and sauté for 2 minutes. Do not let the garlic burn or it will gain a bitter taste.

4 Add the chopped ginger, carrots, broccoli and asparagus tips to the pan and stir-fry for 4 minutes.

5 Add the spring onions and spring greens or collard greens and stir-fry for a further 2 minutes.

6 Add the soy sauce and apple juice and cook for 1–2 minutes until the vegetables are tender. If they appear too dry, simply add a little water to soften them up. Tip the mixture into warmed serviing bowls or four individual dishes, sprinkle the sesame seeds on top and serve.

Mixed Vegetables Monk-style

Chinese monks eat neither meat nor fish, so "Monk-style" dishes are fine for vegetarians.

Ingredients

50g/2 oz dried tofu sticks
115g/4oz fresh lotus root, peeled and sliced
10g/¼oz dried cloud ear (wood ear) mushrooms
8 dried Chinese mushrooms
15ml/1 tbsp vegetable oil
75g/3oz/¾ cup drained, canned straw mushrooms
115g/4oz/1 cup baby corn cobs, cut in half
30ml/2 tbsp light soy sauce
15ml/1 tbsp sake or dry sherry
10ml/2 tsp sugar
150ml/¼ pint/⅔ cup vegetable stock
75g/3oz/¾ cup mangetouts (snow peas)
5ml/1 tsp cornflour (cornstarch)
15ml/1 tbsp cold water
salt

Serves 4

1 Put the tofu sticks in a bowl. Cover them with hot water and leave to soak for 1 hour. The wood ears and dried Chinese mushrooms should be soaked in separate bowls of hot water for 20 minutes.

2 Drain the wood ears, trim off and discard the hard base from each and cut the rest into bitesize pieces. Drain the mushrooms, trim off and discard the stems and slice the caps.

3 Drain the tofu sticks. Cut them into 5cm/2in long pieces, discarding any hard pieces.

4 Heat the oil in a wok and stir-fry the wood ears, Chinese mushrooms and lotus root for about 30 seconds. Add the tofu, straw mushrooms, baby corn cobs, soy sauce, sherry, sugar and stock. Boil, then simmer, covered for 20 minutes.

5 Trim the mangetouts and cut them in half. Add to the vegetable mixture, with salt to taste, and cook, uncovered, for 2 minutes more. Mix the cornflour to a paste with the water and add to the wok. Cook, stirring, until the sauce thickens. Serve immediately.

spring vegetable stir-fry Energy 134kcal/554kJ; Protein 7.8g; Carbohydrate 9.4g, of which sugars 8.6g; Fat 7.4g, of which saturates 1.1g; Cholesterol 0mg; Calcium 195mg; Fibre 6.2g; Sodium 566mg.
mixed veg. monk-style Energy 95kcal/399kJ; Protein 3.3g; Carbohydrate 12g, of which sugars 4.6g; Fat 3.6g, of which saturates 0.4g; Cholesterol 0mg; Calcium 91mg; Fibre 1.4g; Sodium 885mg.

Crisp Deep-fried Vegetables

Stir-fried, steamed or deep-fried vegetables served with a dipping sauce are common fare throughout Asia, and often appear among the delightful "no-name" dishes popular in Thai tourist fare.

Ingredients

6 eggs
1 long aubergine (eggplant), peeled, halved lengthways and sliced into half moons
1 long sweet potato, peeled and sliced into rounds
1 small butternut squash, peeled, seeded, halved lengthways and cut into half moons
salt and ground black pepper
vegetable oil, for deep-frying
chilli sambal or hot chilli sauce for dipping

Serves 4–6

1 Beat the eggs in a wide bowl. Season with salt and pepper. Toss the vegetables in the egg to coat thoroughly.

2 Heat enough oil for deep-frying in a large wok. Cook the vegetables in small batches, making sure there is plenty of egg coating each piece.

3 When they turn golden, lift them out of the oil with a slotted spoon and drain on kitchen paper.

4 Keep the vegetables hot while successive batches are being fried. Serve warm with chilli sambal, hot chilli sauce or a dipping sauce of your choice.

Cook's Tips

- *To encourage the beaten egg coating to adhere to the pieces of aubergine (eggplant) sweet potatoes and butternut squash, toss them in flour or cornflour (cornstarch) first.*
- *Courgettes (zucchini), angled loofah, taro root or pumpkin could also be used.*

Asian-style Courgette Fritters

This is an excellent cultural fusion: a twist on Japanese tempura, using Indian spices and gram flour in the batter. Also known as besan, gram flour is more commonly used in Indian cooking and gives a wonderfully crisp texture, while the courgette baton inside becomes meltingly tender. If you're feeling adventurous, vary the vegetable content by dipping some thinly sliced squash or pumpkin batons with the courgettes. This is an ideal treat for kids.

Ingredients

90g/3½oz/¾ cup gram flour
5ml/1 tsp baking powder
2.5ml/½ tsp ground turmeric
10ml/2 tsp ground coriander
5ml/1 tsp ground cumin
5ml/1 tsp chilli powder
250ml/8fl oz/1 cup beer
600g/1lb 6oz courgettes (zucchini), cut into batons
sunflower oil, for deep-frying
salt
steamed basmati rice, natural (plain) yogurt and pickles, to serve

Serves 4

1 Sift the gram flour, baking powder, turmeric, coriander, cumin and chilli powder into a large bowl. Stir lightly to mix through.

2 Season the mixture with salt and make a hollow in the centre. Pour in a little of the beer, and gradually mix in the surrounding dry ingredients. Add more beer, continuing to mix gently, to make a thick batter. Be careful not to overmix.

3 Fill a large wok, one-third full with sunflower oil and heat to 180°C/350°F or until a cube of bread, dropped into the oil, browns in 45 seconds.

4 Working in batches, dip the courgette batons in the spiced batter and then deep-fry for 1–2 minutes, or until crisp and golden. Lift out of the wok using a slotted spoon. Drain on kitchen paper and keep warm.

5 Serve the courgette fritters on heated plates, or on banana leaves if these are available, with steamed basmati rice, yogurt and pickles.

deep-fried vegetables Energy 280kcal/1164kJ; Protein 8.3g; Carbohydrate 11.9g, of which sugars 5.7g; Fat 22.7g, of which saturates 3.7g; Cholesterol 190mg; Calcium 90mg; Fibre 3.5g; Sodium 84mg.
asian-style fritters Energy 241kcal/999kJ; Protein 7.3g; Carbohydrate 15.3g, of which sugars 4.6g; Fat 15.6g, of which saturates 1.9g; Cholesterol 0mg; Calcium 83mg; Fibre 3.8g; Sodium 15mg.

Seven-spice Aubergines

Seven spice powder is the key ingredient that gives these aubergines a lovely warm flavour, and so well with the light, curry batter.

Ingredients

2 egg whites
90ml/6 tbsp cornflour (cornstarch)
5ml/1 tsp salt
15ml/1 tbsp Thai or Chinese seven-spice powder
15ml/1 tbsp mild chilli powder
500g/1¼lb aubergines (eggplant), thinly sliced
sunflower oil, for deep-frying
fresh mint leaves, to garnish
steamed rice or noodles and hot chilli sauce, to serve

Serves 4

1 Put the egg whites in a large greasefree bowl and beat with an electric whisk until light and foamy, but not dry.

2 Combine the cornflour, salt, seven-spice powder and chilli powder and spread evenly on to a large plate.

3 Fill a wok one-third full of oil and heat to 180°C/350°F or until a cube of day-old bread, dropped into the oil, browns in 40 seconds.

4 Dip the aubergine slices in the egg white and then into the spiced flour mixture to coat. Deep-fry in batches for 3–4 minutes, or until crisp and golden. Drain on kitchen paper and transfer to a platter to keep hot.

5 Serve the aubergine garnished with mint leaves and with hot chilli sauce on the side for dipping.

Cook's Tip

Seven-spice powder is a commercial blend of spices, usually comprising coriander, cumin, cinnamon, star anise, chillli, cloves and lemon peel.

Fried Vegetables with Chilli Sauce

A wok makes the ideal pan for frying slices of aubergine, butternut squash and courgette because they become beautifully tender and succulent. The beaten egg in this recipe gives a satisfyingly substantial batter.

Ingredients

3 large (US extra large) eggs
1 aubergine (eggplant), halved lengthways and cut into long, thin slices
½ small butternut squash, peeled, seeded and cut into long, thin slices
2 courgettes (zucchini), trimmed and cut into long, thin slices
105ml/7 tbsp vegetable or sunflower oil
salt and ground black pepper
sweet chilli sauce, or a dip of your own choice, to serve (see below for suggestion)

Serves 4

1 Beat the eggs in a large bowl. Season the egg mixture with salt and pepper. Add the slices of aubergine, butternut squash and courgette. Toss the vegetables slices until they are coated all over in the egg.

2 Have a warmed dish ready lined with kitchen paper. Heat the oil in a wok. When it is hot, add the vegetables, one strip at a time, making sure that each strip has plenty of egg clinging to it.

3 Do not cook more than eight strips of vegetable at a time or the oil will cool down too much.

4 As each strip turns golden and is cooked, lift it out, using a wire basket or slotted spoon, and transfer to the plate. Keep hot while cooking the remaining vegetables. Serve with the sweet chilli sauce as a dip.

Variation

Instead of sweet chilli sauce, try a simple mix of mango chutney and chilli dip. The spicy fruity flavour goes particularly well with the butternut squash.

seven-spice aubergines Energy 203kcal/850kJ; Protein 2.7g; Carbohydrate 23.5g, of which sugars 2.5g; Fat 11.7g, of which saturates 1.4g; Cholesterol 0mg; Calcium 17mg; Fibre 2.5g; Sodium 45mg.
vegetables w. chilli sauce Energy 113kcal/468kJ; Protein 5.2g; Carbohydrate 3.6g, of which sugars 3.1g; Fat 8.8g, of which saturates 1.6g; Cholesterol 95mg; Calcium 56mg; Fibre 2g; Sodium 36mg.

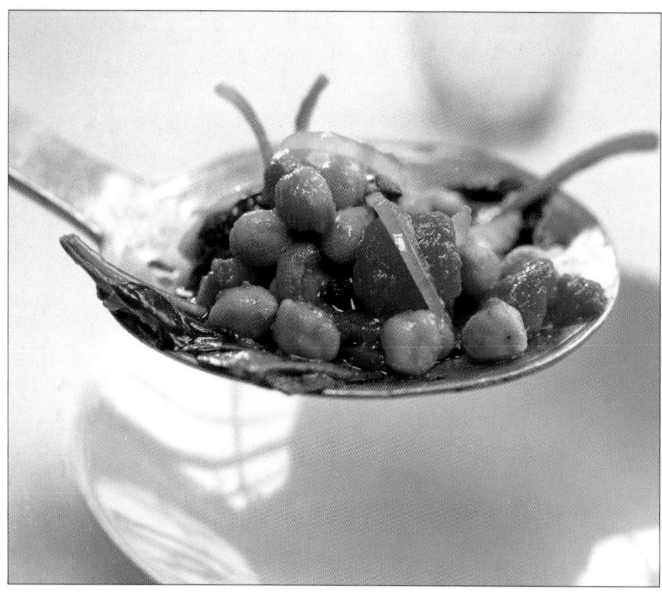

Spinach with Spicy Chickpeas

This richly flavoured dish makes an excellent accompaniment to a dry curry, or with a rice-based stir fry. It is particularly good served drizzled with a little plain yogurt – the sharp, creamy flavour complements the complex spices perfectly.

Ingredients

200g/7oz dried chickpeas
30ml/2 tbsp sunflower oil
2 onions, halved and thinly sliced
10ml/2 tsp ground coriander
10ml/2 tsp ground cumin
5ml/1 tsp hot chilli powder
2.5ml/½ tsp ground turmeric
15ml/1 tbsp medium curry powder
400g/14oz can chopped tomatoes
5ml/1 tsp caster (superfine) sugar
salt and ground black pepper
30ml/2 tbsp chopped mint leaves
115g/4oz baby leaf spinach
steamed rice or bread, to serve

Serves 4

1 Soak the chickpeas in cold water overnight. Drain, rinse and place in a large pan. Cover with water and bring to the boil. Reduce the heat and simmer for 45 minutes to 1¼ hours, or until just tender. Drain and set aside.

2 Heat the oil in a wok, add the onions and cook over a low heat for 15 minutes, until lightly golden.

3 Add the ground coriander and cumin, chilli powder, turmeric and curry powder to the onions in the wok and stir-fry for 1–2 minutes.

4 Add the tomatoes, sugar and 105ml/7 tbsp water to the wok and bring to the boil. Cover, reduce the heat and simmer gently for 15 minutes, stirring occasionally.

5 Add the chickpeas to the wok, season well and cook gently for 8–10 minutes. Stir in the chopped mint.

6 Divide the spinach leaves between shallow bowls, top with the chickpea mixture and serve with some steamed rice or chunks of bread.

Cabbage in Coconut Milk

The idea of cooking cabbage in coconut milk comes from Melaka and Johor, where the culinary culture is influenced by the Chinese, Malay, and Peranakans. With good agricultural ground, there is an abundance of vegetables which, in this part of Malaysia, are often cooked in coconut milk. For this dish, you could use green beans, curly kale, or any type of cabbage, all of which are delicious served with steamed, braised or grilled fish dishes.

Ingredients

4 shallots, chopped
2 garlic cloves, chopped
1 lemon grass stalk, trimmed and chopped
25g/1oz fresh root ginger, peeled and chopped
2 red chillies, seeded and chopped
5ml/1 tsp shrimp paste
5ml/1 tsp turmeric powder
5ml/1 tsp palm sugar (jaggery)
15ml/1 tbsp sesame or groundnut (peanut) oil
400ml/14fl oz/1⅔ cups coconut milk
450g/1lb Chinese leaves (Chinese cabbage) or kale, cut into thick ribbons, or pak choi (bok choy), separated into leaves, or a mixture of the two
salt and ground black pepper

Serves 4

1 Using a mortar and pestle or food processor, grind the shallots, garlic, lemon grass, ginger and chillies to a paste. Scrape into a bowl and add the shrimp paste, turmeric and sugar. Beat well to combine the ingredients.

2 Heat the oil in a wok or heavy pan, and stir in the spice paste. Cook until fragrant and beginning to colour.

3 Pour in the coconut milk, mix well, and let it bubble it up to thicken.

4 Drop in the cabbage leaves, coating them in the coconut milk, and cook for a minute or two until wilted.

5 Season with salt and pepper to taste, spoon into a warmed serving dish and serve immediately.

spinach w. chickpeas Energy 267kcal/1122kJ; Protein 13.3g; Carbohydrate 35.5g, of which sugars 10.2g; Fat 9g, of which saturates 1.1g; Cholesterol 0mg; Calcium 170mg; Fibre 8.2g; Sodium 83mg.
cabbage/coconut Energy 112kcal/469kJ; Protein 2.1g; Carbohydrate 13g, of which sugars 12.6g; Fat 6.1g, of which saturates 1g; Cholesterol 0mg; Calcium 89mg; Fibre 2.6g; Sodium 119mg.

Stir-fried Asparagus with Chillies

Asparagus is one of those vegetables that is still at its best when in season. It tastes best when freshly lifted and cut and is so delicious that it is inevitably snapped up during the brief period when it is available. This is a particularly delightful and simple way of cooking it.

Ingredients

30ml/2 tbsp groundnut (peanut) oil
2 garlic cloves, finely chopped
2 fresh red chillies, seeded and finely chopped
25g/1oz fresh galangal or root ginger, finely shredded
1 lemon grass stalk, trimmed and finely sliced
350g/12oz fresh asparagus spears, trimmed
30ml/2 tbsp fish sauce
30ml/2 tbsp soy sauce
5ml/1 tsp sugar
30ml/2 tbsp unsalted roasted peanuts, finely chopped
1 small bunch fresh coriander (cilantro), finely chopped

Serves 2–4

1 Heat a large wok and add the oil. Stir in the garlic, chillies, galangal or ginger and lemon grass and stir-fry until the ingredients become fragrant and begin to turn golden.

2 Add the asparagus and stir-fry for a further 1–2 minutes, until it is just tender but not too soft.

3 Stir in the fish sauce, soy sauce and sugar. Spoon on to a serving plates, sprinkle with the peanuts and coriander and serve immediately.

Variations

• *This recipe also works well with broccoli, green beans, baby leeks or courgettes (zucchini), cut into strips when the asparagus is not at its best. You may lose a little in bulk if using smaller vegetables, so a medley of all four would work well.*

• *For a touch of sweetness, add a little sweet chilli sauce with the fish sauce when making the dressing for the asparagus.*

Sautéed Green Beans

The smoky flavour of the dried shrimps used in this recipe adds an extra dimension to green beans cooked in this way.

Ingredients

450g/1lb green beans
15ml/1 tbsp vegetable oil
3 garlic cloves, finely chopped
5 spring onions (scallions), cut into 2.5cm/1in lengths
25g/1oz dried shrimps, soaked in warm water and drained
15ml/1 tbsp light soy sauce
salt

Serves 4

1 Trim the green beans. Cut each green bean in half.

2 Bring a pan of lightly salted water to the boil and cook the beans for 3–4 minutes until tender but still crisp. Drain, refresh under cold water and drain again.

3 Heat the oil in a non-stick frying pan or wok until very hot. Stir-fry the garlic and spring onions for 30 seconds, then add the shrimps. Mix lightly.

4 Add the green beans and soy sauce. Toss the mixture over the heat until the beans are hot. Serve immediately.

Variation

For more colour and a contrast in texture, stir-fry sliced red, yellow or orange (bell) peppers in the wok and cook for a few minutes until just tender but still crunch. Add the garlic and spring onions and proceed as above.

Cook's Tip

Don't be tempted to use too many dried shrimps. Their flavour is very strong and could overwhelm the more delicate taste of the green beans.

stir-fried asparagus Energy 79kcal/327kJ; Protein 4g; Carbohydrate 4.9g, of which sugars 4.5g; Fat 4.9g, of which saturates 0.7g; Cholesterol 0mg; Calcium 53mg; Fibre 2.5g; Sodium 540mg.
sautéed green beans Energy 62kcal/254kJ; Protein 2.4g; Carbohydrate 4.2g, of which sugars 3.1g; Fat 4.1g, of which saturates 0.6g; Cholesterol 0mg; Calcium 42mg; Fibre 2.5g; Sodium 534mg.

Stir-fried Chinese Leaves

This simple way of cooking Chinese leaves preserves their delicate flavour and is very quick to prepare.

Ingredients

675g/1½lb Chinese leaves (Chinese cabbage)
15ml/1 tbsp vegetable oil
2 garlic cloves, finely chopped
2.5 m/1in piece of fresh root ginger, finely chopped
2.5ml/½ tsp salt
15ml/1 tbsp oyster sauce
4 spring onions (scallions), cut into 2.5cm/1in lengths

Serves 4

1 Stack the Chinese leaves together and cut them into 2.5cm/1in slices.

2 Heat the oil in a wok or large deep pan. Stir-fry the garlic and ginger for 1 minute.

3 Add the Chinese leaves to the wok or pan and stir-fry for 2 minutes. Sprinkle the salt over and drizzle with the oyster sauce. Toss the leaves over the heat for 2 minutes more.

4 Stir in the spring onions. Toss the mixture well, transfer it to a heated serving plate and serve.

Variation
Use the same treatment for shredded cabbage and leeks. If you want to cut down on preparation time, you can often find this combination of vegetables, ready-prepared, in bags at the supermarket.

Cook's Tip
For guests who are vegetarian, substitute 15 ml/1 tbsp light soy sauce and 5ml/1 tsp of caster (superfine) sugar for the oyster sauce. This rule can be applied to many dishes.

Stir-fried Beansprouts

This fresh and crunchy vegetable, which is synonymous with Chinese restaurants, tastes even better when stir-fried at home.

Ingredients

15ml/1 tbsp vegetable oil
1 garlic clove, finely chopped
5ml/1 tsp grated fresh root ginger
1 small carrot, cut into matchsticks
50g/2oz/½ cup canned bamboo shoots, drained and cut into matchsticks
450g/1lb/2 cups beansprouts
2.5ml/½ tsp salt
large pinch of ground white pepper
15ml/1 tbsp Chinese rice wine or dry sherry
15ml/1 tbsp light soy sauce
2.5ml/½ tsp sesame oil

Serves 4

1 Heat the vegetable oil in a non-stick frying pan or wok. Add the chopped garlic and grated ginger and stir-fry for a few minutes, over a high heat. Add the carrot and bamboo shoot matchsticks to the pan or wok and stir-fry for a few minutes.

2 Add the beansprouts to the pan or wok with the salt and pepper. Drizzle over the rice wine or sherry and toss the beansprouts over the heat for 3 minutes until hot.

3 Sprinkle over the soy sauce and sesame oil, toss to mix thoroughly, then spoon into a bowl and serve immediately.

Variation
Add a handful of almond slices, grilled (broiled) until golden.

Cook's Tip
Beansprouts keep best when stored in the refrigerator or oth cool place in a bowl of cold water, but you must remember change the water daily.

stir-fried chinese leaves Energy 77kcal/321kJ; Protein 2.6g; Carbohydrate 9.8g, of which sugars 9.6g; Fat 3.2g, of which saturates 0.3g; Cholesterol 0mg; Calcium 87mg; Fibre 3.7g; Sodiu
stir-fried beansprouts Energy 76kcal/318kJ; Protein 3.9g; Carbohydrate 6.9g, of which sugars 4.5g; Fat 3.4g, of which saturates 0.5g; Cholesterol 0mg; Calcium 31mg; Fibre 2.3g; Sodium [illegible]

Pak Choi with Lime Dressing

The lime dressing in this dish is usually made using fish sauce, but vegetarians could use mushroom sauce instead. This is a wok recipe that packs a fiery punch so be aware of delicate palates if you are entertaining guests. You can simply use fewer chillies if you prefer, or discard the seeds before you begin stir-frying. Alternatively, simply replace the chillies with red (bell) pepper strips, which will add just as much colour, with a milder impact.

Ingredients

30ml/2 tbsp oil
3 fresh red chillies, cut into thin strips
4 garlic cloves, thinly sliced
6 spring onions (scallions), sliced diagonally
2 pak choi (bok choy), shredded
15ml/1 tbsp crushed peanuts

For the dressing

30ml/2 tbsp fresh lime juice
15–30ml/1–2 tbsp fish sauce
250ml/8fl oz/1 cup whole or low-fat coconut milk

Serves 4

1 Make the dressing. Put the lime juice and fish sauce in a bowl and mix well together, then gradually whisk in the coconut milk until combined.

2 Heat the oil in a wok and stir-fry the chillies for 2–3 minutes, until crisp. Transfer to a plate using a slotted spoon.

3 Add the garlic to the wok and stir-fry for 30–60 seconds, until golden brown. Transfer to the plate.

4 Stir-fry the white parts of the spring onions for about 2–3 minutes, then add the green parts and stir-fry for 1 minute more. Transfer to the plate.

5 Bring a large pan of lightly salted water to the boil and add the pak choi. Stir twice, then drain immediately.

6 Place the pak choi in a large bowl, add the dressing and toss to mix. Spoon into a large serving bowl, sprinkle with the crushed peanuts and the stir-fried ingredients and serve.

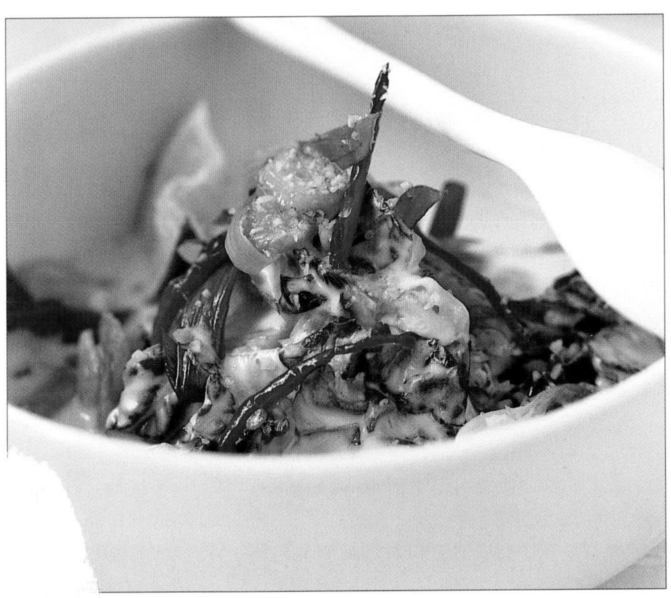

New Potatoes in Dashi Stock

As the stock evaporates in this delicious dish, the onion becomes meltingly soft and caramelized, making a wonderful sauce that coats the potatoes.

Ingredients

15ml/1 tbsp vegetable oil
15ml/1 tbsp toasted sesame oil
1 small onion, thinly sliced
1kg/2¼lb baby new potatoes, unpeeled
200ml/7fl oz/scant 1 cup water with 5ml/1 tsp instant dashi powder
45ml/3 tbsp shoyu, dark soy sauce or kecap manis

Serves 4

1 Heat the vegetable and sesame oils in a wok or large pan. Add the onion slices and stir-fry for 30 seconds, then add the potatoes. Stir constantly, until all the potatoes are well coated in sesame oil, and have begun to sizzle.

2 Pour on the dashi stock and shoyu, dark soy sauce or kecap manis and reduce the heat to the lowest setting. Cover the wok or pan and cook for 15 minutes, using a slotted spoon to turn the potatoes every 5 minutes so that they cook evenly.

3 Uncover the wok or pan for a further 5 minutes to reduce the liquid. If there is already very little liquid remaining, remove the wok or pan from the heat, cover and leave to stand for 5 minutes. Check that the potatoes are cooked, then remove from the heat.

4 Transfer the potatoes and onions to a deep serving bowl. Pour the sauce over the top and serve immediately.

Cook's Tip

Toasted sesame oil is recommended because of its distinctive aroma, but mixing it with vegetable oil not only moderates the flavour, it also lessens the likelihood of the oil burning when heated in the pan.

lime Energy 93kcal/384kJ; Protein 2.9g; Carbohydrate 6.2g, of which sugars 5.7g; Fat 6.4g, of which saturates 0.9g; Cholesterol 0mg; Calcium 157mg; Fibre 2.1g; Sodium 354mg.
e' in dashi stock Energy 210kcal/890kJ; Protein 4.8g; Carbohydrate 42.4g, of which sugars 4.9g; Fat 3.5g, of which saturates 0.7g; Cholesterol 0mg; Calcium 21mg; Fibre 2.7g; Sodium 829mg.

Noodle, Tofu & Beansprout Salad

Bean thread noodles look like spun glass on this stunning salad, which owes its goodness to fresh beansprouts, diced tomato and cucumber in a sweet-sour dressing.

Ingredients

25g/1oz cellophane noodles
500g/1¼lb mixed sprouted beans and pulses (aduki, chickpea, mung, red lentil)
4 spring onions (scallions), finely shredded
115g/4oz firm tofu, diced
1 ripe plum tomato, seeded and diced
½ cucumber, peeled, seeded and diced
60ml/4 tbsp chopped fresh coriander (cilantro)
45ml/3 tbsp chopped fresh mint
60ml/4 tbsp rice vinegar
10ml/2 tsp caster (superfine) sugar
10ml/2 tsp sesame oil
5ml/1 tsp chilli oil
salt and ground black pepper

Serves 4

1 Place the cellophane noodles in a bowl and pour over enough boiling water to cover. Cover and leave to soak for 12–15 minutes.

2 Drain the noodles and then refresh them under cold, running water and drain again. Using a pair of scissors, cut the noodles into roughly 7.5cm/3in lengths and transfer to a bowl.

3 Fill a wok one-third full of boiling water and place over high heat. Add the sprouted beans and pulses and blanch the mixture for 1 minute. Drain, transfer to the noodle bowl and add the spring onions, tofu, tomato, cucumber and herbs.

4 Combine the rice vinegar, sugar, sesame oil and chilli oil and toss into the noodle mixture. Transfer to a serving dish and chill for 30 minutes before serving.

Cook's Tip

If you leave the salad to stand for half an hour to an hour, the flavours will improve as they develop and fuse together.

Fried Tofu Salad with Tangy Sauce

The sweet-sour sauce makes this traditional street snack the perfect foil to grilled meats and stir-fried noodles. If you cannot find kecap manis, simply use dark soy sauce with a little more tomato ketchup to achieve the same balance of flavour.

Ingredients

vegetable oil, for deep-frying
450g/1lb firm rectangular tofu, rinsed, patted dry and cut into blocks
1 small cucumber, partially peeled in strips, seeded and shredded
2 spring onions (scallions), trimmed, halved and shredded
2 handfuls of fresh beansprouts rinsed and drained
fresh coriander (cilantro) leaves, to garnish

For the sauce

30ml/2 tbsp tamarind pulp, soaked in water until soft
15ml/1 tbsp sesame or groundnut (peanut) oil
4 shallots, finely chopped
4 garlic cloves, finely chopped
2 fresh red chillies, seeded
2.5ml/½ tsp shrimp paste
115g/4oz/1 cup roasted peanuts, crushed
30–45ml/2–3 tbsp kecap manis
15ml/1 tbsp tomato ketchup

Serves 4

1 First make the sauce. Squeeze the tamarind pulp to soften it in the water, and then strain through a sieve (strainer). Measure out 120ml/4fl oz/½ cup tamarind pulp.

2 Heat the oil in a wok or heavy pan, and stir in the shallots, garlic and chillies, until fragrant. Stir in the shrimp paste and the peanuts, until they emit a nutty aroma. Add the kecap manis, tomato ketchup and tamarind pulp and blend to form a thick sauce. Set aside and leave to cool.

3 Deep-fry the blocks of tofu in oil until golden brown all over. Pat dry on kitchen paper and cut each block into slices. Arrange the fried tofu slices on a plate with the cucumber, spring onions and beansprouts. Drizzle a little of the sauce over the top and serve the remainder separately in a bowl, garnished with the fresh coriander leaves.

noodle, tofu etc. Energy 126kcal/528kJ; Protein 7.2g; Carbohydrate 14.8g, of which sugars 7.2g; Fat 4.4g, of which saturates 0.6g; Cholesterol 0mg; Calcium 209mg; Fibre 3.1g; Sodium 17mg.
tofu salad Energy 423kcal/1749kJ; Protein 17.9g; Carbohydrate 7.8g, of which sugars 4.5g; Fat 35.8g, of which saturates 5.3g; Cholesterol 0mg; Calcium 607mg; Fibre 2.8g; Sodium 296mg.

Cabbage Salad

This is a simple and delicious way of serving a somewhat mundane vegetable. A wok comes in handy for stir-frying the aromatic vegetables.

Ingredients
30ml/2 tbsp vegetable oil
2 large fresh red chillies, seeded and cut into thin strips
6 garlic cloves, thinly sliced
6 shallots, thinly sliced
1 small cabbage, shredded
30ml/2 tbsp coarsely chopped roasted peanuts, to garnish

For the dressing
30ml/2 tbsp fish sauce
grated rind of 1 lime
30ml/2 tbsp fresh lime juice
120ml/4fl oz/½ cup coconut milk

Serves 4–6

1 Make the dressing by mixing the fish sauce, lime rind, lime juice and coconut milk in a bowl. Whisk until thoroughly combined, then set aside.

2 Heat the oil in a wok. Stir-fry the chillies, garlic and shallots over a medium heat for 3–4 minutes, until the shallots are brown and crisp. Remove with a slotted spoon and set aside.

3 Bring a large pan of lightly salted water to the boil. Add the shredded cabbage and blanch for 2–3 minutes. Tip it into a colander, drain well and put into a bowl.

4 Whisk the dressing again, add it to the warm cabbage and toss to combine. Transfer the salad to a serving dish. Just before serving, sprinkle with the fried shallot mixture and garnish with the chopped peanuts.

Variations
• *Other vegetables, such as cauliflower, broccoli and Chinese leaves (Chinese cabbage), can be cooked in this way.*
• *As a healthier option, use low-fat or light coconut milk if you prefer. You can create your own lighter version by using equal parts full-cream coconut milk and distilled water.*

Fragrant Mushrooms in Lettuce Leaf Saucers

This quick and easy vegetable dish looks great served on lettuce leaves, and it means the mushrooms can be scooped up and eaten with the fingers. It's a lovely treat for children.

Ingredients
30ml/2 tbsp vegetable oil
2 garlic cloves, finely chopped
2 baby cos or romaine lettuces, or 2 Little Gem (Bibb) lettuces
1 lemon grass stalk, chopped
2 kaffir lime leaves, rolled in cylinders and thinly sliced
200g/7oz/3 cups oyster or chestnut mushrooms, or a mixture of the two, sliced
1 small fresh red chilli, seeded and finely chopped
juice of ½ lemon
30ml/2 tbsp light soy sauce
5ml/1 tsp palm sugar (jaggery) or light muscovado (brown) sugar
small bunch fresh mint, leaves removed from the stalks

Serves 2

1 Heat the oil in a wok or frying pan. Add the garlic and cook over a medium heat, stirring occasionally, until golden. Do not let it burn or it will taste bitter.

2 Meanwhile, separate the individual lettuce leaves. Rinse them well, dry in a salad spinner or blot with kitchen paper, and set aside.

3 Increase the heat under the wok or pan and add the chopped lemon grass, sliced lime leaves and sliced mushrooms. Stir-fry for about 2 minutes.

4 Add the chilli, lemon juice, soy sauce and sugar to the wok or pan. Toss the mixture over the heat to combine the ingredients together, then stir-fry for a further 2 minutes.

5 Arrange the lettuce leaves on one large or two individual salad plates. Spoon a small amount of the mushroom mixture on to each leaf, top with a mint leaf and serve.

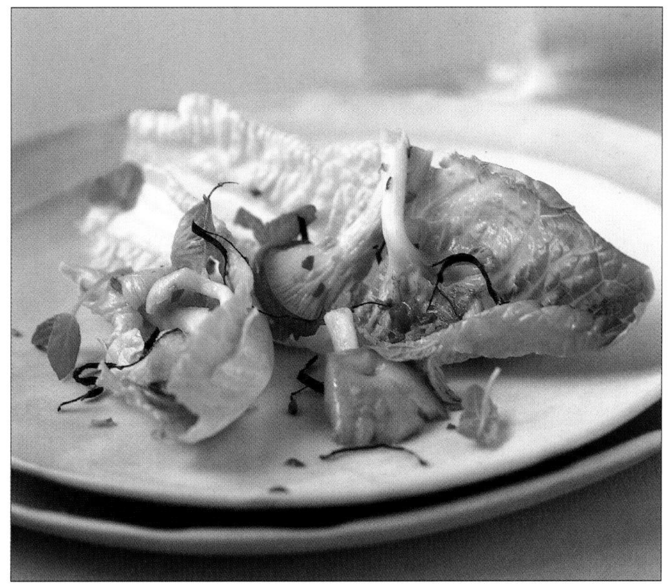

cabbage salad Energy 96kcal/400kJ; Protein 2.7g; Carbohydrate 7.7g, of which sugars 6.6g; Fat 6.2g, of which saturates 0.9g; Cholesterol 0mg; Calcium 50mg; Fibre 2.2g; Sodium 147mg.
mushrooms in lettuce saucers Energy 145kcal/600kJ; Protein 3.6g; Carbohydrate 5.5g, of which sugars 4g; Fat 12.2g, of which saturates 1.5g; Cholesterol 0mg; Calcium 87mg; Fibre 2g; Sodium 12mg.

Mackerel with Black Beans

Shiitake mushrooms, ginger and salted black beans are perfect partners for robustly flavoured mackerel fillets.

Ingredients

20 dried shiitake mushrooms
15ml/1 tbsp finely julienned fresh root ginger
3 star anise
8 x 115g/4oz mackerel fillets
45ml/3 tbsp dark soy sauce
15ml/1 tbsp Chinese rice wine
15ml/1 tbsp salted black beans
6 spring onions (scallions), finely shredded
30ml/2 tbsp sunflower oil
5ml/1 tsp sesame oil
4 garlic cloves, very thinly sliced
sliced cucumber and steamed basmati rice, to serve

Serves 4

1 Place the dried mushrooms in a large bowl and cover with boiling water. Soak for 20 minutes. Drain, reserving the soaking liquid, discard the stems and slice the caps thinly.

2 Place a trivet or a steamer rack in a large wok and pour in 5cm/2in of the mushroom liquid (top up with water if necessary). Add half the ginger and the star anise.

3 Divide the mackerel between two lightly oiled heatproof plates, skin side up. Cut three diagonal slits in each one. Insert the remaining ginger strips and sprinkle over the mushrooms. Bring the liquid to the boil and put one of the plates on the trivet.

4 Cover the wok, reduce the heat and steam for about 10–12 minutes, or until the mackerel is cooked. Repeat with the second plate of fish. Put all the fish on a platter and keep warm.

5 Ladle 105ml/7 tbsp of the steaming liquid from the wok into a pan with the soy sauce, wine and black beans. Place over a gentle heat and bring to a simmer. Spoon over the fish and sprinkle over the spring onions.

6 Heat the oils and stir-fry garlic for a few minutes until lightly golden. Pour over the fish and serve with sliced cucumber and steamed basmati rice.

Grilled Mackerel with Tamarind

Oily fish like mackerel are cheap and nutritious. They go very well with a tart or sour accompaniment, like these tamarind-flavoured lentils. Serve with chopped fresh tomatoes, onion salad and flat bread, or new potatoes and green beans.

Ingredients

250g/9oz/1 cup red lentils, or yellow split peas (soaked overnight in water)
1 litre/1¾ pints/4 cups water
30ml/2 tbsp sunflower oil
2.5ml/½ tsp each mustard seeds, cumin seeds, fennel seeds, and fenugreek or cardamom seeds
5ml/1 tsp ground turmeric
3–4 dried red chillies, crumbled
30ml/2 tbsp tamarind paste
5ml/1 tsp soft brown sugar
30ml/2 tbsp chopped fresh coriander (cilantro)
4 mackerel or 8 large sardines
salt and ground black pepper
fresh red chilli slices and chopped coriander (cilantro), to garnish
flat bread and tomatoes, to serve

Serves 4

1 Rinse the lentils or split peas, drain them and put them in a pan. Pour in the water and bring to the boil. Lower the heat, partially cover the pan and simmer the pulses for 30–40 minutes, stirring occasionally, until they are tender and mushy.

2 Heat the oil in a wok or shallow pan. Add the mustard seeds, then cover and cook for a few seconds, until they pop. Remove the lid, add the rest of the seeds, with the turmeric and chillies and fry for a few more seconds.

3 Stir in the pulses, with salt to taste. Mix well; stir in the tamarind paste and sugar. Bring to the boil, then simmer for 10 minutes, until thick. Stir in the chopped fresh coriander.

4 Meanwhile, clean the fish then heat a ridged grilling pan until very hot. Make six diagonal slashes on either side of each fish and remove the head from each one if you wish.

5 Season inside and out, then cook for 5–7 minutes on each side, until the skin is crisp. Serve with the dhal, flat bread and tomatoes, garnished with red chilli and chopped coriander.

mackerel w. beans Energy 693kcal/2872kJ; Protein 45.5g; Carbohydrate 1.9g, of which sugars 0.5g; Fat 55.9g, of which saturates 10.4g; Cholesterol 128mg; Calcium 35mg; Fibre 0.6g; Sodium 152mg.
mackerel w. tamarind Energy 578kcal/2420kJ; Protein 43.5g; Carbohydrate 35.2g, of which sugars 1.5g; Fat 30.2g, of which saturates 5.7g; Cholesterol 80mg; Calcium 48mg; Fibre 3.1g; Sodium 110mg.

Fried Sea Bass with Leeks

Sea bass tastes sensational when given this simple treatment.

Ingredients

1 sea bass, about 1.4–1.5kg/3–3½ lb, scaled and cleaned
8 spring onions (scallions)
60ml/4 tbsp teriyaki marinade
30ml/2 tbsp cornflour (cornstarch)
juice of 1 lemon
30ml/2 tbsp rice wine vinegar
5ml/1 tsp ground ginger
60ml/4 tbsp groundnut (peanut) oil
2 leeks, shredded
2.5cm/1in piece fresh root ginger, peeled and grated
105ml/7 tbsp fish stock
30ml/2 tbsp dry sherry
5ml/1 tsp caster (superfine) sugar
salt and ground black pepper

Serves 4

1 Make several diagonal slashes on either side of the sea bass, then season the fish inside and out with salt and ground black pepper. Trim the spring onions, cut them in half lengthways, then slice them diagonally into 2cm/¾ in lengths. Put half of the spring onions in the cavity of the fish and reserve the rest.

2 In a shallow dish, mix together the teriyaki marinade, the cornflour, lemon juice, rice wine vinegar and ground ginger to make a smooth, runny paste. Turn the fish in the marinade to coat it thoroughly, working it into the slashes, then leave it to marinate for 20–30 minutes, turning it several times.

3 Heat a wok or frying pan that is large enough to hold the sea bass comfortably. Add the oil, then the leeks and grated ginger. Fry gently for about 5 minutes, until the leeks are tender. Remove the leeks and ginger and drain on kitchen paper.

4 Lift the sea bass out of the marinade and lower it into the hot oil. Fry over a medium heat for 2–3 minutes on each side. Stir the stock, sherry and sugar into the marinade. Season.

5 Pour the mixture over the fish. Return the leeks, ginger and reserved spring onions to the wok. Cover and simmer for about 15 minutes, until the fish is cooked. Serve immediately.

Steamed Sea Bass with Chilli Sauce

By leaving the fish whole and on the bone, maximum flavour is retained.

Ingredients

1 large or 2 medium firm fish such as sea bass or grouper, scaled and cleaned
30ml/2 tbsp rice wine
3 fresh red chillies, seeded and thinly sliced
2 garlic cloves, finely chopped
2cm/¾ in piece fresh root ginger, peeled and finely shredded
2 lemon grass stalks, crushed and finely chopped
2 spring onions (scallions), chopped
30ml/2 tbsp fish sauce
juice of 1 lime
1 fresh banana leaf or baking parchment

For the chilli sauce

10 fresh red chillies, seeded and chopped
4 garlic cloves, chopped
60ml/4 tbsp fish sauce
15ml/1 tbsp sugar
75ml/5 tbsp fresh lime juice

Serves 4

1 Thoroughly rinse the fish under cold running water. Pat it dry with kitchen paper. With a sharp knife, slash the skin of the fish a few times on both sides.

2 Mix together the rice wine, chillies, garlic, shredded ginger, lemon grass and spring onions in a non-metallic bowl. Add the fish sauce and lime juice and mix to a paste. Place the fish on the banana leaf or parchment and spread the spice paste evenly over it, rubbing it into the slashes.

3 Put a rack or a small upturned plate in the base of a wok. Pour in boiling water to a depth of 5cm/2in. Lift the banana leaf or parchment and fish, and place on the rack or plate. Cover and steam for 10–15 minutes, or until the fish is cooked.

4 Meanwhile, make the sauce. Place all the ingredients in a food processor and process until smooth. If the mixture seems to be too thick, add a little cold water. Scrape into a serving bowl.

5 Serve the fish hot, on the banana leaf if you like, with the sweet chilli sauce to spoon over the top.

sea bass w. leeks Energy 300kcal/1253kJ; Protein 31.1g; Carbohydrate 7.5g, of which sugars 6.7g; Fat 15.4g, of which saturates 2g; Cholesterol 120mg; Calcium 229mg; Fibre 2.6g; Sodium 271mg.
sea bass w. chilli Energy 216kcal/910kJ; Protein 36.3g; Carbohydrate 7.5g, of which sugars 5.5g; Fat 4.7g, of which saturates 0.7g; Cholesterol 140mg; Calcium 246mg; Fibre 0.5g; Sodium 1192mg.

Green Hoki Curry

Any firm-fleshed fish can be used for this curry, which gains its rich colour from a mixture of fresh herbs.

Ingredients

4 garlic cloves, roughly chopped
5cm/2in piece fresh root ginger, peeled and roughly chopped
2 fresh green chillies, seeded and roughly chopped
grated rind and juice of 1 lime
5ml/1 tsp coriander seeds
5ml/1 tsp five-spice powder
75ml/5 tbsp sesame oil
2 red onions, finely chopped
900g/2lb hoki fillets, skinned
400ml/14fl oz/1⅔ cups coconut milk
45ml/3 tbsp fish sauce
50g/2oz fresh coriander (cilantro)
50g/2oz fresh mint leaves
50g/2oz fresh basil leaves
6 spring onions (scallions), chopped
150ml/¼ pint/⅔ cup sunflower or groundnut (peanut) oil
sliced fresh green chilli and chopped fresh coriander (cilantro), to garnish
cooked Basmati or Thai fragrant rice and lime wedges, to serve

Serves 4

1 First make the curry paste. Combine the garlic, fresh root ginger, green chillies and the lime juice in a food processor. Add the coriander seeds and five-spice powder, with half the sesame oil. Whiz to a fine paste, then set aside.

2 Heat a wok and stir-fry the red onions in the remaining sesame oil for 2 minutes. Add the fish and stir-fry for 1–2 minutes to seal on all sides.

3 Lift out the red onions and fish and put them on a plate. Add the curry paste to the wok or pan and fry for 1 minute, stirring. Return the hoki fillets and red onions to the wok, pour in the coconut milk and bring to the boil. Lower the heat, add the fish sauce and simmer for 5–7 minutes until the fish is cooked through.

4 Meanwhile, process the herbs, spring onions, lime rind and oil in a food processor to a coarse paste. Stir into the fish curry. Garnish with chilli and coriander and serve with the cooked rice and lime wedges.

Hoki Stir-fry

Any firm white fish, such as monkfish, hake or cod, can be used for this attractive stir-fry. You can vary the vegetables according to what is available, but try to include at least three different colours.

Ingredients

675g/1½ lb hoki fillet, skinned
pinch of five-spice powder
2 carrots
115g/4oz/1 cup small mangetouts (snow peas)
115g/4oz asparagus spears
4 spring onions (scallions)
45ml/3 tbsp groundnut (peanut) oil
2.5cm/1in piece fresh root ginger, peeled and cut into thin slivers
2 garlic cloves, finely chopped
300g/11oz/scant 1½ cups beansprouts
8–12 small baby corn cobs
15–30ml/1–2 tbsp light soy sauce
salt and ground black pepper

Serves 4–6

1 Cut the hoki into finger-size strips and season with salt, pepper and five-spice powder. Cut the carrots diagonally into slices as thin as the mangetouts.

2 Trim the mangetouts. Trim the asparagus spears and cut in half crossways. Trim the spring onions and cut them diagonally into 2cm/¾ in pieces, keeping the white and green parts separate. Set aside.

3 Heat a wok, then pour in the oil. As soon as it is hot, add the ginger and garlic. Stir-fry for 1 minute, then add the white parts of the spring onions and cook for 1 minute more.

4 Add the hoki strips and stir-fry for 2–3 minutes, until all the pieces of fish are opaque. Add the beansprouts and toss them around to coat them in the oil, then put in the carrots, mangetouts, asparagus and corn. Continue to stir-fry for 3–4 minutes, by which time the fish should be cooked, but all the vegetables will still be crunchy.

5 Add soy sauce to taste, toss everything quickly together, then stir in the green parts of the spring onions. Serve immediately.

green hoki curry Energy 608kcal/2527kJ; Protein 41g; Carbohydrate 13.3g, of which sugars 9.5g; Fat 43.8g, of which saturates 5.9g; Cholesterol 0mg; Calcium 168mg; Fibre 1.3g; Sodium 313mg.
hoki stir-fry Energy 183kcal/764kJ; Protein 22.4g; Carbohydrate 5g, of which sugars 3.8g; Fat 8.2g, of which saturates 1.1g; Cholesterol 0mg; Calcium 49mg; Fibre 2.3g; Sodium 295mg.

Trout with Tamarind

Sometimes trout can taste rather bland, but this spicy sauce really gives it a zing.

Ingredients

4 trout, cleaned
6 spring onions (scallions), sliced
60ml/4 tbsp soy sauce
15ml/1 tbsp vegetable oil
30ml/2 tbsp chopped fresh coriander (cilantro) and strips of fresh red chilli, to garnish

For the sauce

50g/2oz tamarind pulp
105ml/7 tbsp boiling water
2 shallots, coarsely chopped
1 fresh red chilli, seeded and chopped
1cm/½in piece fresh root ginger, peeled and chopped
5ml/1 tsp soft light brown sugar
45ml/3 tbsp fish sauce

Serves 4

1 Slash the trout diagonally four or five times on each side. Place them in a shallow dish that is large enough to hold them all in a single layer.

2 Fill the cavity in each trout with spring onions and douse each fish with soy sauce. Carefully turn the fish over to coat both sides with the sauce. Sprinkle any remaining spring onions over the top.

3 To make the sauce, put the tamarind pulp in a small bowl and pour on the boiling water. Mash it well with a fork until it has softened.

4 Tip the tamarind mixture into a food processor or blender, and add the shallots, fresh chilli, ginger, sugar and fish sauce. Process to a coarse pulp. Scrape into a bowl.

5 Heat the oil in a large frying pan or wok and cook the trout, one at a time if necessary, for about 5 minutes on each side, until the skin is crisp and browned and the flesh cooked.

6 If cooking in batches, keep the cooked trout hot until all four fish have been fried. Serve the trout on warmed plates and spoon over some of the sauce. Sprinkle with the coriander and chilli and offer the remaining sauce separately.

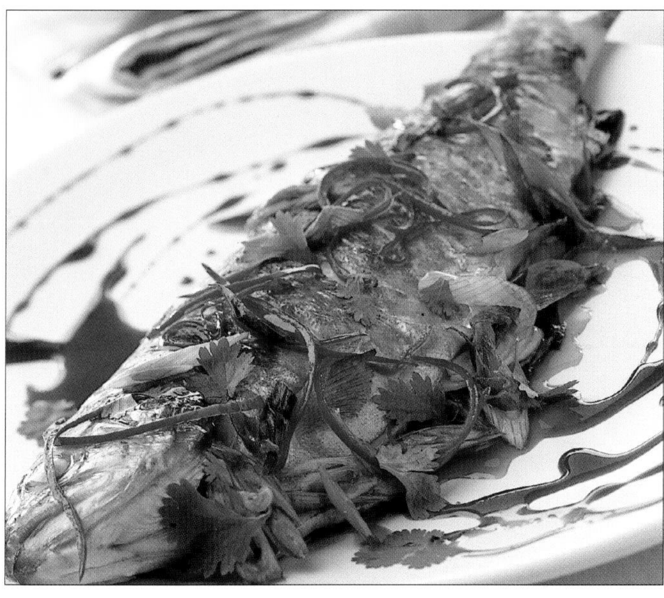

Fish Moolie

This is a very popular South-east Asian fish curry in a coconut sauce, which is truly delicious. Choose a firm-textured fish so that the pieces stay intact during the brief cooking process. Halibut and cod work equally well.

Ingredients

500g/1¼lb monkfish or other firm-textured fish fillets, skinned and cut into 2.5cm/1in cubes
2.5ml/½ tsp salt
50g/2oz/⅔ cup desiccated (dry unsweetened) coconut
6 shallots, chopped
6 blanched almonds
2–3 garlic cloves, roughly chopped
2.5cm/1in piece fresh root ginger, peeled and sliced
2 lemon grass stalks, trimmed
10ml/2 tsp ground turmeric
45ml/3 tbsp vegetable oil
2 × 400ml/14fl oz cans coconut milk
1–3 fresh chillies, seeded and sliced
salt and ground black pepper
fresh chives, to garnish
boiled rice, to serve

Serves 4

1 Put the fish cubes in a shallow dish and sprinkle with the salt. Dry fry the coconut in a wok, turning all the time until it is crisp and golden, then tip into a food processor and process to an oily paste. Scrape into a bowl and reserve.

2 Add the shallots, almonds, garlic and ginger to the food processor. Chop the bulbous part of each lemon grass stalk and add to the processor with the turmeric. Process the mixture to a paste. Bruise the remaining lemon grass stalks.

3 Heat the oil in a wok. Cook the onion mixture for 2–3 minutes. Stir in the coconut milk and bring to the boil, stirring. Add the fish, most of the chilli and the lemon grass stalks. Cook for 3–4 minutes. Stir in the coconut paste and cook for a further 2–3 minutes only. Adjust the seasoning.

4 Remove the lemon grass. Transfer the moolie to a hot serving dish and sprinkle with the remaining slices of chilli. Garnish with chopped and whole chives and serve with rice.

trout w. tamarind Energy 329kcal/1384kJ; Protein 47.9g; Carbohydrate 8.1g, of which sugars 6.3g; Fat 11.9g, of which saturates 2.5g; Cholesterol 192mg; Calcium 96mg; Fibre 1.2g; Sodium 978mg.
fish moolie Energy 319kcal/1335kJ; Protein 22.4g; Carbohydrate 16.7g, of which sugars 14.9g; Fat 18.6g, of which saturates 8.3g; Cholesterol 18mg; Calcium 96mg; Fibre 3g; Sodium 249mg.

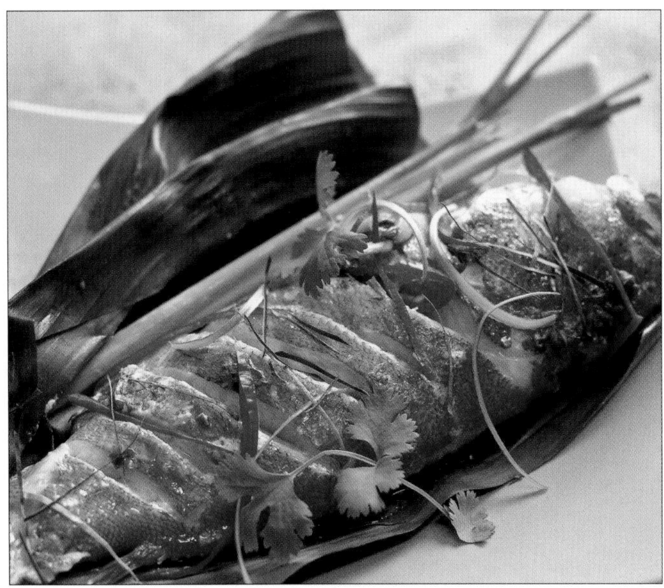

Red Snapper in Banana Leaves

Whole snappers infused with coconut cream, herbs and chilli make an impressive main course.

Ingredients

4 small red snapper, gutted and cleaned
4 large squares of banana leaf
50ml/2fl oz/¼ cup coconut cream
90ml/6 tbsp chopped coriander (cilantro)
90ml/6 tbsp chopped mint
juice of 3 limes
3 spring onions (scallions), finely sliced
4 kaffir lime leaves, finely shredded
2 fresh red chillies, seeded and finely sliced
4 lemon grass stalks, split lengthways
salt and ground black pepper
steamed rice and steamed Asian greens, to serve

Serves 4

1 Using a small sharp knife, score the fish diagonally on each side. Half fill a wok with water and bring to the boil.

2 Dip each square of banana leaf into the boiling water in the wok for 15–20 seconds so they become pliable. Lift out carefully, rinse under cold water and dry with kitchen paper.

3 Place the coconut cream, chopped herbs, lime juice, spring onions, lime leaves and chillies in a bowl and stir. Season well.

4 Lay the banana leaves flat and place a fish and a split lemon grass stalk in the centre of each of them. Spread the herb mixture over each fish and fold over each banana leaf to form a neat parcel. Secure each parcel tightly with a bamboo skewer.

5 Place the parcels in a single layer in one or two tiers of a large bamboo steamer and place over a wok of simmering water. Cover tightly and steam for 15–20 minutes, or until the fish is cooked through.

6 Remove the fish from the steamer and serve in their banana-leaf wrappings, with steamed rice and greens.

Seafood Laksa

A laksa is a Malaysian stew of fish, poultry, meat or vegetables with noodles.

Ingredients

3 medium-hot fresh red chillies, seeded
4–5 garlic cloves
5ml/1 tsp mild paprika
10ml/2 tsp shrimp paste
25ml/1½ tbsp chopped fresh root ginger
250g/9oz small red shallots
25g/1oz fresh coriander (cilantro)
45ml/3 tbsp groundnut (peanut) oil
5ml/1 tsp fennel seeds, crushed
2 fennel bulbs, cut into thin wedges
600ml/1 pint/2½ cups fish stock
450ml/¾ pint/scant 2 cups coconut milk
juice of 1–2 limes
30–45ml/2–3 tbsp fish sauce
450g/1lb firm white fish fillet, cut into chunks
20 large raw prawns (shrimp), shelled and deveined
small bunch of basil
300g/11oz thin vermicelli rice noodles, cooked
2 spring onions (scallions), sliced

Serves 4–5

1 Process the chillies, garlic, paprika, shrimp paste, ginger and two shallots to a paste in a food processor.

2 Set aside the coriander leaves. Add the stems to the paste with 15ml/1 tbsp oil and process again until fairly smooth.

3 Cook the remaining shallots, the fennel seeds and fennel wedges in the remaining oil in a large pan. When lightly browned, add 45ml/3 tbsp of the paste and stir-fry for about 2 minutes. Pour in the fish stock and simmer for 8–10 minutes.

4 Add the coconut milk, the juice of 1 lime and 30ml/2 tbsp of the fish sauce. Bring to a simmer and adjust the flavouring.

5 Add the fish into chunks. Cook for 2–3 minutes, then add the prawns and cook until they turn pink. Chop most of the basil and add to the pan with chopped coriander leaves.

6 Divide the noodles among 4–5 wide bowls, then ladle in the stew. Sprinkle with spring onions and whole basil leaves. Serve.

red snapper Energy 185kcal/781kJ; Protein 39.4g; Carbohydrate 0.9g, of which sugars 0.8g; Fat 2.7g, of which saturates 0.6g; Cholesterol 74mg; Calcium 87mg; Fibre 0.1g; Sodium 168mg.
seafood laksa Energy 524kcal/2199kJ; Protein 43.1g; Carbohydrate 65.1g, of which sugars 6.3g; Fat 10.1g, of which saturates 2g; Cholesterol 233mg; Calcium 162mg; Fibre 1.9g; Sodium 356mg.

Squid with Broccoli

The slightly chewy squid contrasts beautifully with the crisp crunch of the broccoli to give this dish the perfect combination of textures so beloved by the Chinese.

Ingredients
300ml/½ pint/1¼ cups fish stock
350g/12oz prepared squid, cut into large pieces
225g/8oz broccoli
15ml/1 tbsp vegetable oil
2 garlic cloves, finely chopped
15ml/1 tbsp Chinese rice wine or dry sherry
10ml/2 tsp cornflour (cornstarch)
2.5ml/½ tsp caster (superfine) sugar
45ml/3 tbsp cold water
15ml/1 tbsp oyster sauce
2.5ml/½ tsp sesame oil
noodles, to serve

Serves 4

1 Bring the fish stock to the boil in a wok or pan. Add the squid pieces and cook for 2 minutes over medium heat until they are tender and have curled. Drain the squid pieces and set aside until required.

2 Trim the broccoli and cut it into small florets. Bring a pan of lightly salted water to the boil, add the broccoli and cook for 2 minutes until crisp-tender. Drain thoroughly.

3 Heat the vegetable oil in a wok or non-stick frying pan. When the oil is hot, add the garlic, stir-fry for a few seconds, then add the squid, broccoli and rice wine or sherry. Stir-fry the mixture over medium heat for about 2 minutes.

4 Mix the cornflour and sugar to a paste with the water. Stir the mixture into the wok or pan, with the oyster sauce. Cook, stirring, until the sauce thickens slightly. Just before serving, stir in the sesame oil. Serve with noodles.

Variation
Use pak choi (bok choy) instead of broccoli when it is available.

Stuffed Squid with Shiitake Mushrooms

The smaller the squid, the sweeter the dish will taste. Be very careful not to overcook the flesh as it toughens very quickly.

Ingredients
8 small squid
50g/2oz cellophane noodles
30ml/2 tbsp groundnut (peanut) oil
2 spring onions (scallions), finely chopped
8 shiitake mushrooms, halved if large
250g/9oz minced (ground) pork
1 garlic clove, chopped
30ml/2 tbsp fish sauce
5ml/1 tsp caster (superfine) sugar
15ml/1 tbsp finely chopped fresh coriander (cilantro)
5ml/1 tsp lemon juice
salt and ground black pepper

Serves 4

1 Cut off the tentacles of the squid just below the eye. Remove the transparent "quill" from inside the body and rub off the skin on the outside. Wash the squid thoroughly in cold water and set aside on a plate.

2 Bring a pan of water to the boil and add the noodles. Remove from the heat and set aside to soak for 20 minutes.

3 Preheat the oven to 200°C/400°F/Gas 6. Heat 15ml/1 tbsp of the oil in a preheated wok and stir-fry the spring onions, shiitake mushrooms, pork and garlic for 4 minutes until the meat is golden and the spring onions and mushrooms have softened.

4 Drain the noodles and add to the wok, with the fish sauce, sugar, coriander, lemon juice and salt and pepper to taste.

5 Stuff the squid with the mixture and secure with cocktail sticks (toothpicks). Arrange the squid in an ovenproof dish, drizzle over the remaining oil and prick each squid twice.

6 Bake in the preheated oven for 10 minutes. Serve hot.

squid w. broccoli Energy 127kcal/536kJ; Protein 16g; Carbohydrate 4.4g, of which sugars 0.9g; Fat 4.8g, of which saturates 0.8g; Cholesterol 197mg; Calcium 44mg; Fibre 1.5g; Sodium 103mg.
squid w. mushrooms Energy 356kcal/1486kJ; Protein 21.8g; Carbohydrate 15.2g, of which sugars 3.6g; Fat 23.6g, of which saturates 11.1g; Cholesterol 321mg; Calcium 55mg; Fibre 1.9g; Sodium 352mg.

Squid in Hot Yellow Sauce

Simple fishermen's dishes such as this one are cooked in coastal regions throughout Asia. This one includes enough chillies to set your tongue on fire. To temper the heat, the dish is often served with rice or sago porridge, and finely shredded green mango tossed in lime juice.

Ingredients

500g/1¼lb fresh squid
juice of 2 limes
5ml/1 tsp salt
4 shallots, chopped
4 garlic cloves, chopped
25g/1oz galangal, chopped
25g/1oz fresh turmeric, chopped
6–8 fresh red chillies, seeded and chopped
30ml/2 tbsp vegetable oil
7.5ml/1½ tsp palm sugar (jaggery)
2 lemon grass stalks, crushed
4 lime leaves
400ml/14fl oz/1⅔ cups coconut milk
salt and ground black pepper
crusty bread or steamed rice, to serve

Serves 4

1 First prepare the squid. Hold the body sac in one hand and pull off the head with the other. Sever the tentacles just above the eyes, and discard the rest of the head and innards. Clean the body sac inside and out and remove the skin. Pat the squid dry, cut it into thick slices and put them in a bowl, along with the tentacles. Mix the lime juice with the salt and rub it into the squid. Set aside for 30 minutes.

2 Meanwhile, using a mortar and pestle or food processor, grind the shallots, garlic, galangal, turmeric and chillies to a coarse paste.

3 Heat the oil in a wok or heavy pan, and stir in the coarse paste. Cook the paste until fragrant, then stir in the palm sugar, lemon grass and lime leaves. Drain the squid of any juice and toss it around the wok, coating it in the flavourings.

4 Pour in the coconut milk and bring it to the boil. Reduce the heat and simmer for 5–10 minutes, until the squid is tender. Season and serve with crusty bread or steamed rice.

Five-spice Squid

Squid is perfect for stir-frying as it should be cooked quickly. The spicy sauce makes the ideal accompaniment.

Ingredients

450g/1lb small squid, cleaned
45ml/3 tbsp oil
2.5cm/1in fresh root ginger, grated
1 garlic clove, crushed
8 spring onions (scallions), cut into 2.5cm/1in lengths
1 red (bell) pepper, seeded and cut into strips
1 fresh green chilli, seeded and thinly sliced
6 mushrooms, sliced
5ml/1 tsp Chinese five-spice powder
30ml/2 tbsp black bean sauce
30ml/2 tbsp soy sauce
5ml/1 tsp sugar
15ml/1 tbsp Chinese rice wine or dry sherry

Serves 6

1 Rinse the squid and pull away the outer skin. Dry on kitchen paper. Slit the squid open and score the inside into diamonds with a sharp knife. Cut the squid into strips.

2 Heat the oil in a preheated wok. Stir-fry the squid quickly. Remove the squid strips from the wok with a slotted spoon and set aside.

3 Add the ginger, garlic, spring onions, red pepper, chilli and mushrooms to the oil remaining in the wok and stir-fry for 2 minutes.

4 Return the squid to the wok and stir in the five-spice powder. Stir in the black bean sauce, soy sauce, sugar and rice wine or dry sherry. Bring to the boil and cook, stirring, for 1 minute. Serve immediately.

Variation
Use button (white) mushrooms for this recipe, or try a mixture of cultivated and wild mushrooms. Dried shiitake mushrooms would also be good but must be first soaked in water.

squid in hot sauce Energy 185kcal/780kJ; Protein 19.8g; Carbohydrate 9.4g, of which sugars 7.6g; Fat 8g, of which saturates 1.4g; Cholesterol 281mg; Calcium 50mg; Fibre 0.2g; Sodium 739mg.
five-spice squid Energy 134kcal/562kJ; Protein 15.1g; Carbohydrate 4.8g, of which sugars 3.5g; Fat 6.2g, of which saturates 0.9g; Cholesterol 203mg; Calcium 23mg; Fibre 0.9g; Sodium 956mg.

Salt & Pepper Prawns

These succulent shellfish beg to be eaten with the fingers, so provide finger bowls or hot cloths for all your guests.

Ingredients

15–18 large raw prawns (shrimp), in the shell, about 450g/1lb
vegetable oil, for deep-frying
3 shallots or 1 small onion, very finely chopped
2 garlic cloves, crushed
1cm/½in piece fresh root ginger, peeled and very finely grated
1–2 fresh red chillies, seeded and finely sliced
2.5ml/½ tsp caster (superfine) sugar or to taste
3–4 spring onions (scallions), shredded, to garnish

For the fried salt

10ml/2 tsp salt
5ml/1 tsp Sichuan peppercorns

Serves 3–4

1 Make the fried salt by dry-frying the salt and peppercorns in a heavy frying pan over medium heat until the peppercorns begin to release their aroma. Cool the mixture, then tip into a mortar and crush with a pestle.

2 Carefully remove the heads and legs from the raw prawns and discard. Leave the body shells and the tails in place. Pat the prepared prawns dry with sheets of kitchen paper.

3 Heat the oil for deep frying to 190°C/375°F. Fry the prawns for 1 minute, then lift them out and drain thoroughly on kitchen paper. Spoon 30ml/2 tbsp of the hot oil into a wok or large frying pan, leaving the rest of the oil to one side to cool.

4 Heat the oil in the wok or frying pan. Add the fried salt, with the shallots or onion, garlic, ginger, chillies and sugar. Toss together for 1 minute.

5 Add the prawns and toss them over the heat for about 1 minute more until they are coated and the shells are pleasantly impregnated with the seasonings. Spoon the shellfish mixture into heated serving bowls and garnish with the shredded spring onions.

Gong Boa Prawns

A sweet and sour sauce complements tiger prawns perfectly.

Ingredients

350g/12oz raw tiger prawns (jumbo shrimp)
½ cucumber, about 75g/3oz
300ml/½ pint/1¼ cups fish stock
15ml/1 tbsp vegetable oil
2.5ml/½ tsp crushed dried chillies
½ green (bell) pepper, seeded and cut into 2.5cm/1in strips
1 small carrot, thinly sliced
30ml/2 tbsp tomato ketchup
45ml/3 tbsp rice vinegar
15ml/1 tbsp sugar
150ml/¼ pint/⅔ cup vegetable stock
50g/2oz/½ cup drained canned pineapple chunks
10ml/2 tsp cornflour (cornstarch) mixed with 15ml/1 tbsp cold water
salt

Serves 4

1 Peel and devein the prawns. Rub them with 2.5ml/½ tsp salt; leave them for a few minutes, then wash and pat dry.

2 Using a narrow peeler or cannelle knife, pare strips of skin off the cucumber to give a stripy effect.

3 Cut the cucumber in half lengthways and scoop out the seeds with a teaspoon. Cut the flesh into 5mm/¼in crescents.

4 Bring the fish stock to the boil in a pan. Add the prawns, lower the heat and poach the prawns for 2 minutes until they turn pink, then lift them out using a slotted spoon and set aside.

5 Heat the oil in a non-stick frying pan or wok over a high heat. Fry the chillies for a few seconds, then add the pepper strips and carrot slices and stir-fry for 1 minute more.

6 Stir the tomato ketchup, vinegar, sugar, stock and 1.5ml/¼ tsp salt into the pan and cook for 3 minutes more.

7 Add the prawns, cucumber and pineapple and cook for 2 minutes. Add the cornflour paste and cook, stirring constantly, until the sauce thickens. Serve immediately.

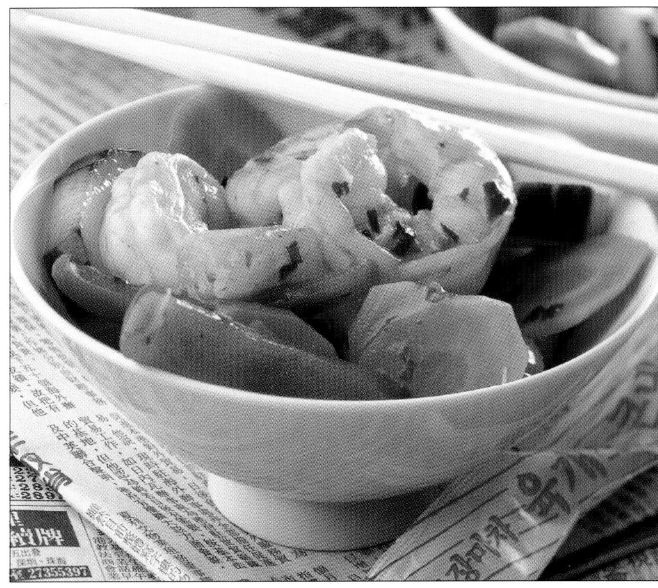

salt & pepper prawns Energy 122kcal/514kJ; Protein 20.1g; Carbohydrate 2.7g, of which sugars 2.4g; Fat 3.5g, of which saturates 0.5g; Cholesterol 219mg; Calcium 97mg; Fibre 0.3g; Sodium 1197mg.
gong boa prawns Energy 147kcal/617kJ; Protein 16.3g; Carbohydrate 13.2g, of which sugars 10.7g; Fat 3.5g, of which saturates 0.5g; Cholesterol 171mg; Calcium 88mg; Fibre 1.1g; Sodium 296mg.

Prawns with Jasmine Rice

Strips of omelette are used to garnish this rice dish. Use your wok for frying the omelette – the sloping sides make it easy to spread the beaten egg thinly and then to slide it out.

Ingredients

45ml/3 tbsp vegetable oil
1 egg, beaten
1 onion, chopped
15ml/1 tbsp chopped garlic
15ml/1 tbsp shrimp paste
1kg/2¼lb/4 cups cooked jasmine rice
350g/12oz cooked shelled prawns (shrimp)
50g/2oz thawed frozen peas
oyster sauce, to taste
2 spring onions (scallions), chopped
15–20 Thai basil leaves, roughly snipped, plus a sprig, to garnish

Serves 4–6

1 Heat 15ml/1 tbsp of the oil in a wok or frying pan. Add the beaten egg and swirl it around to set like a thin pancake.

2 Cook the pancake (on one side only) over a gentle heat until golden. Slide the pancake on to a board, roll up and cut into thin strips. Set aside.

3 Heat the remaining oil in the wok or pan, add the onion and garlic and stir-fry for 2–3 minutes. Stir in the shrimp paste and mix well until thoroughly combined.

4 Add the rice, prawns and peas and toss and stir together, until everything is heated through.

5 Season with oyster sauce to taste, taking great care as the shrimp paste is salty. Mix in the spring onions and basil leaves. Transfer to a serving dish and top with the strips of egg pancake. Serve, garnished with a sprig of basil.

Cook's Tip
Leave a few prawns (shrimp) in their shells for an additional garnish, if you like.

Long Beans with Prawns

Popular in many Asian countries, long beans – like many other vegetables – are often stir-fried with garlic. This Cambodian-style recipe is livened up with prawns, as well as other flavourings, and works well either as a side dish or on its own with rice.

Ingredients

45ml/3 tbsp vegetable oil
2 garlic cloves, finely chopped
25g/1oz galangal or root ginger, finely shredded
450g/1lb fresh prawns (shrimp), shelled and deveined
1 onion, halved and finely sliced
450g/1lb long beans, trimmed and cut into 7.5cm/3in lengths
120ml/4fl oz/½ cup soy sauce

For the marinade

30ml/2 tbsp fish sauce
juice of 2 limes
10ml/2 tsp sugar
2 garlic cloves, crushed
1 lemon grass stalk, trimmed and finely sliced

Serves 4

1 To make the marinade, beat the fish sauce and lime juice in a bowl with the sugar, until it has dissolved. Stir in the garlic and lemon grass. Toss in the prawns, cover, and chill for 1–2 hours.

2 Heat 30ml/2 tbsp of the oil in a wok or heavy pan. Stir in the chopped garlic and galangal or root ginger. Just as they begin to colour, toss in the marinated prawns. Stir-fry for a minute or until the prawns turn pink. Lift the prawns out on to a plate, reserving as much of the oil, garlic and galangal or root ginger as you can.

3 Add the remaining oil to the wok. Add the onion and stir-fry until slightly caramelized. Stir in the beans, then pour in the soy sauce. Cook for 2–3 minutes, until the beans are tender. Add the prawns and stir-fry until heated through. Serve immediately.

Cook's Tip
This recipe uses an unusually large quantity of soy sauce. If you feel it will be too salty for your taste, use less or choose a light variety.

prawns w. rice Energy 354kcal/1494kJ; Protein 17.8g; Carbohydrate 53.4g, of which sugars 0.9g; Fat 9.2g, of which saturates 1.5g; Cholesterol 158mg; Calcium 117mg; Fibre 0.8g; Sodium 233mg.
long beans w. prawns Energy 187kcal/782kJ; Protein 22.6g; Carbohydrate 9.3g, of which sugars 7.9g; Fat 6.9g, of which saturates 0.9g; Cholesterol 219mg; Calcium 156mg; Fibre 3.2g; Sodium 485mg.

Prawns with Tamarind

The sour, tangy flavour that is characteristic of many Asian dishes comes from tamarind. Fresh tamarind pods can sometimes be bought, but preparing them for cooking is a laborious process. It is much easier to use ready-made tamarind paste, which is available in many Asian supermarkets.

Ingredients

6 dried red chillies
30ml/2 tbsp vegetable oil
30ml/2 tbsp chopped onion
30ml/2 tbsp palm sugar (jaggery) or light muscovado (brown) sugar
30ml/2 tbsp chicken stock
15ml/1 tbsp fish sauce
90ml/6 tbsp tamarind juice, made by mixing tamarind paste with warm water
450g/1lb raw prawns (shrimp), peeled
15ml/1 tbsp fried chopped garlic
30ml/2 tbsp fried sliced shallots
2 spring onions (scallions), chopped, to garnish

Serves 4–6

1 Heat a wok or large frying pan, but do not add any oil at this stage. Add the dried chillies and dry-fry them by pressing them against the surface of the wok or pan with a spatula, turning them occasionally.

2 Add the oil to the wok or pan and reheat. Cook the chopped onion over a medium heat, stirring occasionally, for 2–3 minutes, until softened and golden brown.

3 Add the sugar, stock, fish sauce, dry-fried red chillies and the tamarind juice, stirring constantly until the sugar has dissolved. Bring to the boil, then lower the heat slightly.

4 Add the prawns, garlic and shallots. Toss over the heat for 3–4 minutes, until the prawns are cooked. Garnish with the spring onions and serve.

Cook's Tip
Do not let the chillies burn when dry-frying as they will turn bitter.

Mango & Prawn Curry

This sweet, spicy curry is simple to make, and the addition of mango and tamarind produces a very full, rich flavour. If you have time, make the sauce the day before to give the flavours time to develop.

Ingredients

1 green mango
5ml/1 tsp hot chilli powder
15ml/1 tbsp paprika
2.5ml/½ tsp ground turmeric
4 garlic cloves, crushed
10ml/2 tsp finely grated ginger
30ml/2 tbsp ground coriander
10ml/2 tsp ground cumin
15ml/1 tbsp palm sugar (jaggery)
400g/14oz can coconut milk
10ml/2 tsp salt
15ml/1 tbsp tamarind paste
1kg/2¼lb large prawns (shrimp)
chopped coriander (cilantro), to garnish
steamed white rice, chopped tomato, cucumber and onion salad, to serve

Serves 4

1 Wash, stone (pit) and slice the mango and set aside. In a large bowl, combine the chilli powder, paprika, turmeric, garlic, ginger, ground coriander, ground cumin and palm sugar.

2 Add 400ml/14fl oz/1⅔ cups cold water to the bowl and stir to combine the ingredients.

3 Pour the spice mixture into a wok and place over a high heat and bring the mixture to the boil. Cover the wok with a lid, reduce the heat to low and simmer gently for 8–10 minutes.

4 Add the mango, coconut milk, salt and tamarind paste to the wok and stir to combine. Bring to a simmer and then add the whole prawns.

5 Cover the wok and cook gently for 10–12 minutes, or until the prawns have turned pink and are cooked.

6 Serve the curry garnished with chopped coriander, accompanied by steamed white rice and a tomato, cucumber and onion salad.

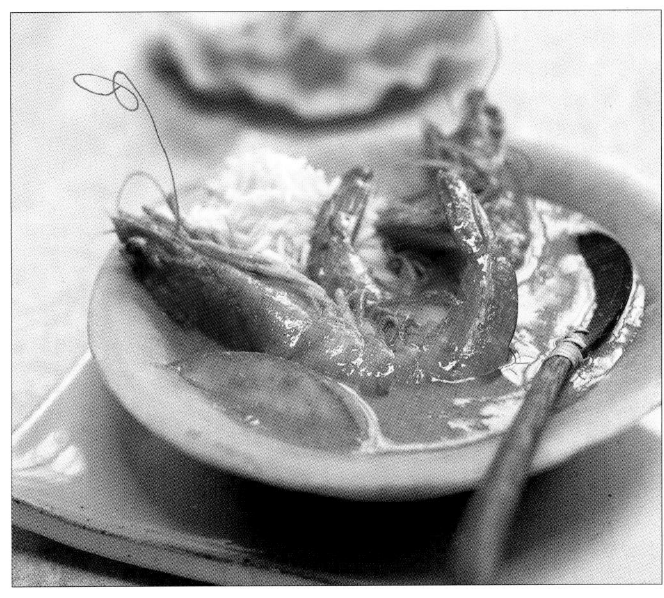

prawns w. tamarind Energy 112kcal/469kJ; Protein 13.4g; Carbohydrate 5.5g, of which sugars 5.2g; Fat 4.1g, of which saturates 0.5g; Cholesterol 146mg; Calcium 65mg; Fibre 0.2g; Sodium 321mg.
mango & prawn Energy 151kcal/648kJ; Protein 22.1g; Carbohydrate 14.1g, of which sugars 14g; Fat 1.1g, of which saturates 0.5g; Cholesterol 263mg; Calcium 143mg; Fibre 1g; Sodium 2102mg.

Chilli & Coconut Prawns

Supply plenty of bread or rice when serving these superb prawns. The sauce is so tasty that diners will want to savour every last drop. Be warned, though, the chilli makes these fiery, even though tamarind has a taming influence.

Ingredients

8 shallots, chopped
4 garlic cloves, chopped
8–10 dried red chillies, soaked in warm water until soft, squeezed dry, seeded and chopped
5ml/1 tsp shrimp paste
30ml/2 tbsp vegetable or groundnut (peanut) oil
250ml/8fl oz/1 cup coconut cream
500g/1 1/4lb fresh prawns (shrimp), peeled and deveined
10ml/2 tsp tamarind paste
15ml/1 tbsp palm sugar (jaggery)
salt and ground black pepper
2 fresh red chillies, seeded and finely chopped, and fresh coriander (cilantro) leaves, finely chopped, to garnish
crusty bread or steamed rice and pickles, to serve

Serves 4

1 Using a mortar and pestle or food processor, grind the shallots, garlic and dried chillies to a coarse paste. Beat in the shrimp paste.

2 Heat the oil in a wok and stir in the paste until fragrant. Add the coconut cream and let it bubble up until it separates. Toss in the prawns, reduce the heat and simmer for 3 minutes.

3 Stir in the tamarind paste and the sugar and cook for a further 2 minutes until the sauce is very thick. Season with salt and pepper and scatter the chopped chillies and coriander over the top. Serve immediately with chunks of fresh, crusty bread to mop up the sauce, or with steamed rice and pickles.

Cook's Tip
Tamarind used to be an exotic ingredient, available only as pods which needed to be processed before use. Fortunately the paste is now a stocked supermarket item.

Stir-fried Prawns with Mangetouts

Mangetout means "eat all" and you'll want to do just that when a recipe is as good as this one is. The prawns remain beautifully succulent and the sauce is delicious.

Ingredients

300ml/1/2 pint/1 1/4 cups fish stock
350g/12oz raw tiger prawns (jumbo shrimp), peeled and deveined
15ml/1 tbsp vegetable oil
1 garlic clove, finely chopped
225g/8oz/2 cups mangetouts (snow peas)
1.5ml/1/4 tsp salt
15ml/1 tbsp mirin (sweet rice wine) or dry sherry
15ml/1 tbsp oyster sauce
5ml/1 tsp cornflour (cornstarch)
5ml/1 tsp caster (superfine) sugar
15ml/1 tbsp cold water
1.5ml/1/4 tsp sesame oil

Serves 4

1 Bring the fish stock to the boil in a frying pan. Add the prawns. Cook gently for 2 minutes until the prawns have turned pink, then lift them out on a slotted spoon and set aside.

2 Heat the vegetable oil in a non-stick frying pan or wok. When the oil is very hot, add the chopped garlic and cook for a few seconds, then add the mangetouts. Sprinkle with the salt. Stir-fry for 1 minute.

3 Add the prawns and mirin or sherry to the pan or wok. Toss the ingredients together over the heat for a few seconds, then add the oyster sauce and toss again.

4 Mix the cornflour and sugar to a paste with the water. Add to the pan and cook, stirring constantly, until the sauce thickens slightly. Drizzle with sesame oil.

Cook's Tip
Mirin is a sweet rice wine from Japan. It has quite a delicate flavour and is used for cooking. Rice wine for drinking is called sake. Both are available from Asian food stores. If you cannot locate mirin, dry sherry can be used instead.

chilli & prawns Energy 211kcal/886kJ; Protein 23.6g; Carbohydrate 14.8g, of which sugars 13.1g; Fat 6.8g, of which saturates 1g; Cholesterol 244mg; Calcium 152mg; Fibre 1.1g; Sodium 351mg.
prawns w. mangetouts Energy 125kcal/524kJ; Protein 17.6g; Carbohydrate 5.2g, of which sugars 3.6g; Fat 3.4g, of which saturates 0.4g; Cholesterol 171mg; Calcium 96mg; Fibre 1.3g; Sodium 436mg.

Spiced Scallops & Sugar Snap

This is a great dish for special-occasion entertaining.

Ingredients
45ml/3 tbsp oyster sauce
10ml/2 tsp soy sauce
5ml/1 tsp sesame oil
5ml/1 tsp golden caster (superfine) sugar
30ml/2 tbsp sunflower oil
2 fresh red chillies, finely sliced
4 garlic cloves, finely chopped
10ml/2 tsp finely chopped fresh root ginger
250g/9oz sugar snap peas, trimmed
500g/1¼lb king scallops, cleaned and halved, roes discarded
3 spring onions (scallions), finely shredded

For the noodle cakes
250g/9oz fresh thin egg noodles
10ml/2 tsp sesame oil
120ml/4fl oz/½ cup sunflower oil

Serves 4

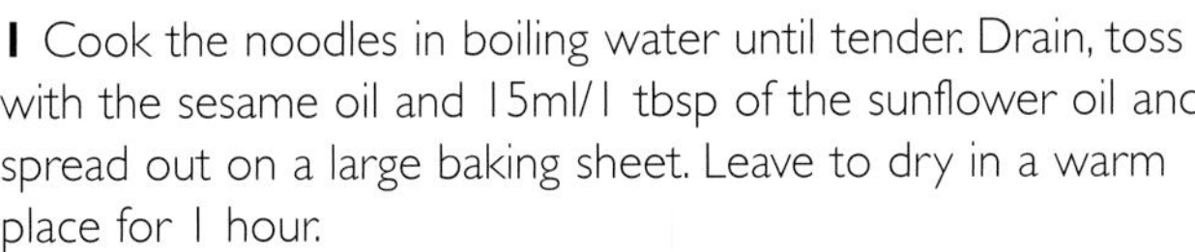

1 Cook the noodles in boiling water until tender. Drain, toss with the sesame oil and 15ml/1 tbsp of the sunflower oil and spread out on a large baking sheet. Leave to dry in a warm place for 1 hour.

2 Heat 15ml/1 tbsp of the oil in a wok. Add a quarter of the noodle mixture, flatten it and shape it into a cake.

3 Cook the cake for about 5 minutes on each side until crisp and golden. Drain on kitchen paper and keep hot while you make the remaining three noodle cakes in the same way.

4 Mix the oyster sauce, soy sauce, sesame oil and sugar, stirring until the sugar has dissolved completely.

5 Heat a wok, add the sunflower oil, then stir-fry the chillies, garlic, ginger and sugar snaps for 1–2 minutes. Add the scallops and spring onions and stir-fry for 1 minute, then add the sauce mixture and cook for 1 minute.

6 Place a noodle cake on each plate, top with the scallop mixture and serve immediately.

Lemon Grass Snails

Served straight from the steamer, these taste great.

Ingredients
24 fresh snails in their shells
225g/8oz lean minced (ground) pork, passed through the mincer (grinder) twice
3 lemon grass stalks, trimmed and finely chopped or ground (reserve the outer leaves)
2 spring onions (scallions), finely chopped
25g/1oz fresh root ginger, peeled and finely grated
1 fresh red chilli, seeded and finely chopped
10ml/2 tsp sesame or groundnut (peanut) oil
sea salt and ground black pepper
chilli sauce or other sauce, for dipping

Serves 4

1 Pull the snails out of their shells and place them in a colander. Rinse the snails thoroughly in plenty of cold water and pat dry with kitchen paper. Rinse the shells and leave to drain.

2 Chop the snails finely and put them in a bowl. Add the minced pork, lemon grass, spring onions, ginger, chilli and oil. Season with salt and pepper and mix well.

3 Select the best of the lemon grass leaves and tear each one into thin ribbons, roughly 7.5cm/3in long. Bend each ribbon in half and put it inside a snail shell, so that the ends are poking out. The idea is that each diner pulls the ends of the lemon grass ribbon to gently prize the steamed morsel out of its shell.

4 Using your fingers, stuff each shell with the snail and pork mixture, gently pushing it between the lemon grass ends to the back of the shell so that it fills the shell completely.

5 Fill a wok a third of the way up with water and bring it to the boil. Arrange the snail shells, open side up, in a steamer that fits the wok. Cover and steam for about 10 minutes, until the mixture is cooked.

6 Serve hot with a dipping sauce of your choice.

spiced scallops Energy 689kcal/2888kJ; Protein 41.4g; Carbohydrate 59.9g, of which sugars 6.2g; Fat 33.3g, of which saturates 5.4g; Cholesterol 78mg; Calcium 73mg; Fibre 5g; Sodium 700mg.
lemon grass snails Energy 136kcal/573kJ; Protein 24.2g; Carbohydrate 0.2g, of which sugars 0.2g; Fat 4.3g, of which saturates 1.1g; Cholesterol 70mg; Calcium 9mg; Fibre 0.1g; Sodium 70mg.

Steamed Mussels in Coconut Milk

Mussels steamed in coconut milk and fresh aromatic herbs and spices make an ideal dish for informal entertaining. A wok makes short work of the cooking and the dish is great for a relaxed dinner with friends.

Ingredients

15ml/1 tbsp sunflower oil
6 garlic cloves, roughly chopped
15ml/1 tbsp finely chopped fresh root ginger
2 large fresh red chillies, seeded and finely sliced
6 spring onions (scallions), finely chopped
400ml/14fl oz/1⅔ cups coconut milk
45ml/3 tbsp light soy sauce
2 limes
5ml/1 tsp caster (superfine) sugar
1.6kg/3½lb mussels, scrubbed and beards removed
a large handful of chopped coriander (cilantro)
salt and ground black pepper

Serves 4

1 Heat the wok over a high heat and then add the oil. Stir in the garlic, ginger, chillies and spring onions and stir-fry for 30 seconds. Pour in the coconut milk, then add the soy sauce.

2 Grate the zest of the limes into the coconut milk mixture and add the sugar. Stir to mix and bring to the boil. Add the mussels. Return to the boil, cover and cook briskly for about 5–6 minutes, or until all the mussels have opened. Discard any mussels that remain closed.

3 Remove the wok from the heat and stir the chopped coriander into the mussel mixture. Season the mussels well with salt and pepper. Ladle into warmed bowls and serve.

Cook's Tip

For an informal supper with friends, take the wok straight to the table rather than serving in individual bowls. A wok makes a great serving dish, and there's something utterly irresistible about eating the mussels straight from it.

Mussels & Clams with Lemon Grass

Wine is seldom used in green curies but in this recipe it adds depth of flavour to the sauce.

Ingredients

1.8kg/4lb fresh mussels
450g/1lb baby clams
120ml/4fl oz/½ cup dry white wine
1 bunch spring onions (scallions), chopped
2 lemon grass stalks, chopped
6 kaffir lime leaves, chopped
10ml/2 tsp green curry paste
200ml/7fl oz/scant 1 cup coconut cream
30ml/2 tbsp chopped fresh coriander (cilantro)
salt and ground black pepper
garlic chives, to garnish

Serves 6

1 Clean the mussels by pulling off the beards, scrubbing the shells well and scraping off any barnacles with the blade of a knife. Scrub the clams. Discard any mussels or clams that are damaged or broken or which do not close immediately when tapped sharply.

2 Put the wine in a wok or large pan with the spring onions, lemon grass and lime leaves. Stir in the curry paste. Simmer until the wine has almost evaporated.

3 Add the mussels and clams to the wok or pan and increase the heat to high. Cover tightly and steam the shellfish for 5–6 minutes, until they open.

4 Using a slotted spoon, transfer the mussels and clams to a heated serving bowl, cover and keep hot. Discard any shellfish that remain closed. Strain the cooking liquid into a clean pan through a sieve (strainer) lined with muslin (cheesecloth) and simmer briefly to reduce to about 250ml/8fl oz/1 cup.

5 Stir the coconut cream and chopped coriander into the sauce and season with salt and pepper to taste. Heat through. Pour the sauce over the mussels and clams, garnish with the garlic chives and serve immediately.

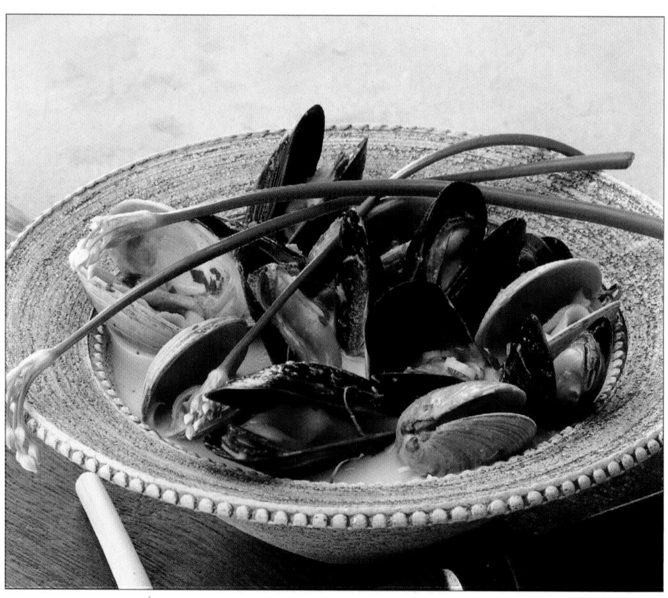

steamed mussels Energy 165kcal/701kJ; Protein 22.1g; Carbohydrate 7.3g, of which sugars 7.2g; Fat 5.6g, of which saturates 1g; Cholesterol 48mg; Calcium 276mg; Fibre 0.2g; Sodium 1165mg.
mussels w. lemon grass Energy 237kcal/993kJ; Protein 22.5g; Carbohydrate 2.8g, of which sugars 1.7g; Fat 13.8g, of which saturates 10.3g; Cholesterol 58mg; Calcium 238mg; Fibre 0.9g; Sodium 606mg.

Asparagus with Crab Meat Sauce

The subtle flavour of fresh asparagus is enhanced by the equally delicate taste of the crab meat in this classic dish, which is relatively low in saturated fat.

Ingredients

450g/1lb asparagus spears, trimmed
4 thin slices of peeled fresh root ginger
15ml/1 tbsp vegetable oil
2 garlic cloves, finely chopped
115g/4oz/⅔ cup fresh or thawed frozen white crab meat
5ml/1 tsp sake or dry sherry
150ml/¼ pint/⅔ cup semi-skimmed (low-fat) milk
15ml/1 tbsp cornflour (cornstarch)
45ml/3 tbsp cold water
salt and ground white pepper
1 spring onion (scallion), thinly shredded, to garnish

Serves 4

1 Bring a large pan of lightly salted water to the boil. Poach the asparagus for about 5 minutes until just crisp-tender.

2 Drain well and keep hot in a shallow serving dish.

3 Bruise the slices of ginger with a rolling pin. Heat the oil in a non-stick frying pan or wok. Add the ginger and garlic for 1 minute and cook to release their flavour, then lift them out with a slotted spoon and discard them.

4 Add the crab meat to the flavoured oil and toss to mix. Drizzle over the sake or sherry, then pour in the milk. Cook, stirring often, for 2 minutes.

5 Meanwhile, put the cornflour in a small bowl with the water and mix to a smooth paste.

6 Add the cornflour paste to the pan, stirring constantly, then cook the mixture, continuing to stir, until it forms a thick and creamy sauce.

7 Season to taste with salt and pepper, spoon over the asparagus, garnish with shreds of spring onion and serve.

Chilli Crab

This dish is based on a popular dish from Singapore. An all-time favourite at hawker stalls and coffee shops, steaming woks of crab deep-frying are a common sight. The crabs are placed in the middle of the table with a bowl for the discarded pieces of shell, and small bowls of water for cleaning your fingers. Crack the shells, then dip the meat into the cooking sauce. Mop up the spicy sauce with lots of crusty bread.

Ingredients

vegetable oil, for deep-frying
4 fresh crabs, about 250g/9oz each, cleaned
30ml/2 tbsp sesame oil
30–45ml/2–3 tbsp chilli sauce
45ml/3 tbsp tomato ketchup
15ml/1 tbsp soy sauce
15ml/1 tbsp sugar
250ml/8fl oz/1 cup chicken stock
2 eggs, beaten
salt and ground black pepper
finely sliced spring onions (scallions), and chopped coriander (cilantro) leaves, to garnish

For the spice paste

4 garlic cloves, chopped
25g/1oz fresh root ginger, chopped
4 fresh red chillies, seeded and chopped

Serves 4

1 Using a mortar and pestle or food processor, grind the ingredients for the spice paste and set aside.

2 Deep-fry the crabs in hot oil until the shells turn bright red. Remove from the oil and drain.

3 Heat the sesame oil in a wok and stir in the spice paste. Fry until fragrant and stir in the chilli sauce, ketchup, soy sauce and sugar. Toss in the fried crab and coat well. Pour in the chicken stock, bring to the boil, then simmer for 5 minutes. Season.

4 Pour in the eggs, stirring gently, to let them set in the sauce. Serve immediately, garnished with spring onions and coriander.

asparagus w. crab Energy 121kcal/507kJ; Protein 10.4g; Carbohydrate 7.5g, of which sugars 3.9g; Fat 5.6g, of which saturates 1.1g; Cholesterol 23mg; Calcium 84mg; Fibre 1.9g; Sodium 126mg.
singapore chilli crab Energy 276kcal/1144kJ; Protein 12.1g; Carbohydrate 8.6g, of which sugars 8.1g; Fat 21.7g, of which saturates 3.1g; Cholesterol 126mg; Calcium 23mg; Fibre 0.3g; Sodium 674mg

Beef with Tomatoes

This colourful and fresh-tasting mixture is the perfect way of serving sun-ripened tomatoes from the garden or farmers' market.

Ingredients

350g/12oz lean rump (round) steak, trimmed of fat
15ml/1 tbsp vegetable oil
300ml/½ pint/1¼ cups beef stock
1 garlic clove, finely chopped
1 small onion, sliced into rings
5 tomatoes, quartered
15ml/1 tbsp tomato purée (paste)
5ml/1 tsp caster (superfine) sugar
15ml/1 tbsp dry sherry
salt and ground white pepper
noodles, to serve

Serves 4

1 Slice the rump steak thinly. Place the steak slices in a bowl, add 5ml/1 tsp of the vegetable oil and stir to coat.

2 Bring the stock to the boil in a large pan. Add the beef and cook for 2 minutes, stirring constantly. Lift out the beef and set it aside on a plate.

3 Heat the remaining oil in a non-stick frying pan or wok until very hot. Stir-fry the garlic and onion for a few seconds.

4 Add the beef to the pan or wok, then tip in the tomatoes. Stir-fry for 1 minute more over high heat.

5 Mix the tomato purée, sugar, sherry and 15ml/1 tbsp cold water in a cup or small bowl. Stir into the beef and tomato mixture in the pan or wok, add salt and pepper to taste and mix thoroughly. Cook for 1 minute until the sauce is hot. Serve in heated bowls, with noodles.

Variation

Add 5–10ml/1–2 tsp soy sauce to the tomato purée (paste). You will not need to add any extra salt.

Stir-fried Beef & Mushrooms

Garlic and salted black beans is a classic Cantonese seasoning for beef.

Ingredients

30ml/2 tbsp soy sauce
30ml/2 tbsp Chinese rice wine
10ml/2 tsp cornflour (cornstarch)
10ml/2 tsp sesame oil
450g/1lb beef fillet (tenderloin), trimmed of fat
12 dried shiitake mushrooms
25ml/1½ tbsp salted black beans
5ml/1 tsp sugar
45ml/3 tbsp groundnut (peanut) oil
4 garlic cloves, thinly sliced
2.5cm/1in piece fresh root ginger, cut into fine strips
200g/7oz open cap mushrooms, sliced
1 bunch spring onions (scallions), sliced diagonally
1 fresh red chilli, seeded and finely shredded
salt and ground black pepper

Serves 4

1 In a large bowl, mix half the soy sauce, half the rice wine, half the cornflour and all the sesame oil with 15ml/1 tbsp cold water until smooth. Add a good pinch of salt and pepper. Slice the beef very thinly and add to the cornflour mixture. Rub the mixture into the beef. Set aside for 30 minutes.

2 Pour boiling water over the dried mushrooms and soak for 25 minutes. Drain, reserving 45ml/3 tbsp of the soaking water. Remove and discard the hard stalks and cut the caps in half. Mash the black beans with the sugar in a small bowl. Stir the remaining cornflour, soy sauce and rice wine together in another bowl.

3 Heat the oil in a wok and stir-fry the beef for 30–45 seconds, until just brown. Transfer it to a plate, then stir-fry the garlic, ginger, dried and fresh mushrooms for 2 minutes. Add half the spring onions with the mashed black beans and stir-fry for another 1–2 minutes.

4 Stir the beef back into the mixture in the wok, then add the reserved shiitake soaking water. Add the cornflour mixture and simmer, stirring until the sauce thickens. Sprinkle the chilli and reserved spring onions over the beef and serve.

beef w. tomatoes Energy 172kcal/723kJ; Protein 20.5g; Carbohydrate 6.7g, of which sugars 6.4g; Fat 6.8g, of which saturates 1.9g; Cholesterol 52mg; Calcium 18mg; Fibre 1.6g; Sodium 74mg.
beef & mushrooms Energy 208kcal/873kJ; Protein 25.9g; Carbohydrate 4.7g, of which sugars 1.5g; Fat 8.8g, of which saturates 3.5g; Cholesterol 69mg; Calcium 20mg; Fibre 1.1g; Sodium 590mg.

Sichuan Beef with Tofu

China's western province is famous for its spicy cuisine, full of strong flavours. Sichuan peppercorns, which feature in this meat dish are not, in fact, peppercorns, but the dried berries of a type of ash tree. But, they do have a very peppery flavour.

Ingredients

200g/7oz/1 cup fragrant jasmine or basmati rice
30ml/2 tbsp groundnut (peanut) or soya oil
4 garlic cloves, finely chopped
600g/1lb 6oz beef rump (round) steak or fillet (tenderloin), cut into thin strips
500g/1 ¼lb firm tofu, drained and diced
1 head broccoli, coarsely chopped
90ml/6 tbsp soy sauce
pinch of sugar
juice of 1 lime
ground Sichuan peppercorns
sweet chilli sauce or another dipping sauce, to serve

Serves 4

1 Cook the rice in a large pan of salted boiling water until tender, following the instructions on the packet, then put it into a bowl and keep it hot.

2 Heat the oil in a large non-stick wok or frying pan, then add the garlic and stir-fry for a few seconds, until golden. Increase the heat to high, add the strips of steak and stir-fry for 1–2 minutes to seal.

3 Add the tofu cubes and broccoli and stir-fry for a few seconds. Stir in the soy sauce, sugar, lime juice and ground Sichuan peppercorns, then stir-fry for about 2 minutes. Transfer to warm serving plates or bowls and serve immediately with the rice and chilli sauce or other sauce.

Cook's Tip
Tofu, also known as bean curd, is a form of vegetable protein based on soya beans. There are two basic types: soft or silken tofu, which has a very light texture, and firm tofu, which is the type used in the recipe above.

Stir-fried Beef with Sesame Sauce

Similar to stir-fried beef with saté, the spicy peanut sauce, this recipe has a deliciously rich, spicy and nutty flavour.

Ingredients

450g/1lb beef sirloin or fillet (tenderloin), cut into thin strips
15ml/1 tbsp groundnut (peanut) or sesame oil
2 garlic cloves, finely chopped
2 fresh red chillies, seeded and finely chopped
7.5ml/1 ½ tsp sugar
30ml/2 tbsp sesame paste
30–45ml/2–3 tbsp beef stock or water
sea salt and ground black pepper
red chilli strips, to garnish
1 lemon, cut into quarters, to serve

For the marinade

15ml/1 tbsp groundnut (peanut) oil
30ml/2 tbsp fish sauce
30ml/2 tbsp soy sauce

Serves 4

1 In a bowl, mix together the ingredients for the marinade. Toss in the beef, making sure it is well coated. Leave to marinate for 30 minutes.

2 Heat the groundnut or sesame oil in a wok. Add the garlic and chillies and cook until golden and fragrant. Stir in the sugar. Add the beef, tossing it around the wok to sear it.

3 Stir in the sesame paste and enough stock or water to thin it down. Cook for 1–2 minutes, making sure the beef is coated with the sauce.

4 Season the sauce with salt and pepper. Spoon into warmed bowls, garnish with chilli strips and serve with lemon wedges.

Variations
Chicken breast fillet or pork fillet can be used instead of beef, but extend the cooking time to ensure that the poultry or pork is fully coated. Serve chicken or pork with orange wedges instead of lemon.

sichuan beef Energy 646kcal/2694kJ; Protein 55g; Carbohydrate 46.9g, of which sugars 4.1g; Fat 26.2g, of which saturates 7.6g; Cholesterol 87mg; Calcium 731mg; Fibre 3.8g; Sodium 1714mg.
beef w. sesame sauce Energy 269kcal/1119kJ; Protein 26.2g; Carbohydrate 0g, of which sugars 0g; Fat 18.2g, of which saturates 5.2g; Cholesterol 65mg; Calcium 31mg; Fibre 0.3g; Sodium 73mg.

Spicy Meat Balls

Serve these spicy little beef and chilli patties with egg noodles and chilli sambal.

Ingredients

1cm/½in cube shrimp paste
1 large onion, roughly chopped
1–2 fresh red chillies, seeded and chopped
2 garlic cloves, crushed
15ml/1 tbsp coriander seeds
5ml/1 tsp cumin seeds
450g/1lb lean minced (ground) beef
10ml/2 tsp dark soy sauce
5ml/1 tsp soft dark brown sugar
juice of 1½ lemons
a little beaten egg
vegetable oil, for shallow frying
salt and ground black pepper
1 green and 2 fresh red chillies, to garnish
chilli sambal, to serve

Serves 4–6

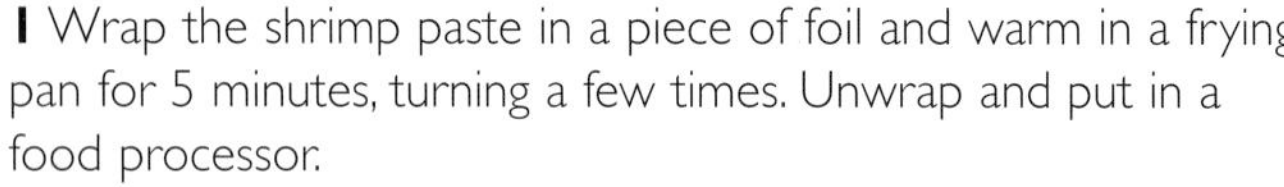

1 Wrap the shrimp paste in a piece of foil and warm in a frying pan for 5 minutes, turning a few times. Unwrap and put in a food processor.

2 Add the onion, chillies and garlic to the food processor and process until finely chopped. Set aside. Dry-fry the coriander and cumin seeds in a hot frying pan for 1 minute, to release the aroma. Tip the seeds into a mortar and grind with a pestle.

3 Put the meat in a large bowl. Stir in the onion mixture, ground spices, soy sauce, brown sugar, lemon juice and beaten egg. Season to taste.

4 Heat the oil in a wok or large frying pan and fry the meat balls for 4–5 minutes, turning often, until cooked through and browned. You may have to do this in batches.

5 Drain the meat balls on kitchen paper, and then pile them on to a warm serving platter or into a large serving bowl.

6 Finely slice the green chilli and one of the red chillies and sprinkle over the meat balls. Garnish with the remaining red chilli, if you like. Serve with the chilli sambal.

Beef with Charred Aubergines

To obtain the unique, smoky flavour that is integral to this dish, aubergines are charred over a flame, or charcoal grill, then skinned, chopped to a pulp and added to a minced meat mixture. Although popular in parts of South-east Asia, the method is more associated with the cooking of India, the Middle East, and North Africa.

Ingredients

2 aubergines (eggplant)
15ml/1 tbsp vegetable or groundnut (peanut) oil
2 shallots, finely chopped
4 garlic cloves, peeled and finely chopped
1 fresh red chilli, finely chopped
350g/12oz minced (ground) beef
30ml/2 tbsp fish sauce
sea salt and ground black pepper
crusty bread or rice and salad, to serve

Serves 4

1 Place the aubergines directly over an open flame. Turn them over from time to time, until the skin is charred all over. Put the aubergines into a plastic bag to sweat for a few minutes.

2 Hold each aubergine by its stalk under running cold water, while you peel off the skin. Squeeze out the excess water and chop the aubergines roughly on a board.

3 Heat the oil in a wok or a large pan. Stir in the shallots, garlic and chilli and fry until golden. Add the minced beef and stir-fry for about 5 minutes.

4 Stir in the fish sauce and the aubergine and cook gently, stirring frequently, for about 20 minutes, until the meat is tender. Season with salt and pepper and serve with crusty bread or rice and a salad.

Variation

This dish can also be made with beef or pork – either way it is delicious served with chunks of fresh, crusty bread.

spicy meat balls Energy 213kcal/881kJ; Protein 13.2g; Carbohydrate 3.4g, of which sugars 2.6g; Fat 16.3g, of which saturates 5.1g; Cholesterol 41mg; Calcium 23mg; Fibre 0.5g; Sodium 180mg.
beef w. aubergines Energy 251kcal/1050kJ; Protein 27.2g; Carbohydrate 7.2g, of which sugars 6.2g; Fat 12.8g, of which saturates 2.9g; Cholesterol 75mg; Calcium 29mg; Fibre 3g; Sodium 87mg.

Citrus Beef Curry

This superbly aromatic curry is not too hot but nonetheless full of flavour. For a special meal, it goes perfectly with fried noodles.

Ingredients

450g/1lb rump (round) steak
30ml/2 tbsp sunflower oil
30ml/2 tbsp medium curry paste
2 bay leaves
400ml/14fl oz/1⅔ cups coconut milk
300ml/½ pint/1¼ cups beef stock
30ml/2 tbsp lemon juice
45ml/3 tbsp fish sauce
15ml/1 tbsp sugar
115g/4oz baby (pearl) onions, peeled but left whole
225g/8oz new potatoes, halved
115g/4oz/1 cup unsalted roasted peanuts, roughly chopped
115g/4oz fine green beans, halved
1 red (bell) pepper, seeded and thinly sliced
unsalted roasted peanuts, to garnish

Serves 4

1 Trim any fat off the beef and use a sharp knife to cut it into 5cm/2in strips.

2 Heat the oil in a work or large pan, add the curry paste and cook over a medium heat for 30 seconds, stirring constantly.

3 Add the beef and cook, stirring, for 2 minutes until it is beginning to brown and is thoroughly coated with the spices.

4 Stir in the bay leaves, coconut milk, stock, lemon juice, fish sauce and sugar, and bring to the boil, stirring.

5 Add the onions and potatoes, then bring back to the boil, reduce the heat and simmer, uncovered, for 5 minutes.

6 Stir in the peanuts, beans and pepper and simmer for a further 10 minutes, or until the beef and potatoes are tender. Serve in warmed shallow bowls, with a spoon and fork, to enjoy all the rich and creamy juices. Sprinkle with extra unsalted roasted peanuts, to garnish.

Chilli Beef & Butternut

Stir-fried beef and sweet, orange-fleshed squash flavoured with warm spices, oyster sauce and fresh herbs makes a robust main course when served with rice or egg noodles. The addition of chilli and fresh root ginger gives the dish a wonderful vigorous bite.

Ingredients

30ml/2 tbsp sunflower oil
2 onions, cut into thick slices
500g/1¼lb butternut squash, peeled, seeded and cut into thin strips
675g/1½lb fillet steak (beef tenderloin)
60ml/4 tbsp soy sauce
90g/3½oz/½ cup golden caster (superfine) sugar
1 fresh bird's eye chilli or a milder red chilli, seeded and chopped
15ml/1 tbsp finely shredded fresh root ginger
30ml/2 tbsp fish sauce
5ml/1 tsp ground star anise
5ml/1 tsp five-spice powder
15ml/1 tbsp oyster sauce
4 spring onions (scallions), shredded
a small handful of sweet basil leaves
a small handful of mint leaves

Serves 4

1 Heat a wok over a medium-high heat and add the oil. When hot, stir in the onions and squash. Stir-fry for 2–3 minutes, then reduce the heat, cover and cook gently for 5–6 minutes, or until the vegetables are just tender.

2 Place the beef between two sheets of clear film (plastic wrap) and beat, with a mallet or rolling pin, until thin. Using a sharp knife, cut into thin strips.

3 In a separate wok, mix the soy sauce, sugar, chilli, ginger, fish sauce, star anise, five-spice powder and oyster sauce. Cook for 3–4 minutes, stirring frequently.

4 Add the beef to the soy sauce mixture in the wok and cook over a high heat for 3–4 minutes. Remove from the heat. Add the onion and squash slices to the beef and toss well with the spring onions and herbs. Serve immediately.

citrus beef curry Energy 476kcal/1990kJ; Protein 33.8g; Carbohydrate 27.5g, of which sugars 16.3g; Fat 26.4g, of which saturates 6.6g; Cholesterol 69mg; Calcium 77mg; Fibre 4.1g; Sodium 169mg.
chilli beef Energy 500kcal/2093kJ; Protein 41.3g; Carbohydrate 36.9g, of which sugars 33.8g; Fat 21.7g, of which saturates 7.2g; Cholesterol 98mg; Calcium 91mg; Fibre 2.9g; Sodium 1243mg.

Stir-fried Beef with Oyster Sauce

Another simple but very tasty recipe. It is often made with just straw mushrooms, when these are available fresh, but oyster mushrooms make a good substitute and using a mixture makes the dish extra interesting.

Ingredients

450g/1lb rump (round) steak
30ml/2 tbsp soy sauce
15ml/1 tbsp cornflour (cornstarch)
45ml/3 tbsp vegetable oil
15ml/1 tbsp chopped garlic
15ml/1 tbsp chopped fresh root ginger
225g/8oz/3¼ cups mixed mushrooms such as shiitake, oyster and straw
30ml/2 tbsp oyster sauce
5ml/1 tsp sugar
4 spring onions (scallions), cut into short lengths
ground black pepper
2 fresh red chillies, seeded and cut into strips, to garnish

Serves 4–6

1 Place the steak in the freezer for 30–40 minutes, until firm, then slice it on the diagonal into long thin strips. Mix together the soy sauce and cornflour in a large bowl. Add the steak, turning to coat well, cover with clear film (plastic wrap) and marinate at room temperature for 1–2 hours.

2 Heat half the oil in a wok. Add the garlic and ginger and cook for 1–2 minutes, until fragrant. Drain the steak, add it to the wok and stir-fry for a further 1–2 minutes, until the steak is tender. Remove from the wok and set aside.

3 Heat the remaining oil in the wok and stir-fry the mushrooms until golden brown. Return the steak to the wok and mix it with the mushrooms.

4 Spoon the oyster sauce and sugar into the wok, mix well, then add ground black pepper to taste. Toss over the heat until all the ingredients are thoroughly combined, then stir in the spring onions.

5 Tip the mixture on to a heated serving platter, garnish with the strips of red chilli and serve.

Beef with Black Bean Sauce

The black bean sauce gives this low-fat dish a lovely rich flavour. The beef is first simmered in stock and then stir-fried with garlic, ginger, chilli and green pepper.

Ingredients

350g/12oz rump (round) steak, trimmed and thinly sliced
15ml/1 tbsp vegetable oil
300ml/½ pint/1¼ cups beef stock
2 garlic cloves, finely chopped
5ml/1 tsp grated fresh root ginger
1 fresh red chilli, seeded and finely chopped
15ml/1 tbsp black bean sauce
1 green (bell) pepper, seeded and cut into 2.5cm/1in squares
15ml/1 tbsp dry sherry
5ml/1 tsp cornflour (cornstarch)
5ml/1 tsp caster (superfine) sugar
45ml/3 tbsp cold water
salt
rice noodles, to serve

Serves 4

1 Place the sliced steak in a bowl. Add 5ml/1 tsp of the oil and stir to coat.

2 Bring the stock to the boil in a large pan. Add the sliced steak and cook for 2 minutes, stirring constantly to prevent the slices from sticking together. Lift out the beef and set aside.

3 Heat the remaining oil in a wok. Stir-fry the garlic, ginger and chilli with the black bean sauce for a few seconds.

4 Add the pepper and a little water. Cook for about 2 minutes more, then stir in the sherry. Add the beef slices to the pan and spoon the sauce over to coat them.

5 Mix the cornflour and sugar to a paste with the water. Pour the mixture into the pan. Cook, stirring, until the sauce has thickened. Season and serve immediately, with rice noodles.

Cook's Tip

For extra colour, use half each of a green and red pepper.

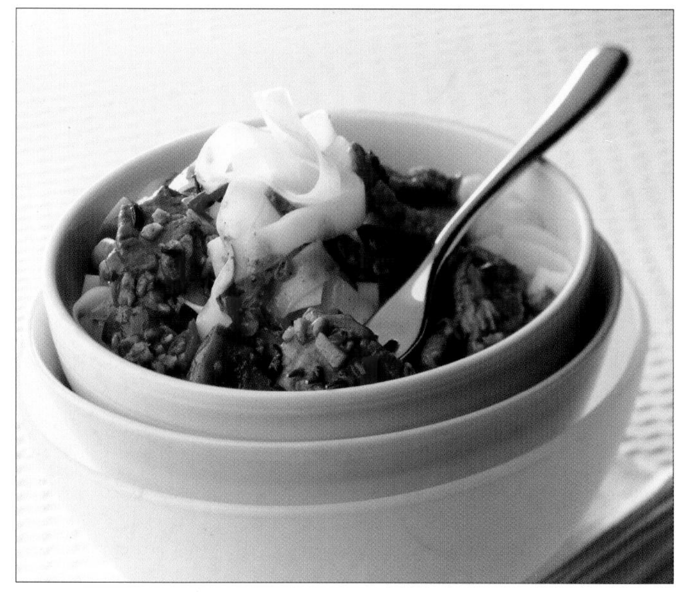

beef w. oyster sauce Energy 205kcal/852kJ; Protein 18.4g; Carbohydrate 3.5g, of which sugars 1g; Fat 13.1g, of which saturates 3.7g; Cholesterol 45mg; Calcium 10mg; Fibre 0.5g; Sodium 53mg.
beef w. black bean Energy 219kcal/912kJ; Protein 19.5g; Carbohydrate 8.4g, of which sugars 5.8g; Fat 12g, of which saturates 3.1g; Cholesterol 33mg; Calcium 69mg; Fibre 4.5g; Sodium 907mg.

Dry Beef & Peanut Butter Curry

Although this is called a dry curry, the method of cooking keeps the beef succulent.

Ingredients

400g/14oz can coconut milk
900g/2lb stewing beef, finely chopped
300ml/½ pint/1¼ cups beef stock
30–40ml/2–3 tbsp red curry paste
30ml/2 tbsp crunchy peanut butter
juice of 2 limes
lime slices, shredded coriander (cilantro) and fresh red chilli slices, to garnish

Serves 4–6

1 Strain the coconut milk into a bowl, retaining the thicker coconut milk in the strainer or sieve.

2 Pour the thin coconut milk from the bowl into a large, heavy pan, then scrape in half the residue from the sieve. Reserve the remaining thick coconut milk. Add the chopped beef. Pour in the beef stock and bring to the boil. Reduce the heat, cover the pan and simmer gently for 50 minutes.

3 Strain the beef, reserving the cooking liquid, and place a cupful of liquid in a wok. Stir in 30–45ml/2–3 tbsp of the curry paste, according to taste. Boil rapidly until all the liquid has evaporated. Stir in the reserved thick coconut milk, the peanut butter and the beef. Simmer, uncovered, for 15–20 minutes, adding a little more cooking liquid if the mixture starts to stick to the pan, but keep the curry dry.

4 Just before serving, stir in the lime juice. Serve in warmed bowls, garnished with the lime slices, shredded coriander and sliced red chillies.

Variation

The curry is equally delicious made with lean leg or shoulder of lamb, or with pork fillet (tenderloin).

Green Beef Curry

Use good-quality meat for this quick-cook curry. Sirloin steak is recommended, but tender rump steak could be used instead. If you buy the curry paste, there's very little additional preparation.

Ingredients

450g/1lb sirloin steak
15ml/1 tbsp vegetable oil
45ml/3 tbsp green curry paste
600ml/1 pint/2½ cups coconut milk
4 kaffir lime leaves, torn
15–30ml/1–2 tbsp fish sauce
5ml/1 tsp palm sugar (jaggery) or light muscovado (brown) sugar
150g/5oz small Thai aubergines (eggplants), halved
small handful of fresh Thai basil leaves
2 fresh green chillies, finely shredded, to garnish

Serves 4–6

1 Trim off any excess fat from the beef. Using a sharp knife, cut it into long, thin strips. Set the beef strips aside on a plate.

2 Heat the oil in a wok. Add the curry paste and cook for 1–2 minutes, until it you can smell the fragrances.

3 Stir in half the coconut milk, a little at a time. Cook, stirring frequently, for about 5–6 minutes, until an oily sheen appears on the surface of the liquid.

4 Add the beef to the pan with the kaffir lime leaves, fish sauce, sugar and aubergine halves. Cook for 2–3 minutes, then stir in the remaining coconut milk.

5 Bring back to a simmer and cook until the meat and aubergines are tender. Stir in the Thai basil just before serving. Garnish with the shredded green chillies.

Cook's Tip

It's easiest to slice the beef if you place it in the freezer for about 20 minutes to firm up first.

beef & peanut butter Energy 296kcal/1238kJ; Protein 35.2g; Carbohydrate 4.9g, of which sugars 4.5g; Fat 15.2g, of which saturates 4.8g; Cholesterol 103mg; Calcium 66mg; Fibre 0.7g; Sodium 262mg.
green beef curry Energy 176kcal/738kJ; Protein 17.6g; Carbohydrate 6.2g, of which sugars 6.1g; Fat 9.2g, of which saturates 3.3g; Cholesterol 44mg; Calcium 36mg; Fibre 0.5g; Sodium 159mg.

Sweet & Sour Pork

This is a modern Chinese classic. The delicate flavour of pork combines beautifully with the tangy flavour of this easy-to-make sweet and sour sauce. Serve this dish very simply, accompanied by plain boiled rice and steamed Asian greens.

Ingredients

45ml/3 tbsp light soy sauce
15ml/1 tbsp Chinese rice wine
15ml/1 tbsp sesame oil
5ml/1 tsp ground black pepper
500g/1 ¼lb pork loin, cut into 1cm/½in cubes
65g/2½oz/9 tbsp cornflour (cornstarch)
1 carrot
1 red (bell) pepper
4 spring onions (scallions)
65g/2½oz/9 tbsp plain (all-purpose) flour
5ml/1 tsp bicarbonate of soda (baking soda)
sunflower oil, for deep-frying
10ml/2 tsp finely grated garlic
5ml/1 tsp finely grated fresh root ginger
60ml/4 tbsp tomato ketchup
30ml/2 tbsp sugar
15ml/1 tbsp rice vinegar
15ml/1 tbsp cornflour (cornstarch) blended with 120ml/4fl oz/½ cup water

Serves 4

1 In a large mixing bowl, combine 15ml/1 tbsp of the soy sauce with the rice wine, sesame oil and pepper. Add the pork and toss to mix. Cover and chill for 3–4 hours. Meanwhile, cut the carrots, pepper and spring onions in shreds, and set aside.

2 Combine the cornflour, plain flour and bicarbonate of soda in a bowl. Add a pinch of salt and mix in 150ml/¼ pint/⅔ cup cold water to make a thick batter. Add the pork and mix well.

3 Separate the pork cubes and deep-fry them, in batches in hot oil, for 1–2 minutes, or until golden. Drain on kitchen paper.

4 Mix the garlic, ginger, tomato ketchup, sugar, the remaining soy sauce, rice vinegar and cornflour mixture in a wok or pan. Stir over a medium heat for 2–3 minutes, until thickened. Add the carrot, red pepper and spring onions, stir and remove from the heat.

5 Reheat the deep-frying oil and then re-fry the pork pieces in batches for 1–2 minutes, until golden and crisp. Drain and add to the sauce and toss to mix well. Serve solo or with egg-fried rice or noodles.

Aromatic Pork with Basil

The combination of moist, juicy pork and mushrooms, crisp green mangetouts and fragrant basil in this ginger- and garlic-infused stir-fry is absolutely delicious.

Ingredients

40g/1½oz cornflour (cornstarch)
500g/1¼lb pork fillet (tenderloin), thinly sliced
15ml/1 tbsp sunflower oil
10ml/2 tsp sesame oil
15ml/1 tbsp very finely shredded fresh root ginger
3 garlic cloves, thinly sliced
200g/7oz/scant 2 cups mangetouts (snow peas), halved
300g/11oz/generous 4 cups mixed mushrooms, sliced if large
120ml/4fl oz/½ cup Chinese cooking wine
45ml/3 tbsp soy sauce
a small handful of sweet basil leaves
salt and ground black pepper
steamed jasmine rice, to serve

Serves 4

1 Place the cornflour in a strong plastic bag. Season well and add the sliced pork. Shake the bag to coat the pork in flour and then remove the pork and shake off any excess flour. Set aside.

2 Preheat the wok over a high heat and add the oils. When very hot, stir in the ginger and garlic and cook for 30 seconds. Add the pork and cook over a high heat for about 5 minutes, stirring often, until sealed.

3 Add the mangetouts and mushrooms to the wok and stir-fry for 2–3 minutes. Add the Chinese cooking wine and soy sauce, stir-fry for 2–3 minutes and remove from the heat.

4 Just before serving, stir the sweet basil leaves into the pork. Serve with steamed jasmine rice.

Cook's Tip
For the mushroom medley, try to include fresh shiitake and oyster mushrooms as well as cultivated button (white) ones.

sweet & sour pork Energy 727kcal/3035kJ; Protein 32.7g; Carbohydrate 76.5g, of which sugars 39.4g; Fat 32.8g, of which saturates 5.8g; Cholesterol 272mg; Calcium 85mg; Fibre 2.7g; Sodium 1048mg.
aromatic pork Energy 298kcal/1248kJ; Protein 30.4g; Carbohydrate 14.6g, of which sugars 4.8g; Fat 9.8g, of which saturates 2.4g; Cholesterol 79mg; Calcium 41mg; Fibre 2g; Sodium 903mg.

Pork Chops with Field Mushrooms

Barbecued pork chops are delicious with noodles.

Ingredients
4 pork chops
4 large field (portabello) mushrooms
45ml/3 tbsp vegetable oil
4 fresh red chillies, seeded and thinly sliced
45ml/3 tbsp fish sauce
90ml/6 tbsp fresh lime juice
4 shallots, chopped
5ml/1 tsp roasted ground rice
60ml/4 tbsp spring onions (scallions), shredded
coriander (cilantro) leaves, to garnish

For the marinade
2 garlic cloves, chopped
15ml/1 tbsp sugar
15ml/1 tbsp fish sauce
30ml/2 tbsp soy sauce
15ml/1 tbsp sesame oil
15ml/1 tbsp whisky or dry sherry
2 lemon grass stalks, finely chopped
2 spring onions (scallions), chopped

Serves 4

1 Make the marinade. Combine the garlic, sugar, sauces, oil and whisky or sherry in a large, shallow dish. Stir in the lemon grass and the chopped spring onions.

2 Add the pork chops, turning to coat them in the marinade. Cover and leave to marinate for 1–2 hours.

3 Lift the chops out of the marinade and place them on a barbecue grid over hot coals or on a grill (broiler) rack. Add the mushrooms and brush them with 15ml/1 tbsp of the oil.

4 Cook the pork chops for 5–7 minutes on each side and the mushrooms for about 2 minutes. Brush both with the marinade while cooking.

5 Heat the remaining oil in a wok or small frying pan, then remove the pan from the heat and stir in the chillies, fish sauce, lime juice, shallots, ground rice and half the shredded spring onions. Put the pork chops and mushrooms on a large serving plate and spoon over the sauce. Garnish with the coriander leaves and remaining shredded spring onion.

Pork Belly with Five Spices

This recipe originated in China, but travelled to Thailand when colonists from southern China settled in the country. Over the centuries, the dish has evolved and Thai cooks have provided their own unique imprint.

Ingredients
1 large bunch fresh coriander (cilantro) with roots
30ml/2 tbsp vegetable oil
1 garlic clove, crushed
30ml/2 tbsp five-spice powder
500g/1¼lb pork belly, cut into 2.5cm/1in pieces
400g/14oz can chopped tomatoes
150ml/¼ pint/⅔ cup hot water
30ml/2 tbsp dark soy sauce
45ml/3 tbsp fish sauce
30ml/2 tbsp sugar
1 lime, halved

Serves 4

1 Cut off the coriander roots. Chop five of them finely and freeze the remainder for another occasion. Chop the coriander stalks and leaves and set them aside. Keep the roots separate.

2 Heat the oil in a wok or large pan and cook the garlic until golden brown. Stirring constantly, add the chopped coriander roots and then the five-spice powder.

3 Add the pork and stir-fry until the meat is thoroughly coated in spices and has browned. Stir in the tomatoes and hot water. Bring to the boil, then stir in the soy sauce, fish sauce and sugar.

4 Reduce the heat, cover the wok or pan and simmer for 30 minutes. Stir in the chopped coriander stalks and leaves, squeeze over the lime juice and ladle into bowls. Serve.

Cook's Tip
Make sure that you buy Chinese five-spice powder, as the Indian variety is made up from quite different spices.

chops w. mushrooms Energy 342kcal/1423kJ; Protein 34g; Carbohydrate 1.7g, of which sugars 1.2g; Fat 22.1g, of which saturates 5.3g; Cholesterol 110mg; Calcium 21mg; Fibre 1.2g; Sodium 89mg.
pork belly Energy 581kcal/2405kJ; Protein 20.6g; Carbohydrate 11.6g, of which sugars 11.5g; Fat 50.5g, of which saturates 17.1g; Cholesterol 90mg; Calcium 71mg; Fibre 2.3g; Sodium 109mg.

Braised Pork Belly with Greens

Pork belly becomes meltingly tender in this slow-braised dish flavoured with orange, cinnamon, star anise and ginger. The flavours meld and mellow during cooking to produce a rich, complex, rounded taste. Serve simply with rice and steamed greens.

Ingredients

800g/1¾lb pork belly, trimmed and cut into 12 pieces
400ml/14fl oz/1⅔ cups beef stock
75ml/5 tbsp soy sauce
finely grated rind and juice of 1 large orange
15ml/1 tbsp finely shredded fresh root ginger
2 garlic cloves, sliced
15ml/1 tbsp hot chilli powder
15ml/1 tbsp muscovado (molasses) sugar
3 cinnamon sticks
3 cloves
10 black peppercorns
2–3 star anise
steamed greens and rice, to serve

Serves 4

1 Place the pork in a wok and pour over water to cover. Bring the water to the boil. Cover, reduce the heat and cook gently for 30 minutes.

2 Drain the pork and return to the wok with the stock, soy sauce, orange rind and juice, ginger, garlic, chilli powder, muscovado sugar, cinnamon sticks, cloves, peppercorns and star anise. Pour over enought water to just cover the pork belly pieces and cook on a high heat until the mixture comes to a boil.

3 Cover the wok tightly with a lid, then reduce the heat to low and cook gently for 1½ hours, stirring occasionally to prevent the pork from sticking to the base of the wok.

4 Taste the sauce and season to taste. You are unlikely to need pepper, with peppercorns a prime ingredient, but may wish to add a little salt. Serve in warmed bowls.

Stir-fried Pork Ribs

Sweet-and-sour spare ribs, a Chinese classic adopted by culinary cultures the world over, has given rise to some interesting variations. This version includes basil leaves and fish sauce. This is finger food at its finest, requiring finger bowls and plenty of napkins, and is perfect served with sticky rice and a salad.

Ingredients

45ml/3 tbsp hoisin sauce
45ml/3 tbsp fish sauce
10ml/2 tsp five-spice powder
45ml/3 tbsp vegetable or sesame oil
900g/2lb pork ribs
3 garlic cloves, crushed
4cm/1½in fresh root ginger, peeled and grated
1 bunch fresh basil, stalks removed, leaves shredded

Serves 4–6

1 In a bowl, mix together the hoisin sauce, fish sauce and five-spice powder with 15ml/1 tbsp of the oil.

2 Bring a large wok or pan of water to the boil, then add the pork ribs, bring back to the boil and blanch for 10 minutes. Lift the pork ribs out with a slotted spoon and drain well, then set them aside. Discard the liquid.

3 Heat the remaining oil in a clean wok. Add the crushed garlic and grated ginger and cook, stirring, until fragrant, then add the blanched pork ribs.

4 Stir-fry for about 5 minutes, or until the pork ribs are well browned, then add the hoisin sauce mixture, turning the ribs so that each one is thoroughly coated. Continue stir-frying for 10–15 minutes, or until there is almost no liquid in the wok and the ribs are caramelized and slightly blackened.

5 Add the shredded basil leaves and stir. Serve the ribs straight from the pan or in individual warmed dishes.

6 Offer dinner guests finger bowls containing water and slices of lemon or lime, and plenty of napkins to wipe sticky fingers.

pork belly w. greens Energy 543kcal/2260kJ; Protein 38.9g; Carbohydrate 6.6g, of which sugars 6.4g; Fat 40.4g, of which saturates 14.6g; Cholesterol 142mg; Calcium 19mg; Fibre 0g; Sodium 1475mg.
stir-fried ribs Energy 633kcal/2638kJ; Protein 42.9g; Carbohydrate 11.5g, of which sugars 11.2g; Fat 45.2g, of which saturates 14.1g; Cholesterol 149mg; Calcium 43mg; Fibre 0.5g; Sodium 250mg.

Curried Pork with Pickled Garlic

This very rich curry is best accompanied by lots of plain rice and perhaps a light vegetable dish. It could serve four with a vegetable curry on the side, and perhaps some steamed greeens, such as pak choi (bok choy) or curly kale.

Ingredients

130g/4½oz lean pork steaks
30ml/2 tbsp vegetable oil
1 garlic clove, crushed
15ml/1 tbsp red curry paste
130ml/4½fl oz/generous ½ cup coconut cream
2.5cm/1in piece fresh root ginger, finely chopped
30ml/2 tbsp vegetable or chicken stock
30ml/2 tbsp fish sauce
5ml/1 tsp sugar
2.5ml/½ tsp ground turmeric
10ml/2 tsp lemon juice
4 pickled garlic cloves, finely chopped
strips of lemon and lime rind, to garnish

Serves 2

1 Place the pork steaks in the freezer for 30–40 minutes, until firm, then, using a sharp knife, cut the meat into fine slivers, trimming off any excess fat.

2 Heat the oil in a wok or large, heavy frying pan and cook the garlic over a low to medium heat until golden brown. Do not let it burn. Add the curry paste and stir it in well.

3 Add the coconut cream and stir until the liquid begins to reduce and thicken. Stir in the pork. Cook for 2 minutes more, until the pork is cooked through.

4 Add the ginger, stock, fish sauce, sugar and turmeric, stirring constantly, then add the lemon juice and pickled garlic and heat through. Serve in warmed bowls, garnished with strips of rind.

Cook's Tip
Asian stores sell pickled garlic. It is well worth investing in, as the taste is sweet and delicious.

Pork & Butternut Curry

This curry can be made with butternut squash, pumpkin or winter melon. It is delicious served with rice and a fruit-based salad, or even just with chunks of fresh crusty bread to mop up the tasty sauce.

Ingredients

30ml/2 tbsp groundnut (peanut) oil
25g/1oz galangal, finely sliced
2 fresh red chillies, peeled, seeded and finely sliced
3 shallots, halved and finely sliced
30ml/2 tbsp kroeung or magic paste
10ml/2 tsp ground turmeric
5ml/1 tsp ground fenugreek
10ml/2 tsp palm sugar (jaggery)
450g/1lb pork loin, cut into bitesize chunks
30ml/2 tbsp fish sauce
900ml/1½ pints/3¾ cups coconut milk
1 butternut squash, peeled, seeded and cut into bitesize chunks
4 kaffir lime leaves
sea salt and ground black pepper
1 small bunch fresh coriander (cilantro), coarsely chopped and 1 small bunch fresh mint, stalks removed, to garnish
rice or noodles and salad, to serve

Serves 4–6

1 Heat the oil in a large wok or heavy pan. Stir in the galangal, chillies and shallots and stir-fry until fragrant. Add the kroeung or magic paste and stir-fry until it begins to colour. Add the turmeric, fenugreek and sugar and stir to combine.

2 Stir in the chunks of pork loin and stir-fry until golden brown on all sides. Stir in the fish sauce and pour in the coconut milk.

3 Bring to the boil, add the squash and the lime leaves, and reduce the heat. Cook gently, uncovered, for 15–20 minutes, until the squash and pork are tender and the sauce has reduced. Season to taste. Garnish the curry with the coriander and mint, and serve with rice or noodles and salad.

Cook's Tip
Increase the number of chillies if you want a really hot curry.

curried pork w. garlic Energy 227kcal/947kJ; Protein 16.3g; Carbohydrate 9.8g, of which sugars 6.1g; Fat 14g, of which saturates 2.4g; Cholesterol 41mg; Calcium 30mg; Fibre 1g; Sodium 474mg.
pork & butternut Energy 149kcal/628kJ; Protein 17g; Carbohydrate 10.6g, of which sugars 10.2g; Fat 4.6g, of which saturates 1.5g; Cholesterol 47mg; Calcium 71mg; Fibre 0.7g; Sodium 221mg.

Chicken with Lemon Sauce

Succulent chicken with a refreshing lemony sauce and just a hint of lime is a sure winner as a family meal that is quick and easy to prepare.

Ingredients
4 small skinless chicken breast fillets
5ml/1 tsp sesame oil
15ml/1 tbsp dry sherry
1 egg white, lightly beaten
30ml/2 tbsp cornflour (cornstarch)
15ml/1 tbsp vegetable oil
salt and ground white pepper
chopped coriander (cilantro) leaves and spring onions (scallions) and lemon wedges, to garnish

For the sauce
45ml/3 tbsp fresh lemon juice
30ml/2 tbsp sweetened lime juice
45ml/3 tbsp caster (superfine) sugar
10ml/2 tsp cornflour (cornstarch)
90ml/6 tbsp cold water

Serves 4

1 Arrange the chicken fillets in a single layer in a bowl. Mix the sesame oil with the sherry and add 2.5ml/½ tsp salt and 1.5ml/¼ tsp pepper. Pour over the chicken, cover and marinate for 15 minutes at room temperature.

2 Mix together the egg white and cornflour. Add the mixture to the chicken and turn the chicken with tongs until thoroughly coated.

3 Heat the vegetable oil in a non-stick frying pan or wok and fry the chicken fillets for about 15 minutes until they are golden brown on both sides.

4 Meanwhile, make the sauce. Combine the lemon juice, lime juice, sugar, cornflour and water in a small pan. Add 1.5ml/¼ tsp salt. Bring to the boil over a low heat, stirring constantly until the sauce is smooth and has thickened.

5 Cut the chicken into pieces and place on a warm serving plate. Pour the sauce over, garnish with the coriander leaves, spring onions and lemon wedges.

Chicken with Mixed Vegetables

Far East Asian cooks are experts in making delicious dishes from a relatively small amount of meat and a lot of vegetables. Good news for anyone trying to eat less fat.

Ingredients
350g/12oz skinless chicken breast fillets
20ml/4 tsp vegetable oil
300ml/½ pint/1¼ cups chicken stock
75g/3oz/¾ cup drained, canned straw mushrooms
50g/2oz/½ cup sliced, drained, canned bamboo shoots
50g/2oz/⅓ cup drained, canned water chestnuts, sliced
1 small carrot, sliced
50g/2oz/½ cup mangetouts (snow peas)
15ml/1 tbsp dry sherry
15ml/1 tbsp oyster sauce
5ml/1 tsp caster (superfine) sugar
5ml/1 tsp cornflour (cornstarch)
15ml/1 tbsp cold water
salt and ground white pepper

Serves 4

1 Put the chicken in a shallow bowl. Add 5ml/1 tsp of the oil, 1.5ml/¼ tsp salt and a pinch of pepper. Cover and set aside for 10 minutes in a cool place.

2 Bring the stock to the boil in a pan. Add the chicken fillets and cook for 12 minutes, or until tender. Drain and slice, reserving 75ml/5 tbsp of the chicken stock.

3 Heat the remaining oil in a non-stick frying pan or wok, add all the vegetables and stir-fry for 2 minutes. Stir in the sherry, oyster sauce, caster sugar and reserved stock. Add the chicken to the pan and cook for 2 minutes more.

4 Mix the cornflour to a paste with the water. Add the mixture to the pan and cook, stirring, until the sauce thickens slightly. Season to taste with salt and pepper and serve immediately.

Cook's Tip
Water chestnuts give a dish great texture as they remain crunchy, no matter how long you cook them for.

chicken w. lemon Energy 235kcal/995kJ; Protein 30.9g; Carbohydrate 23.3g, of which sugars 14.1g; Fat 2.2g, of which saturates 0.5g; Cholesterol 88mg; Calcium 15mg; Fibre 0g; Sodium 97mg.
chicken w. vegetables Energy 154kcal/646kJ; Protein 22.2g; Carbohydrate 4.9g, of which sugars 3.4g; Fat 4.3g, of which saturates 0.7g; Cholesterol 61mg; Calcium 17mg; Fibre 1g; Sodium 61mg.

Chicken & Lemon Grass Curry

A tasty curry in less than 20 minutes – what more can anyone ask?

Ingredients

45ml/3 tbsp vegetable oil
2 garlic cloves, crushed
500g/1¼lb skinless, boneless chicken thighs, diced
45ml/3 tbsp fish sauce
120ml/4fl oz/½ cup chicken stock
5ml/1 tsp sugar
1 lemon grass stalk, chopped into 4 sticks and lightly crushed
5 kaffir lime leaves, rolled into cylinders and thinly sliced across, plus extra to garnish

For the curry paste

1 lemon grass stalk, coarsely chopped
2.5cm/1in piece fresh galangal, peeled and coarsely chopped
2 kaffir lime leaves, chopped
3 shallots, coarsely chopped
6 coriander (cilantro) roots, coarsely chopped
2 garlic cloves
2 fresh green chillies, seeded and coarsely chopped
5ml/1 tsp shrimp paste
5ml/1 tsp ground turmeric
chopped roasted peanuts and chopped fresh coriander (cilantro), to garnish

Serves 4

1 Make the curry paste. Place all the ingredients in a large mortar or food processor and pound with a pestle or process to a smooth paste.

2 Heat the vegetable oil in a wok, add the garlic and cook over a low heat, stirring frequently, until golden brown. Be careful not to let the garlic burn or it will taste bitter. Add the curry paste and stir-fry for 30 seconds more.

3 Add the chicken pieces to the pan and stir until thoroughly coated with the curry paste. Stir in the fish sauce and chicken stock, then add the sugar, and cook, stirring constantly, for 2 minutes more.

4 Add the lemon grass and lime leaves, reduce the heat and simmer for 10 minutes. Spoon the curry into four warmed dishes, garnish and serve immediately.

Red Chicken Curry

Bamboo shoots give this a lovely crunchy texture.

Ingredients

1 litre/1¾ pints/4 cups coconut milk
30ml/2 tbsp red curry paste
450g/1lb skinless chicken breast fillets, cut into bitesize pieces
30ml/2 tbsp fish sauce
15ml/1 tbsp sugar
225g/8oz drained canned bamboo shoots, rinsed and sliced
5 kaffir lime leaves, torn
salt and ground black pepper
chopped fresh red chillies and kaffir lime leaves, to garnish

Serves 4–6

1 Pour half of the coconut milk into a wok or large heavy pan. Bring to the boil, stirring constantly until it has separated.

2 Stir in the red curry paste and cook the mixture for about 2–3 minutes, stirring constantly.

Add the chicken pieces, fish sauce and sugar to the wok or pan. Stir well, then cook for 5–6 minutes until the chicken changes colour and is cooked through, stirring constantly to prevent the mixture from sticking to the bottom of the pan.

4 Pour the remaining coconut milk into the pan, then add the sliced bamboo shoots and torn kaffir lime leaves. Bring back to the boil over a medium heat, stirring constantly to prevent the mixture sticking, then taste and season if necessary.

5 To serve, spoon the curry into a warmed serving dish and garnish with chopped chillies and kaffir lime leaves.

Cook's Tip

It is essential to use chicken breast fillets, rather than any other cut, for this curry, as it is cooked very quickly. Look out for diced chicken or strips of chicken (which are often labelled "stir-fry chicken") in the supermarket.

chicken & lemon grass Energy 122kcal/512kJ; Protein 17.4g; Carbohydrate 3.7g, of which sugars 3g; Fat 4.3g, of which saturates 0.8g; Cholesterol 85mg; Calcium 77mg; Fibre 1.6g; Sodium 131mg.
red chicken curry Energy 261kcal/1105kJ; Protein 29.6g; Carbohydrate 19.6g, of which sugars 18.3g; Fat 7.8g, of which saturates 1.5g; Cholesterol 79mg; Calcium 95mg; Fibre 1.1g; Sodium 837mg.

Jungle Curry of Guinea Fowl

A traditional wild food country curry, this dish can be made using any game, fish or chicken.

Ingredients

1 guinea fowl or similar game bird
15ml/1 tbsp vegetable oil
10ml/2 tsp green curry paste
15ml/1 tbsp fish sauce
2.5cm/1in piece fresh galangal, peeled and finely chopped
15ml/1 tbsp fresh green peppercorns
3 kaffir lime leaves, torn
15ml/1 tbsp whisky
300ml/½ pint/1¼ cups chicken stock
50g/2oz snake beans or yard-long beans, cut into 2.5cm/1in lengths (about ½ cup)
225g/8oz/3¼ cups chestnut mushrooms, sliced
1 piece drained canned bamboo shoot, about 50g/2oz, shredded

Serves 4

1 Cut up the guinea fowl, remove and discard the skin, then take all the meat off the bones. Chop the meat into bitesize pieces and set aside on a plate.

2 Heat the oil in a wok or frying pan and add the curry paste. Stir-fry over a medium heat for 30 seconds, until the paste gives off its aroma. Add the fish sauce and the guinea fowl meat and stir-fry until the meat is browned all over. Add the galangal, peppercorns, lime leaves and whisky, then pour in the stock.

3 Bring to the boil. Add the vegetables, return to a simmer and cook gently for 2–3 minutes, until they are just cooked. Spoon into a dish, and serve.

Cook's Tip
Fresh green peppercorns are simply unripe berries. They are sold on the stem and look rather like miniature Brussels sprout stalks. Look for them at Thai supermarkets. If unavailable, substitute bottled green peppercorns, but rinse well and drain them before adding them to the curry.

Cashew Chicken

One of the most popular items on any Chinese restaurant menu, Cashew Chicken is easy to recreate at home.

Ingredients

450g/1lb skinless chicken breast fillets
1 red (bell) pepper
2 garlic cloves
4 dried red chillies
30ml/2 tbsp vegetable oil
30ml/2 tbsp oyster sauce
15ml/1 tbsp soy sauce
pinch of sugar
1 bunch spring onions (scallions), cut into 5cm/2in lengths
175g/6oz/1½ cups cashew nuts, roasted
coriander (cilantro) leaves, to garnish

Serves 4–6

1 Remove and discard the skin from the chicken breast fillets and trim off any excess fat. With a sharp knife, cut the chicken into bitesize pieces and set aside.

2 Halve the red pepper, scrape out the seeds and membranes and discard, then cut the flesh into 2cm/¾ in dice. Peel and thinly slice the garlic and chop the dried red chillies.

3 Preheat a wok and then heat the oil. The best way to do this is to drizzle a "necklace" of oil around the inner rim of the wok, so that it drops down to coat the entire inner surface. Make sure the coating is even by swirling the wok.

4 Add the garlic and dried chillies to the wok and stir-fry over a medium heat until golden. Do not let the garlic burn, otherwise it will taste bitter.

5 Add the chicken to the wok and stir-fry until it is cooked through, then add the red pepper. If the mixture is very dry, add a little water.

6 Stir in the oyster sauce, soy sauce and sugar. Add the spring onions and cashew nuts. Stir-fry for 1–2 minutes more, until heated through. Spoon into a warm dish and serve immediately, garnished with the coriander leaves.

curry of guinea fowl Energy 321kcal/1345kJ; Protein 42.2g; Carbohydrate 1.1g, of which sugars 0.7g; Fat 15g, of which saturates 4.4g; Cholesterol 0mg; Calcium 72mg; Fibre 1.1g; Sodium 136mg.
cashew chicken Energy 314kcal/1307kJ; Protein 24.7g; Carbohydrate 10.2g, of which sugars 6.2g; Fat 19.6g, of which saturates 3.7g; Cholesterol 53mg; Calcium 24mg; Fibre 1.7g; Sodium 268mg.

Spicy Fried Chicken

You cannot visit South-east Asia without trying the famous Malaysian-style fried chicken. Indonesian in origin, ayam goreng puts Western fried chicken to shame. First the chicken is cooked in spices and flavourings to ensure a depth of taste, then it is simply deep-fried to form a crisp, golden skin.

Ingredients

2 shallots, chopped
4 garlic cloves, chopped
50g/2oz fresh root ginger or galangal, peeled and chopped
25g/1oz fresh turmeric, chopped
2 lemon grass stalks, chopped
6 whole chicken legs, separated into drumsticks and thighs
30ml/2 tbsp kecap manis
salt and ground black pepper
vegetable oil, for deep-frying

Serves 4

1 Using a mortar and pestle or food processor, grind the shallots, garlic, ginger or galangal, turmeric and lemon grass to a paste. Scrape into a bowl and set aside.

2 Place the chicken pieces in a heavy pan or flameproof pot and smear with the spice paste. Add the kecap manis and 150ml/¼ pint/⅔ cup water. Bring to the boil, reduce the heat and cook the chicken for about 25 minutes, turning it from time to time, until the liquid has evaporated. The chicken should be dry before deep-frying, but the spices should be sticking to it. Season with salt and pepper.

3 Heat enough oil for deep-frying in a wok. Fry the chicken pieces in batches until golden brown and crisp. Drain them on kitchen paper and serve hot.

Cook's Tips

- *Served with a sambal, or pickle, this makes a delicious snack, but for a main course serve with Thai fragrant rice and a salad.*
- *If you cannot find kecap manis, use soy sauce sweetened with palm sugar (jaggery).*

Chicken & Sweet Potato Curry

Ho Chi Minh City is home to many stalls specializing in curries like this one. They all use Indian curry powder and coconut milk.

Ingredients

45ml/3 tbsp Indian curry powder
15ml/1 tbsp ground turmeric
500g/1¼lb skinless boneless chicken thighs or chicken breast fillets
25ml/1½ tbsp raw cane sugar
30ml/2 tbsp sesame oil
2 shallots, chopped
2 garlic cloves, chopped
4cm/1½in galangal, peeled and chopped
2 lemon grass stalks, chopped
10ml/2 tsp chilli paste or dried chilli flakes
2 medium sweet potatoes, peeled and cubed
45ml/3 tbsp chilli sambal
600ml/1 pint/2½ cups coconut milk
1 small bunch each fresh basil and coriander (cilantro), stalks removed
salt and ground black pepper

Serves 4

1 In a small bowl, mix together the curry powder and turmeric. Put the chicken in a bowl and coat with half of the spice. Set aside.

2 Heat the sugar in a small pan with 7.5ml/1½ tsp water, until the sugar dissolves and the syrup turns golden. Remove from the heat and set aside.

3 Heat a wok or heavy pan and add the oil. Stir-fry the shallots, garlic, galangal and lemon grass. Stir in the rest of the turmeric and curry powder with the chilli paste or flakes, followed by the chicken, and stir-fry for 2–3 minutes.

4 Add the sweet potatoes, then the chilli sambal, syrup, coconut milk and 150ml/¼ pint/⅔ cup water, mixing thoroughly to combine the flavours.

5 Bring to the boil, reduce the heat and cook for about 15 minutes until the chicken is cooked through. Season and stir in half the basil and coriander. Spoon into warmed bowls, garnish with the remaining herbs and serve immediately.

spicy fried chicken Energy 300kcal/1250kJ; Protein 31.9g; Carbohydrate 2.1g, of which sugars 0.9g; Fat 18.3g, of which saturates 2.9g; Cholesterol 158mg; Calcium 19mg; Fibre 0.2g; Sodium 136mg.
chicken & potato Energy 384kcal/1621kJ; Protein 29.5g; Carbohydrate 39.7g, of which sugars 20.7g; Fat 13.1g, of which saturates 2.5g; Cholesterol 131mg; Calcium 181mg; Fibre 5.8g; Sodium 373mg.

Chicken Rendang

This makes a marvellous dish for a buffet. Serve it with prawn crackers.

Ingredients

1 chicken, about 1.4kg/3lb
5ml/1 tsp sugar
75g/3oz/1 cup desiccated (dry unsweetened) coconut
4 small onions, chopped
2 garlic cloves, chopped
2.5cm/1in piece fresh root ginger, peeled and sliced
1–2 lemon grass stalks, root trimmed
2.5cm/1in piece fresh galangal, peeled and sliced
75ml/5 tbsp vegetable oil
10–15ml/2–3 tsp chilli powder
400ml/14fl oz can coconut milk
10ml/2 tsp salt
fresh chives and deep-fried anchovies, to garnish

Serves 4

1 Joint the chicken into eight pieces and remove the skin, sprinkle with the sugar and leave to stand for 1 hour. Meanwhile, dry-roast the coconut in a wok, turning all the time until it is crisp and golden. Tip into a food processor and process to an oily paste. Set aside.

2 Add the onions, garlic and ginger to the processor. Cut off the lower 5cm/2in of the lemon grass, chop and add to the processor with the galangal. Process to a fine paste.

3 Heat the oil in a wok or large pan and fry the onion mixture for a few minutes. Reduce the heat, stir in the chilli powder and cook for 2–3 minutes, stirring constantly. Spoon in 120ml/4fl oz/½ cup of the coconut milk and add salt to taste.

4 As soon as the mixture bubbles, add the chicken pieces, turning them until they are well coated with the spices. Pour in the coconut milk, stirring constantly to prevent curdling. Bruise the top of the lemon grass stalks and add to the wok or pan. Cover and cook for 45 minutes until the chicken is tender.

5 Just before serving stir in the coconut paste. Bring to just below boiling point, then simmer for 5 minutes. Garnish with fresh chives and deep-fried anchovies and serve.

Lemon & Sesame Chicken

These delicate strips of chicken are at their best if you leave them to marinate overnight.

Ingredients

4 large chicken breast fillets, skinned and cut into strips
15ml/1 tbsp light soy sauce
15ml/1 tbsp Chinese rice wine
2 garlic cloves, crushed
10ml/2 tsp finely grated fresh root ginger
1 egg, lightly beaten
150g/5oz cornflour (cornstarch)
sunflower oil, for deep-frying
toasted sesame seeds, to sprinkle
rice or noodles, to serve

For the sauce

15ml/1 tbsp sunflower oil
2 spring onions (scallions), finely sliced
1 garlic clove, crushed
10ml/2 tsp cornflour (cornstarch)
90ml/6 tbsp chicken stock
10ml/2 tsp finely grated lemon rind
30ml/2 tbsp lemon juice
10ml/2 tsp sugar
2.5ml/½ tsp sesame oil
salt

Serves 4

1 Mix the chicken strips with the soy sauce, wine, garlic and ginger in a bowl. Toss together to combine, then cover and marinate in the refrigerator for 8–10 hours.

2 When ready to cook, add the beaten egg to the chicken and mix well, then drain off any excess liquid. Put the cornflour in a plastic bag, add the chicken pieces and shake to coat the strips.

3 Deep-fry the chicken in hot oil for 3–4 minutes for each batch. As each batch cooks, lift it out and drain on kitchen paper. Reheat the oil and deep-fry all the chicken in batches for a second time, for 2–3 minutes. Remove and drain well.

4 To make the sauce, add the oil to a hot wok and stir-fry the spring onions and garlic for 1–2 minutes. Add the remaining ingredients and cook for 2–3 minutes until thickened.

5 Return the chicken to the wok, toss lightly to coat with sauce, and sprinkle over the sesame seeds. Serve with rice or noodles.

chicken rendang Energy 501kcal/2098kJ; Protein 55.4g; Carbohydrate 7.2g, of which sugars 7.2g; Fat 28.1g, of which saturates 12.5g; Cholesterol 158mg; Calcium 45mg; Fibre 2.6g; Sodium 1233mg.
lemon & sesame Energy 450kcal/1892kJ; Protein 38.2g; Carbohydrate 37.1g, of which sugars 2.5g; Fat 17.6g, of which saturates 2.6g; Cholesterol 157mg; Calcium 25mg; Fibre 0.1g; Sodium 397mg.

Bang Bang Chicken

Toasted sesame paste gives this dish an authentic flavour, although crunchy peanut butter can be used instead.

Ingredients
3 chicken breast fillets
1 garlic clove, crushed
2.5ml/½ tsp black peppercorns
1 small onion, halved
1 large cucumber, peeled, seeded and cut into thin strips
salt and ground black pepper

For the sauce
45ml/3 tbsp toasted sesame paste
15ml/1 tbsp light soy sauce
15ml/1 tbsp wine vinegar
2 spring onions (scallions), chopped
2 garlic cloves, crushed
5 × 1cm/2 × ½in piece fresh root ginger, peeled and cut into matchsticks
15ml/1 tbsp Sichuan peppercorns, dry-fried and crushed
5ml/1 tsp soft light brown sugar

For the chilli oil
60ml/4 tbsp groundnut (peanut) oil
5ml/1 tsp chilli powder

Serves 4

1 Place the chicken in a wok or pan. Just cover with water, add the garlic, peppercorns and onion and bring to the boil. Skim the surface, season to taste, then cover. Cook for 25 minutes or until the chicken is just tender. Drain, reserving the stock.

2 Make the sauce by mixing the toasted sesame paste with 45ml/3 tbsp of the chicken stock, saving the rest for soup. Add the soy sauce, vinegar, spring onions, garlic, ginger and crushed peppercorns to the sesame mixture. Stir in sugar to taste.

3 Make the chilli oil by gently heating the oil and chilli powder together until foaming. Simmer for 2 minutes, cool, then strain off the red-coloured oil and discard the sediment.

4 Spread out the cucumber batons on a platter. Cut the chicken into pieces the same size as the batons and arrange on top. Pour over the sauce, drizzle on the chilli oil and serve.

Chicken with Hijiki Seaweed

The taste of hijiki – a type of seaweed – is somewhere between rice and vegetable. It goes well with meat or tofu products, especially when stir-fried in the wok first with a little oil.

Ingredients
90g/3½oz dried hijiki seaweed
150g/5oz chicken breast fillet
½ small carrot, about 5cm/2in
15ml/1 tbsp vegetable oil
100ml/3fl oz/scant ½ cup instant dashi powder plus 1.5ml/¼ tsp dashi-no-moto
30ml/2 tbsp sake
30ml/2 tbsp caster (superfine) sugar
45ml/3 tbsp shoyu
a pinch of cayenne pepper

Serves 2

1 Soak the hijiki in cold water for about 30 minutes. It will be ready to cook when it can be easily crushed between the fingers. Pour into a sieve (strainer) and wash under running water. Drain.

2 Peel the skin from the chicken and par-boil the skin in rapidly boiling water for 1 minute, then drain. With a sharp knife, shave off all the yellow fat from the skin. Discard the clear membrane between the fat and the skin as well. Cut the skin into thin strips about 5mm/¼in wide and 2.5cm/1in long. Cut the meat into small, bitesize chunks.

3 Peel and chop the carrot into long, narrow matchsticks.

4 Heat the oil in a wok or frying pan and stir-fry the strips of chicken skin for 5 minutes, or until golden and curled up. Add the chicken meat and keep stirring until the colour changes.

5 Add the hijiki and carrot, then stir-fry for a further minute. Add the remaining ingredients. Lower the heat and toss over the heat for 5 minutes more.

6 Remove the wok from the heat and stand for 10 minutes. Season and serve in small individual bowls.

bang bang chicken Energy 200kcal/838kJ; Protein 29.5g; Carbohydrate 2.8g, of which sugars 2.4g; Fat 7.9g, of which saturates 1.3g; Cholesterol 79mg; Calcium 89mg; Fibre 1.2g; Sodium 338mg.
chicken w. hijiki Energy 154kcal/644kJ; Protein 10g; Carbohydrate 10.4g, of which sugars 10.2g; Fat 8.4g, of which saturates 2g; Cholesterol 39mg; Calcium 76mg; Fibre 1.1g; Sodium 884mg.

Stir-fried Crispy Duck

This stir-fry is delicious wrapped in steamed mandarin pancakes, with a little extra plum sauce.

Ingredients

350g/12oz duck breast fillets
30ml/2 tbsp plain (all-purpose) flour
60ml/4 tbsp oil
1 bunch spring onions (scallions), cut in strips, plus extra to garnish
275g/10oz/2½ cups finely shredded green cabbage
225g/8oz can water chestnuts, drained and sliced
50g/2oz/½ cup unsalted cashew nuts
cucumber, cut in strips
45ml/3 tbsp plum sauce
15ml/1 tbsp soy sauce
salt and ground black pepper

Serves 2

1 Remove any skin from the duck breast, then trim off a little of the fat. Thinly slice the meat. Season the flour with plenty of salt and pepper and use it to coat the pieces of duck all over.

2 Heat the oil in a wok and cook the duck slices in batches over a high heat until golden and crisp. Keep stirring to prevent the duck from sticking. As each batch cooks, remove the duck with a slotted spoon and drain on kitchen paper.

3 Add the spring onions to the wok and cook for 2 minutes, then stir in the cabbage and cook for 5 minutes, or until it has softened.

4 Return the duck to the pan with the water chestnuts, cashews and cucumber. Stir-fry for 2 minutes. Add the plum sauce and soy sauce, season with salt and black pepper to taste, then heat for 2 minutes. Serve in individual bowls, garnished with the sliced spring onions.

Cook's Tip
Water chestnuts are the perfect foil for the rich duck in this stir-fry, remaining crisp and crunchy after cooking.

Duck with Pineapple

Duck and pineapple is a favourite combination, but the fruit must not be allowed to dominate as you will upset the delicate balance in sweet-sour flavour.

Ingredients

15ml/1 tbsp dry sherry
15ml/1 tbsp dark soy sauce
2 small skinless duck breast fillets
15ml/1 tbsp vegetable oil
2 garlic cloves, finely chopped
1 small onion, sliced
1 red (bell) pepper, seeded and cut into 2.5cm/1in squares
75g/3oz/½ cup drained, canned pineapple chunks
90ml/6 tbsp pineapple juice
15ml/1 tbsp rice vinegar
5ml/1 tsp cornflour (cornstarch)
15ml/1 tbsp cold water
5ml/1 tsp sesame oil
salt and ground white pepper
1 spring onion (scallion), shredded, to garnish

Serves 4

1 Mix together the sherry and soy sauce. Stir in 2.5ml/½ tsp salt and 1.5ml/¼ tsp white pepper. Put the duck fillets in a bowl and add the marinade. Cover with clear film (plastic wrap) and leave in a cool place for 1 hour.

2 Drain the duck fillets and place them on a rack in a grill (broiler) pan, or on a preheated griddle pan. Cook using medium to high heat, for 10 minutes on each side. Leave to cool for 10 minutes, then cut the duck into bitesize pieces.

3 Heat the vegetable oil in a non-stick frying pan or wok and stir-fry the garlic and onion for 1 minute. Add the red pepper, pineapple chunks, duck, pineapple juice and vinegar and toss over the heat for 2 minutes.

4 Mix the cornflour to a paste with the water. Add the mixture to the pan with 1.5ml/¼ tsp salt. Cook, stirring, until the sauce thickens. Stir in the sesame oil. Spoon the duck and pineapple mixture into four warmed bowls, garnish with the spring onion shreds, and serve.

stir-fried duck Energy 682kcal/2846kJ; Protein 36.9g; Carbohydrate 41.3g, of which sugars 26.3g; Fat 44.4g, of which saturates 7.5g; Cholesterol 151mg; Calcium 174mg; Fibre 5.8g; Sodium 844mg.
duck w. pineapple Energy 682kcal/2861kJ; Protein 62.6g; Carbohydrate 40.3g, of which sugars 33.7g; Fat 34.4g, of which saturates 5.8g; Cholesterol 330mg; Calcium 83mg; Fibre 4g; Sodium 1419mg.

Chinese Duck Curry

The duck used in this dish is best marinated for as long as possible – preferably overnight – although it tastes good even if you only marinate it briefly.

Ingredients

4 duck breast portions, skin and bones removed
30ml/2 tbsp five-spice powder
30ml/2 tbsp sesame oil
grated rind and juice of 1 orange
1 medium butternut squash, peeled and cubed
10ml/2 tsp red curry paste
30ml/2 tbsp fish sauce
15ml/1 tbsp palm sugar (jaggery) or soft light brown sugar
300ml/½ pint/1 ¼ cups coconut milk
2 fresh red chillies, seeded
4 kaffir lime leaves, torn
small bunch coriander (cilantro), chopped, to garnish

Serves 4

1 Cut the duck meat into bitesize pieces and place in a bowl with the five-spice powder, sesame oil, and orange rind and juice. Stir well to mix all the ingredients and coat the duck in the marinade. Cover the bowl with clear film (plastic wrap) and set aside in a cool place to marinate for at least 15 minutes.

2 Meanwhile, bring a pan of water to the boil. Add the squash and cook for 10–15 minutes, until just tender. Drain well and set aside in a bowl.

3 Pour the marinade from the duck into a wok and heat until boiling. Stir in the curry paste and cook for 2–3 minutes, until well blended and fragrant. Add the duck and cook for 3–4 minutes, stirring constantly, until browned on all sides.

4 Add the fish sauce and sugar and cook for 2 minutes more. Stir in the coconut milk until the mixture is smooth, then add the cooked squash, with the chillies and lime leaves.

5 Simmer gently, stirring frequently, for 5 minutes, then spoon into a dish, sprinkle with the coriander and serve.

Red Duck Curry

Slow simmering is the secret of this wonderful duck curry.

Ingredients

4 skinless duck breast fillets
400ml/14fl oz can coconut milk
200ml/7fl oz/scant 1 cup chicken stock
30ml/2 tbsp red curry paste
8 spring onions (scallions), finely sliced
10ml/2 tsp grated fresh root ginger
30ml/2 tbsp Chinese rice wine
15ml/1 tbsp fish sauce
15ml/1 tbsp soy sauce
2 lemon grass stalks, halved lengthways
3–4 kaffir lime leaves
300g/11oz pea aubergines (eggplants)
10ml/2 tsp sugar
salt and ground black pepper
10–12 fresh basil and mint leaves, to garnish
steamed jasmine rice, to serve

Serves 4

1 Using a sharp knife, cut the duck breast portions into neat bitesize pieces and set aside on a plate.

2 Place a wok over a low heat and add the coconut milk, stock, curry paste, spring onions, ginger, rice wine, fish and soy sauces, lemon grass and lime leaves. Stir well to mix, then bring to the boil over a medium heat.

3 Add the duck, aubergines and sugar to the wok and simmer for 25–30 minutes, stirring occasionally.

4 Remove the wok from the heat and leave to stand, covered, for about 15 minutes. Season to taste.

5 Ladle the duck curry into shallow bowls, garnish with fresh mint and basil leaves, and serve with steamed jasmine rice.

Cook's Tip

Tiny pea aubergines (eggplants) are sold in Asian stores. If you can't find them, use regular aubergines, cut into neat chunks.

chinese duck Energy 295kcal/1241kJ; Protein 31.4g; Carbohydrate 13.3g, of which sugars 12.3g; Fat 15.9g, of which saturates 3.1g; Cholesterol 165mg; Calcium 102mg; Fibre 2g; Sodium 427mg.
red duck curry Energy 241kcal/1017kJ; Protein 31.1g; Carbohydrate 10.2g, of which sugars 10g; Fat 10.5g, of which saturates 2.3g; Cholesterol 165mg; Calcium 65mg; Fibre 1.8g; Sodium 546mg.

Steamed Sticky Rice

Sticky rice requires a long soak in water before being cooked in a bamboo steamer. It is used for savoury and sweet dishes, especially rice cakes, and is available in Chinese and Asian stores, as well as some supermarkets.

Ingredients

350g/12oz/1¾ cups sticky rice

Serves 4

1 Put the rice into a large bowl and fill the bowl with cold water. Leave the rice to soak for at least 6 hours, then drain, rinse thoroughly, and drain again.

2 Fill a wok or heavy pan one-third full with water. Place a bamboo steamer, with the lid on, over the wok or pan and bring the water to the boil.

3 Uncover the steamer and place a dampened piece of muslin (cheesecloth) over the rack. Tip the rice into the middle and spread it out. Fold the muslin over the rice, cover and steam for 25 minutes until the rice is tender but firm. The measured quantity of rice grains doubles when cooked.

Cook's Tip

The measured quantity of rice grains doubles when cooked, which is a useful point to remember when planning to cook sticky rice for a meal. The grains clump together when cooked, making this type of rice ideal for moulding. It is fairly bulky, so is often served with a dipping sauce.

Variation

Sticky rice can be enjoyed as a sweet, filling snack with sugar and coconut milk.

Rice Cakes with Dipping Sauce

Easy to make, these rice cakes will keep almost indefinitely in an airtight container. Start making them at least a day before you plan to serve them, so the rice can dry out overnight.

Ingredients

175g/6oz/1 cup Thai jasmine rice
oil, for deep-frying and greasing
dipping sauce, for serving

Serves 4–6

1 Preheat the oven to the lowest setting. Grease a baking sheet. Wash the rice in several changes of water. Put it in a pan, add 350ml/12fl oz/1½ cups water and cover tightly. Bring to the boil, reduce the heat and simmer gently for about 15 minutes.

2 Remove the lid and fluff up the rice. Spoon it on to the baking sheet and press it down with the back of a spoon. Leave in the oven to dry out overnight.

3 Break the rice into bitesize pieces. Heat the oil in a wok or deep-fryer to 190°C/375°F or until a cube of bread, added to oil, browns in 40 seconds. Deep-fry the rice cakes, in batches, for about 1 minute, until they puff up but are not browned. Remove and drain well. Serve with the dipping sauce.

Cook's Tip

For a spicy meat-based dipping sauce to serve with the rice cakes, soak 6 dried red chillies in warm water, drain, then grind to a paste with 2 chopped shallots, 2.5ml/½ tsp salt, 2 chopped garlic cloves, 4 chopped coriander (cilantro) roots and 10 white peppercorns. Heat 250ml/8fl oz/1 cup coconut milk. When it starts to separate, stir in the chilli paste and cook for 3 minutes. Add 15ml/1 tbsp shrimp paste and 115g/4oz minced (ground) pork. Cook, stirring, for 10 minutes, then stir in 4 chopped cherry tomatoes, 15ml/1 tbsp each fish sauce and brown sugar, 30ml/2tbsp each tamarind juice and chopped roasted peanuts, and 2 chopped spring onions (scallions). Cook until thick, then pour into a bowl and cool.

steamed sticky rice Energy 314kcal/1314kJ; Protein 6.5g; Carbohydrate 69.8g, of which sugars 0g; Fat 0.5g, of which saturates 0g; Cholesterol 0mg; Calcium 17mg; Fibre 0g; Sodium 0mg.
rice cakes Energy 180kcal/750kJ; Protein 2.3g; Carbohydrate 25.7g, of which sugars 2.3g; Fat 7.5g, of which saturates 0.9g; Cholesterol 0mg; Calcium 7mg; Fibre 0.1g; Sodium 136mg.

Chicken & Basil Coconut Rice

For this dish, the rice is partially boiled before being simmered with coconut so that it fully absorbs the additional flavours.

Ingredients

350g/12oz/1¾ cups jasmine rice, rinsed
30–45ml/2–3 tbsp groundnut (peanut) oil
1 large onion, finely sliced into rings
1 garlic clove, crushed
1 fresh red chilli, seeded and finely sliced
1 fresh green chilli, seeded and finely sliced
generous handful of basil leaves
3 skinless chicken breast fillets, about 350g/12oz, finely sliced
5mm/¼in piece of lemon grass, pounded or finely chopped
600ml/1 pint/2½ cups coconut cream
salt and ground black pepper

Serves 4

1 Bring a pan of lightly salted water to the boil. Add the rice to the pan and boil for about 6 minutes, until partially cooked. Drain and set aside.

2 Heat the oil in a wok or frying pan and fry the onion rings for 5–10 minutes until golden and crisp. Lift out, drain on kitchen paper and set aside.

3 Fry the garlic and chillies in the same oil for 2–3 minutes, then add the basil leaves and fry briefly until they begin to wilt.

4 Remove a few basil leaves and set them aside for the garnish, then add the chicken slices to the pan with the lemon grass and fry for 2–3 minutes until golden.

5 Add the rice and stir-fry for a few minutes to coat the grains, then pour in the coconut cream. Cook for 4–5 minutes or until the rice is tender, adding a little more water if necessary. Adjust the seasoning.

6 Pile the rice into a warmed serving dish, sprinkle with the fried onion rings and basil leaves, and serve immediately.

Savoury Fried Rice

The title makes this sound like rather an ordinary dish, but it is nothing of the kind. Chilli, nuts and toasted coconut give the mixture of rice and beans and wilted greens plenty of flavour, and the egg that is stirred in provides the protein. For a tangy contrast, lime juice is poured over.

Ingredients

30ml/2 tbsp vegetable oil
2 garlic cloves, finely chopped
1 small fresh red chilli, seeded and finely chopped
50g/2oz/½ cup cashew nuts, toasted
50g/2oz/⅔ cup desiccated (dry unsweetened) coconut, toasted
2.5ml/½ tsp palm sugar (jaggery) or light muscovado (brown) sugar
30ml/2 tbsp light soy sauce
15ml/1 tbsp rice vinegar
1 egg
115g/4oz/1 cup green beans, sliced
½ spring cabbage or 115g/4oz spring greens (collards) or pak choi (bok choy), shredded
90g/3½oz/½ cup jasmine rice, cooked
lime wedges, to serve

Serves 2

1 Heat the oil in a wok or large, heavy frying pan. Add the garlic and cook over a medium to high heat until golden. Do not let it burn or it will taste bitter.

2 Add the red chilli, cashew nuts and toasted coconut to the wok or pan and stir-fry briefly, taking care to prevent the coconut from scorching. Stir in the sugar, soy sauce and rice vinegar. Toss over the heat for 1–2 minutes.

3 Push the stir-fry to one side of the wok or pan and break the egg into the empty side. When the egg is almost set, stir it into the garlic and chilli mixture with a wooden spatula or spoon.

4 Add the green beans, greens and cooked rice. Stir over the heat until the greens have just wilted, then spoon into a dish to serve. Offer the lime wedges separately, for squeezing over the rice.

chicken & basil rice Energy 492kcal/2064kJ; Protein 28.8g; Carbohydrate 83.1g, of which sugars 11.6g; Fat 4.8g, of which saturates 0.9g; Cholesterol 61mg; Calcium 83mg; Fibre 1.1g; Sodium 220mg.
savoury fried rice Energy 571kcal/2368kJ; Protein 16.1g; Carbohydrate 30.5g, of which sugars 8.7g; Fat 43.7g, of which saturates 18.2g; Cholesterol 95mg; Calcium 187mg; Fibre 8.5g; Sodium 1197mg.

Brown Rice with Lime

It is unusual to find brown rice in Chinese recipes, but the nutty flavour of the grains is enhanced by the fragrance of limes and lemon grass in this delicious dish.

Ingredients

2 limes
1 lemon grass stalk
225g/8oz/generous 1 cup brown long grain rice
15ml/1 tbsp olive oil
1 onion, chopped
2.5cm/1in piece fresh root ginger, peeled and finely chopped
7.5ml/1½ tsp coriander seeds
7.5ml/1½ tsp cumin seeds
750ml/1¼ pints/3 cups vegetable stock
60ml/4 tbsp chopped fresh coriander (cilantro)
spring onion (scallion) green and toasted coconut strips, to garnish
1 lime cut into 4 wedges, to serve

Serves 4

1 Pare the limes, using a cannelle knife (zester) or fine grater, taking care to avoid cutting the bitter pith. Set the rind aside. Finely chop the lower bulbous portion of the lemon grass stalk and set it aside.

2 Rinse the rice in plenty of cold water until the water runs clear. Tip it into a sieve (strainer) and drain thoroughly.

3 Heat the oil in a wok or large pan. Add the onion, ginger, coriander and cumin seeds, lemon grass and lime rind and cook over a low heat for 2–3 minutes.

4 Add the rice to the wok or pan and cook, stirring it constantly, for 1 minute, then pour in the stock and bring to the boil. Reduce the heat to very low and cover. Cook gently for 30 minutes, then check the rice. If it is still crunchy, cover and cook for 3–5 minutes more. Remove from the heat.

5 Stir in the fresh coriander, fluff up the rice grains with a fork, cover the wok or pan and leave to stand for 10 minutes. Transfer to a warmed dish, garnish with spring onion green and toasted coconut strips, and serve with lime wedges.

Chinese Leaves & Black Rice

The slightly nutty, chewy black glutinous rice contrasts beautifully with the Chinese leaves in this tasty stir-fry, which looks very dramatic. It is a good dish for dieters as it is low in saturated fat.

Ingredients

225g/8oz/1⅓ cups black glutinous rice or brown rice
900ml/1½ pints/3¾ cups vegetable stock
15ml/1 tbsp vegetable oil
225g/8oz Chinese leaves (Chinese cabbage), cut into 1cm/½in strips
4 spring onions (scallions), thinly sliced
salt and ground white pepper
2.5ml/½ tsp sesame oil

Serves 4

1 Rinse the rice until the water runs clear, then drain and tip into a pan. Add the stock and bring to the boil. Lower the heat, cover the pan and cook gently for 30 minutes.

2 Remove the pan from the heat and leave it to stand for 15 minutes without lifting the lid.

3 Heat the vegetable oil in a non-stick frying pan or wok. Stir-fry the Chinese leaves over medium heat for 2 minutes, adding a little water to prevent them from burning.

4 Drain the rice, stir it into the pan and cook for 4 minutes, using two spatulas or spoons to toss it with the Chinese leaves over the heat.

5 Add the spring onions, with salt and white pepper to taste. Drizzle over the sesame oil. Cook for 1 minute more, stirring constantly. Serve immediately.

Variation
This works well with any type of cabbage. It's particularly good with thinly-sliced Brussels sprouts, and you can add some chopped Chinese or purple-sprouting broccoli for good measure.

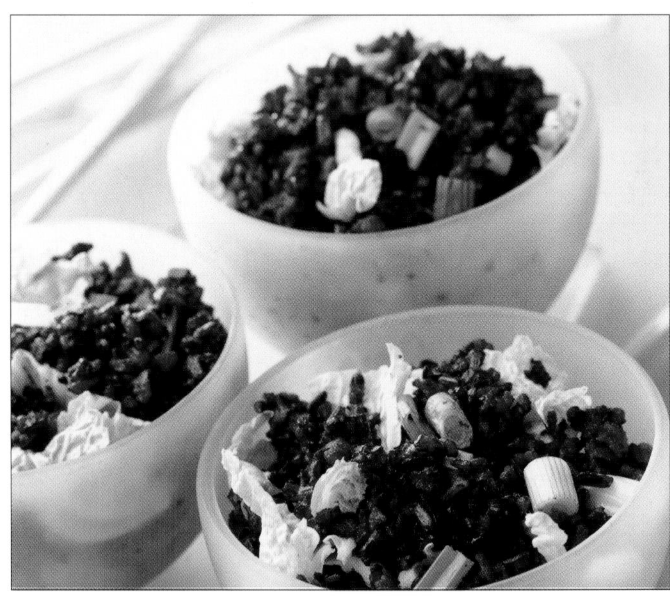

brown rice w. lime Energy 235kcal/996kJ; Protein 4.3g; Carbohydrate 47.3g, of which sugars 1.9g; Fat 4.5g, of which saturates 0.8g; Cholesterol 0mg; Calcium 35mg; Fibre 1.9g; Sodium 6mg.
Chinese black rice Energy 243Kcal/1029kJ; Protein 4.8g; Carbohydrate 48.9g, of which sugars 3.8g; Fat 4.5g, of which saturates 0.7g; Cholesterol 0mg; Calcium 37mg; Fibre 2.4g; Sodium 6mg.

Chinese Jewelled Rice

Another fried rice medley, this time with crab meat and water chestnuts, providing contrasting textures and flavours.

Ingredients

350g/12oz/1¾ cups white long grain rice
45ml/3 tbsp vegetable oil
1 onion, roughly chopped
4 dried black Chinese mushrooms, soaked for 10 minutes in warm water to cover
115g/4oz cooked ham, diced
175g/6oz drained canned white crab meat
75g/3oz/½ cup drained canned water chestnuts
115g/4oz/1 cup peas, thawed if frozen
30ml/2 tbsp oyster sauce
5ml/1 tsp granulated sugar
salt

Serves 4

1 Rinse the rice in cold water, drain well, then add to a pan of lightly salted boiling water. Cook for 10–12 minutes. Drain, refresh under cold water, drain again and cool quickly.

2 Heat half the oil in a wok. When very hot, stir-fry the rice for 3 minutes. Transfer the cooked rice to a bowl and set aside.

3 Heat the remaining oil in the wok and cook the onion until softened but not coloured. Drain the mushrooms, cut off and discard the stems, then chop the caps.

4 Add the chopped mushrooms to the wok, with all the remaining ingredients except the rice. Stir-fry for 2 minutes, then add the rice and stir-fry for about 3 minutes more. Spoon into heated bowls and serve.

Cook's Tip
Always preheat a wok before stir-frying. When you add the oil, drizzle it in a "necklace" just below the rim of the hot wok. As the oil runs down, it will coat the inner surface evenly as it heats through.

Jewelled Rice with Fried Eggs

This vibrant, colourful stir-fry makes a tasty light meal, or can be served as an accompaniment to simply grilled meat or fish.

Ingredients

2 fresh corn on the cob
60ml/4 tbsp sunflower oil
2 garlic cloves, finely chopped
4 red Asian shallots, thinly sliced
1 small fresh red chilli, finely sliced
90g/3½oz carrots, cut into thin matchsticks
90g/3½oz fine green beans, cut into 2cm/¾in lengths
1 red (bell) pepper, seeded and cut into 1cm/½in dice
90g/3½oz/1¼ cups baby button (white) mushrooms
500g/1¼lb/5 cups cooked long grain rice, completely cooled
45ml/3 tbsp light soy sauce
10ml/2 tsp green curry paste
4 eggs
crisp green salad leaves and lime wedges, to serve

Serves 4

1 First shuck the corn cobs. Remove all the papery leaves, and the silky threads, then with a sharp knife cut at the base of the kernels right down the length of the cob.

2 Heat 30ml/2 tbsp of the sunflower oil in a wok over a high heat. When hot, add the garlic, shallots and chilli. Stir-fry for about 2 minutes.

3 Add the carrots, green beans, corn, red pepper and mushrooms to the wok and stir-fry for 3–4 minutes. Add the cooked, cooled rice and stir-fry for a further 4–5 minutes.

4 Mix together the light soy sauce and curry paste and add to the wok. Toss to mix well and stir-fry for 2–3 minutes.

5 Meanwhile, fry the eggs one at a time in the remaining oil in a frying pan. As each egg is cooked, remove it from the pan and place on a plate. Keep the cooked eggs hot.

6 Ladle the rice into four bowls or plates and top each portion with a fried egg. Serve with crisp green salad leaves and wedges of lime to squeeze over.

chinese jewelled rice Energy 474kcal/1979kJ; Protein 22.5g; Carbohydrate 77.5g, of which sugars 4.3g; Fat 7.8g, of which saturates 1.1g; Cholesterol 48mg; Calcium 86mg; Fibre 1.9g; Sodium 710mg.
jewelled rice w. eggs Energy 392kcal/1648kJ; Protein 13.6g; Carbohydrate 51.4g, of which sugars 8.2g; Fat 16.1g, of which saturates 3.6g; Cholesterol 261mg; Calcium 79mg; Fibre 2.2g; Sodium 968mg.

Festive Rice

This pretty rice dish is traditionally shaped into a cone and surrounded by a variety of accompaniments before being served.

Ingredients

450g/1lb/2⅔ cups jasmine rice
60ml/4 tbsp oil
2 garlic cloves, crushed
2 onions, thinly sliced
2.5ml/½ tsp ground turmeric
750ml/1¼ pints/3 cups water
400ml/14fl oz can coconut milk
1–2 lemon grass stalks, bruised

For the accompaniments

omelette strips
2 fresh red chillies, seeded and shredded
cucumber chunks
tomato wedges
deep-fried onions
prawn (shrimp) crackers

Serves 8

1 Put the jasmine rice in a large strainer and rinse it thoroughly under cold water. Drain well.

2 Heat the oil in a wok or frying pan with a lid. Cook the garlic, onions and turmeric over a low heat for 2–3 minutes, until the onions have softened. Add the rice and stir well to coat in oil.

3 Pour in the water and coconut milk and add the lemon grass. Bring to the boil, stirring. Cover and cook gently for 12 minutes, or until all the liquid has been absorbed by the rice.

4 Remove the wok or pan from the heat and lift the lid. Cover with a clean dish towel, replace the lid and leave to stand in a warm place for 15 minutes.

5 Remove the lemon grass, mound the rice mixture in a cone on a platter and garnish with the accompaniments, then serve.

Cook's Tip

Jasmine rice is widely available in most supermarkets and Asian stores. It is also known as Thai fragrant rice. It has a delicately scented, almost milky, aroma.

Garlic & Ginger Rice

Throughout China and South-east Asia, when rice is served on the side, it is usually steamed and plain, or fragrant with the flavours of ginger and herbs. The combination of garlic and ginger is popular in both countries and compliments almost any vegetable, fish or meat dish.

Ingredients

15ml/1 tbsp vegetable or groundnut (peanut) oil
2–3 garlic cloves, finely chopped
25g/1oz fresh root ginger, finely chopped
225g/8oz/generous 1 cup long grain rice, rinsed in several bowls of water and drained
900ml/1½ pints/3¾ cups chicken stock
a bunch of fresh coriander (cilantro) leaves, finely chopped
a bunch of fresh basil and mint, (optional), finely chopped

Serves 4–6

1 Heat the oil in a wok or heavy pan. Stir in the garlic and ginger and fry until golden. Stir in the rice and allow it to absorb the flavours for 1–2 minutes.

2 Pour in the stock and stir to make sure the rice doesn't stick. Bring the stock to the boil, then reduce the heat. Sprinkle the coriander over the surface of the stock with the finely chopped basil and mint, if using. Cover the wok or pan, and leave to cook gently for 20–25 minutes, until the rice has absorbed all the liquid.

3 Turn off the heat and gently fluff up the rice to mix in the herbs. Cover and leave to infuse for 10 minutes before serving.

Cook's Tip

Use homemade chicken stock if possible. It has a superior flavour to stock made using cubes and you can control the level of salt. Whenever you have a chicken carcass – after a roast chicken dinner, for instance – make and freeze the stock.

festive rice Energy 303kcal/1263kJ; Protein 6.4g; Carbohydrate 49.5g, of which sugars 4.2g; Fat 8.6g, of which saturates 2g; Cholesterol 53mg; Calcium 41mg; Fibre 0.5g; Sodium 212mg.
garlic & ginger rice Energy 165kcal/658kJ; Protein 3.9g; Carbohydrate 31.7g, of which sugars 0.5g; Fat 2.3g, of which saturates 0.2g; Cholesterol 0mg; Calcium 40mg; Fibre 1.1g; Sodium 8mg.

Fragrant Harbour Fried Rice

This tasty rice dish celebrates the Chinese name for Hong Kong, which is Fragrant Harbour.

Ingredients

about 90ml/6 tbsp vegetable oil
2 eggs, beaten
8 shallots, sliced
115g/4oz peeled cooked prawns (shrimp)
3 garlic cloves, crushed
115g/4oz cooked pork, cut into thin strips
4 Chinese dried mushrooms, soaked, stems removed and sliced
115g/4oz Chinese sausage, cooked and sliced at an angle
225g/8oz/generous 1 cup long grain rice, cooked, cooled quickly and chilled
30ml/2 tbsp light soy sauce
115g/4oz/1 cup frozen peas, thawed
2 spring onions (scallions), shredded
salt and ground black pepper
coriander (cilantro) leaves, to garnish

Serves 4

1 Heat about 15ml/1 tbsp of the oil in a frying pan, add the eggs and make an omelette. Slide the omelette out, roll it up and cut into strips. Set aside.

2 Heat a wok, add 15ml/1 tbsp of the remaining oil and stir-fry the shallots until crisp and golden. Remove and set aside. Add the prawns and garlic to the wok, with a little more oil if needed, fry for 1 minute, then remove.

3 Heat 15ml/1 tbsp more oil in the wok and stir-fry the pork and mushrooms for 2 minutes; add the cooked Chinese sausage slices and heat for a further 2 minutes. Lift the ingredients out of the wok and keep warm.

4 Reheat the wok with the remaining oil and stir-fry the rice until it glistens. Stir in the soy sauce, salt and pepper, plus half the cooked ingredients. Add the peas and half the spring onions and toss over the heat until the peas are cooked. Pile the fried rice on a heated platter, top with the remaining cooked ingredients and garnish with the coriander leaves.

Fried Rice with Beef

One of the joys of cooking Chinese food is the ease and speed with which a really good meal can be prepared. This delectable beef and rice stir-fry can be on the table in 15 minutes.

Ingredients

200g/7oz beef steak, chilled
15ml/1 tbsp vegetable oil
2 garlic cloves, finely chopped
1 egg
250g/9oz/2¼ cups cooked jasmine rice
½ medium head broccoli, coarsely chopped
30ml/2 tbsp dark soy sauce
15ml/1 tbsp light soy sauce
5ml/1 tsp light muscovado (brown) sugar
15ml/1 tbsp fish sauce
ground black pepper
chilli sauce, to serve

Serves 4

1 Trim the steak and cut into very thin strips with a sharp knife.

2 Heat the oil in a wok or frying pan and cook the garlic over a low to medium heat until golden. Do not let it burn. Increase the heat to high, add the steak and stir-fry for 2 minutes.

3 Move the pieces of beef to the edges of the wok or pan and break the egg into the centre. When the egg starts to set, break it up with chopsticks and then stir-fry it with the meat.

4 Add the rice and toss all the contents of the wok together, scraping up any residue on the base, then add the broccoli, soy sauces, sugar and fish sauce and stir-fry for 2 minutes more. Season to taste with pepper, spoon into heated bowls and serve immediately with chilli sauce.

Cook's Tip

Soy sauce is made from fermented soya beans. The first extraction is sold as light soy sauce and has a delicate, "beany" fragrance. Dark soy sauce is more intensely flavoured and has been allowed to mature for longer. The darker kind is also traditionally used to intensify the colour of a dish.

fragrant fried rice Energy 450kcal/1872kJ; Protein 14.5g; Carbohydrate 51g, of which sugars 4.4g; Fat 20.9g, of which saturates 3.1g; Cholesterol 113mg; Calcium 48mg; Fibre 1.1g; Sodium 58mg.
fried rice w. beef Energy 385kcal/1606kJ; Protein 20.7g; Carbohydrate 52.7g, of which sugars 2.5g; Fat 9.8g, of which saturates 2.8g; Cholesterol 81mg; Calcium 59mg; Fibre 1.6g; Sodium 590mg.

Sticky Rice Parcels

It is a pleasure to cut these parcels open and discover the delicious filling inside.

Ingredients

450g/1lb/2⅔ cups glutinous rice
20ml/4 tsp vegetable oil
15ml/1 tbsp dark soy sauce
1.5ml/¼ tsp five-spice powder
15ml/1 tbsp dry sherry
4 skinless, boneless chicken thighs, each cut into 4 pieces
8 dried Chinese mushrooms, soaked, stems removed and caps diced
25g/1oz dried shrimps, soaked and drained
50g/2oz/½ cup canned bamboo shoots, drained and sliced
300ml/½ pint/1¼ cups chicken stock
10ml/2 tsp cornflour (cornstarch), mixed with 15ml/1 tbsp cold water
4 lotus leaves, soaked in warm water until soft
salt and ground white pepper

Serves 4

1 Rinse the rice in a colander until the water runs clear, then soak in a bowl of water for 2 hours. Drain the rice and tip it into a bowl. Stir in 5ml/1 tsp of the oil and 2.5ml/½ tsp salt.

2 Line a large steamer with muslin or cheesecloth. Add the soaked rice, cover and steam for 45 minutes, stirring occasionally. Leave to cool.

3 Mix the soy sauce, five-spice powder and sherry in a bowl, stir in the chicken pieces, cover and marinate for 20 minutes.

4 Heat the remaining oil in a wok, stir-fry the chicken for 2 minutes, then add the mushrooms, shrimps, bamboo shoots and stock. Mix well, bring to the boil, then simmer for 10 minutes. Add the cornflour paste and cook, stirring, until the sauce has thickened. Season to taste.

5 Spread one-eighth of the rice to a round in the centre of each lotus leaf. Divide the chicken mixture among the leaves, putting it on top of the rice, and then top with more rice. Fold the leaves around the filling to make four neat parcels. Steam, seam side down, for 30 minutes over a high heat. Serve.

Fried Rice with Chicken

This substantial and tasty supper dish is based on jasmine rice cooked in coconut milk. Diced chicken, red pepper and corn kernels add colour and extra flavour.

Ingredients

475ml/16fl oz/2 cups water
50g/2oz/½ cup coconut milk powder
350g/12oz/1¾ cups jasmine rice, rinsed
30ml/2 tbsp groundnut (peanut) oil
2 garlic cloves, chopped
1 small onion, finely chopped
2.5cm/1in piece fresh root ginger, peeled and grated
225g/8oz skinned chicken breast fillets, cut into 1cm/½in pieces
1 red (bell) pepper, seeded and sliced
115g/4oz/1 cup drained canned whole kernel corn
5ml/1 tsp chilli oil
5ml/1 tsp hot curry powder
2 eggs, beaten
salt
spring onion (scallion) shreds, to garnish

Serves 4

1 Pour the water into a pan and whisk in the coconut milk powder. Add the rice and bring to the boil. Reduce the heat, cover and cook for 12 minutes, or until the rice is tender and the liquid has been absorbed. Spread the rice on a baking sheet and cool down as quickly as possible.

2 Heat the oil in a wok, add the garlic, onion and ginger and stir-fry over a medium heat for 2 minutes.

3 Push the onion mixture to the sides of the wok, add the chicken to the centre and stir-fry for 2 minutes. Add the rice and toss well. Stir-fry over a high heat for about 3 minutes more, until the chicken is cooked through.

4 Stir in the sliced red pepper, corn, chilli oil and curry powder, with salt to taste. Toss over the heat for 1 minute. Stir in the beaten eggs and cook for 1 minute more.

5 Garnish with the spring onion shreds and serve.

sticky rice parcels Energy 565kcal/2369kJ; Protein 37.3g; Carbohydrate 87.1g, of which sugars 0.3g; Fat 6.1g, of which saturates 0.7g; Cholesterol 102mg; Calcium 101mg; Fibre 0.2g; Sodium 336mg.
fried rice w. chicken Energy 489kcal/2044kJ; Protein 16.3g; Carbohydrate 82.9g, of which sugars 7.5g; Fat 10.1g, of which saturates 1.7g; Cholesterol 95mg; Calcium 50mg; Fibre 1.4g; Sodium 249mg.

Special Fried Rice

More colourful and elaborate than other fried rice dishes, special fried rice is a meal in itself.

Ingredients
50g/2oz/⅓ cup cooked peeled prawns (shrimp)
3 eggs
5ml/1 tsp salt
2 spring onions (scallions), finely chopped
60ml/4 tbsp vegetable oil
115g/4oz lean pork, finely diced
15ml/1 tbsp light soy sauce
15ml/1 tbsp Chinese rice wine
450g/1lb/6 cups cooked rice
115g/4oz green peas

Serves 4

1 Pat the prawns dry with kitchen paper. Put the eggs in a bowl with a pinch of the salt and a few pieces of spring onion. Whisk lightly.

2 Heat half the oil in a wok, add the pork and stir-fry until golden. Add the prawns and cook for 1 minute, then add the soy sauce and rice wine. Spoon the pork and prawn mixture into a bowl and keep hot.

3 Heat the remaining oil in the wok and lightly scramble the eggs. Add the rice and stir well with chopsticks.

4 Add the remaining salt and spring onions, the stir-fried prawns, pork and peas. Toss well over the heat to combine and serve either hot or cold.

Variation
If you don't have any Chinese rice wine, substitute dry sherry.

Cook's Tip
The weight of rice increases about two and a half times after cooking. When a recipe calls for cooked rice, use just under half the weight in uncooked rice.

Stir-fried Rice with Vegetables

The ginger gives this rice dish a wonderful flavour. Serve it as a vegetarian main course or as an unusual vegetable accompaniment.

Ingredients
115g/4oz/generous ½ cup brown basmati rice, rinsed and drained
350ml/12fl oz/1½ cups vegetable stock
2.5cm/1in piece of fresh root ginger, finely sliced
1 garlic clove, halved
5cm/2in piece of pared lemon rind
115g/4oz/1½ cups shiitake mushrooms
15ml/1 tbsp groundnut (peanut) oil
15ml/1 tbsp ghee or butter
175g/6oz baby carrots, trimmed
225g/8oz baby courgettes (zucchini), halved
175–225g/6–8oz/about 1½ cups broccoli, broken into florets
6 spring onions (scallions), sliced
15ml/1 tbsp light soy sauce
10ml/2 tsp toasted sesame oil

Serves 2–4

1 Put the rice in a pan and pour in the stock. Add the ginger, garlic and lemon rind. Slowly bring to the boil, then cover and cook very gently for 20–25 minutes until the rice is tender.

2 Remove the pan from the heat. Discard the flavourings and keep the pan covered with a clean dish towel and the lid so that the rice stays warm.

3 Slice the mushrooms, discarding the stems. Heat the oil and ghee or butter in a wok and stir-fry the carrots for 4–5 minutes until partially tender.

4 Add the mushrooms and courgettes, stir-fry for 2–3 minutes, then add the broccoli and spring onions and cook for a further 3 minutes, by which time all the vegetables should be tender but should still retain a bit of "bite".

5 Add the cooked rice to the vegetables, and toss briefly over the heat to mix and heat through. Toss with the soy sauce and sesame oil. Spoon into a bowl and serve immediately.

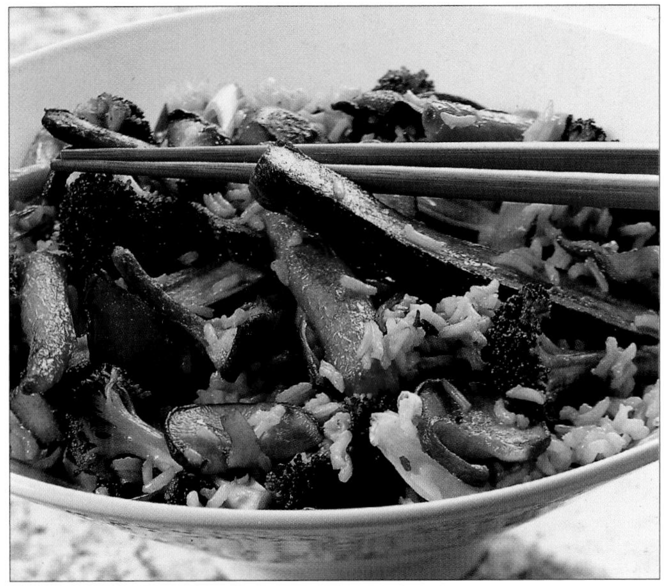

special fried rice Energy 343kcal/1434kJ; Protein 20.2g; Carbohydrate 40.5g, of which sugars 4.2g; Fat 11.2g, of which saturates 1.6g; Cholesterol 124mg; Calcium 91mg; Fibre 2.4g; Sodium 632mg.
stir-fried rice Energy 430kcal/1788kJ; Protein 12.5g; Carbohydrate 58.2g, of which sugars 11.2g; Fat 16.2g, of which saturates 2.2g; Cholesterol 0mg; Calcium 127mg; Fibre 6.5g; Sodium 569mg.

Nasi Goreng

This Indonesian-style dish is a marvellous way to use up left-over rice and meats.

Ingredients

350g/12oz/1¾ cups basmati rice (dry weight), cooked and cooled
2 eggs
30ml/2 tbsp water
105ml/7 tbsp sunflower oil
10ml/2 tsp shrimp paste
2–3 fresh red chillies
2 garlic cloves, crushed
1 onion, sliced
225g/8oz fillet (tenderloin) of pork or beef, cut into strips
115g/4oz cooked, peeled prawns
225g/8oz cooked chicken, chopped
30ml/2 tbsp dark soy sauce
salt and ground black pepper
deep-fried onions, to serve

Serves 4–6

1 Separate the grains of the cooked rice with a fork. Cover and set aside. Beat the eggs with the water and seasoning.

2 Heat 15ml/1 tbsp of the oil in a frying pan or wok, pour in about half the egg mixture and cook until set, without stirring.

3 Roll up the omelette, slide it on to a plate, cut into strips and set aside. Make another omelette in the same way.

4 Put the shrimp paste and half the shredded chillies into a food processor. Add the garlic and onion. Process to a paste.

5 Heat the remaining oil in a wok. Fry the paste, without browning, until it gives off a spicy aroma.

6 Add the strips of pork or beef and toss the meat over the heat, to seal in the juices. Cook the meat in the wok for about 2 minutes, stirring constantly.

7 Add the prawns, cook for 2 minutes, then add the chicken, rice, and soy sauce, with salt and pepper to taste, stirring constantly. Serve in individual bowls, garnished with omelette strips, shredded chilli and deep-fried onions.

Stir-fried Noodles with Beansprouts

Beansprouts are highly nutritious and make a valuable contribution to this low-fat dish, which combines egg noodles with peppers and soy sauce.

Ingredients

175g/6oz dried egg noodles
15ml/1 tbsp vegetable oil
1 garlic clove, finely chopped
1 small onion, halved and sliced
225g/8oz/1 cup beansprouts
1 small red (bell) pepper, seeded and cut into strips
1 small green (bell) pepper, seeded and cut into strips
2.5ml/½ tsp salt
1.5ml/¼ tsp ground white pepper
30ml/2 tbsp light soy sauce

Serves 4

1 Bring a pan of water to the boil. Cook the noodles for 4 minutes until just tender, or according to the instructions on the packet. Drain, refresh under cold water and drain again.

2 Heat the oil in a non-stick frying pan or wok. When the oil is very hot, add the garlic, stir briefly, then add the onion slices. Cook, stirring, for 1 minute, then add the beansprouts and peppers. Stir-fry for 2–3 minutes.

3 Stir in the cooked noodles and toss over the heat, using two spatulas or wooden spoons, for 2–3 minutes or until the ingredients are well mixed and have heated through.

4 Season to taste with salt and ground white pepper. Add the soy sauce and stir thoroughly before serving the noodle mixture in heated bowls.

Cook's Tip

Store beansprouts in the refrigerator and use within a day of purchase, as they tend to lose their crispness and become slimy and unpleasant quite quickly. The most commonly used beansprouts are sprouted mung beans, but you could use other types of beansprouts instead.

nasi goreng Energy 463kcal/1929kJ; Protein 27.3g; Carbohydrate 49.4g, of which sugars 2.1g; Fat 17.1g, of which saturates 2.7g; Cholesterol 151mg; Calcium 49mg; Fibre 0.5g; Sodium 288mg.
noodles w. beansprouts Energy 244kcal/1030kJ; Protein 8g; Carbohydrate 39.9g, of which sugars 7.8g; Fat 7g, of which saturates 1.5g; Cholesterol 13mg; Calcium 34mg; Fibre 3.5g; Sodium 352mg.

Crispy Fried Rice Vermicelli

This crisp tangle of fried rice vermicelli is tossed in a piquant sauce.

Ingredients

vegetable oil, for deep and shallow frying
175g/6oz rice vermicelli
15ml/1 tbsp chopped garlic
4–6 small dried red chillies
30ml/2 tbsp chopped shallots
15ml/1 tbsp dried shrimps, rinsed
115g/4oz minced (ground) pork
115g/4oz raw peeled prawns, (shrimp), chopped
30ml/2 tbsp brown bean sauce
30ml/2 tbsp rice wine vinegar
45ml/3 tbsp fish sauce
75g/3oz soft light brown sugar
30ml/2 tbsp lime juice
115g/4oz/½ cup beansprouts

For the garnish

2 spring onions, shredded
30ml/2 tbsp fresh coriander (cilantro) leaves
2-egg omelette, rolled and sliced
2 fresh red chillies, seeded and cut into thin strips

Serves 4–6

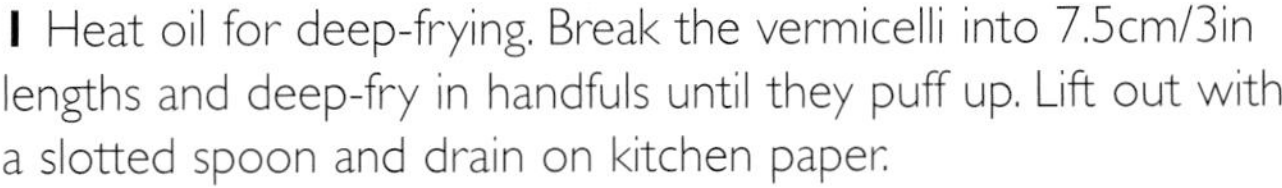

1 Heat oil for deep-frying. Break the vermicelli into 7.5cm/3in lengths and deep-fry in handfuls until they puff up. Lift out with a slotted spoon and drain on kitchen paper.

2 Heat 30ml/2 tbsp oil in a wok and fry the garlic, chillies, shallots and shrimps for about 1 minute. Add the pork and stir-fry for 3–4 minutes, until no longer pink. Add the prawns and fry for 2 minutes. Spoon into a bowl and set aside.

3 Add the brown bean sauce, vinegar, fish sauce and sugar. Bring to a gentle boil, stir to dissolve the sugar and cook until thick and syrupy.

4 Add the lime juice and adjust the seasoning. The sauce should be sweet, sour and salty. Add the pork and prawn mixture with the beansprouts and stir them into the sauce.

5 Add the fried rice noodles to the wok and toss gently to coat them in the sauce. Serve in warmed bowls, garnished with the spring onions, coriander leaves, omelette strips and chillies.

Spicy Fried Noodles

This is a wonderfully versatile dish as you can adapt it to include your favourite ingredients.

Ingredients

225g/8oz egg thread noodles
60ml/4 tbsp vegetable oil
2 garlic cloves, finely chopped
175g/6oz pork fillet (tenderloin), sliced into thin strips
1 skinless, boneless chicken breast portion (about 175g/6oz), sliced into thin strips
115g/4oz/1 cup cooked peeled prawns (shelled shrimp), rinsed if canned
45ml/3 tbsp fresh lemon juice
45ml/3 tbsp fish sauce
30ml/2 tbsp soft light brown sugar
2 eggs, beaten
½ fresh red chilli, seeded and finely chopped
50g/2oz/¼ cup beansprouts
60ml/4 tbsp roasted peanuts, chopped
3 spring onions (scallions), cut into 5cm/2in lengths and shredded
45ml/3 tbsp chopped fresh coriander (cilantro)

Serves 4

1 Bring a large pan of water to the boil. Add the noodles, remove the pan from the heat and leave for 5 minutes.

2 Heat 45ml/3 tbsp of the oil in a wok and cook the garlic for 30 seconds. Add the pork and chicken and stir-fry until lightly browned, then add the prawns; stir-fry for 2 minutes. Stir in the lemon juice, then add the fish sauce and sugar.

3 Drain the noodles and add to the wok or pan with the remaining 15ml/1 tbsp oil. Toss all the ingredients together, then pour the beaten eggs over the noodles. Stir-fry until almost set, then add the chilli and beansprouts.

4 Divide the roasted peanuts, spring onions and coriander leaves into two equal portions, add one portion to the pan and stir-fry for about 2 minutes.

5 Tip the noodles on to a serving platter. Sprinkle on the remaining peanuts, spring onions and chopped coriander; serve.

fried rice vermicelli Energy 204kcal/854kJ; Protein 10.6g; Carbohydrate 33.9g, of which sugars 4.3g; Fat 2.9g, of which saturates 0.6g; Cholesterol 76mg; Calcium 38mg; Fibre 1.2g; Sodium 206mg.
spicy fried noodles Energy 597kcal/2504kJ; Protein 39.3g; Carbohydrate 50.8g, of which sugars 10.3g; Fat 27.8g, of which saturates 5.5g; Cholesterol 226mg; Calcium 76mg; Fibre 2.9g; Sodium 250mg.

Cellophane Noodles with Pork

Simple, speedy and very satisfying, this is an excellent way of using mung bean noodles. It scores high on presentation too, thanks to the contrast between the translucent, thread-like noodles and the vibrant colour of the vegetables.

Ingredients

200g/7oz cellophane noodles
30ml/2 tbsp vegetable oil
15ml/1 tbsp magic paste
200g/7oz minced (ground) pork
1 fresh green or red chilli, seeded and finely chopped
300g/11oz/scant 1½ cups beansprouts
bunch spring onions (scallions), finely chopped
30ml/2 tbsp soy sauce
30ml/2 tbspfish sauce
30ml/2 tbsp sweet chilli sauce
15ml/1 tbsp light brown sugar
30ml/2 tbsp rice vinegar
30ml/2 tbsp roasted peanuts, chopped, to garnish
small bunch fresh coriander (cilantro), chopped, to garnish

Serves 2

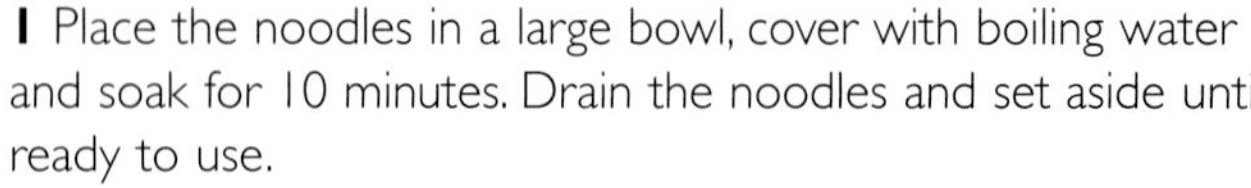

1 Place the noodles in a large bowl, cover with boiling water and soak for 10 minutes. Drain the noodles and set aside until ready to use.

2 Heat the oil in a wok or large, heavy frying pan. Add the magic paste and stir-fry for 2–3 seconds, then add the pork. Stir-fry the meat, breaking it up with a wooden spatula, for 2–3 minutes, until browned all over.

3 Add the chopped chilli to the meat and stir-fry for 3–4 seconds, then add the beansprouts and chopped spring onions, stir-frying for a few seconds after each addition.

4 Snip the noodles into 5cm/2in lengths and add to the wok or pan, with the soy sauce, fish sauce, sweet chilli sauce, sugar and rice vinegar.

5 Toss the ingredients together over the heat until the noodles have warmed through. Pile on to a platter or into a large bowl. Sprinkle the peanuts and coriander over the top and serve.

Rice Rolls Stuffed with Pork

Steamed rice sheets are very tasty when filled with pork, rolled up, drizzled in herb oil, and then dipped in a hot chilli sauce. Generally, they are eaten as a snack, or served as a starter.

Ingredients

25g/1oz dried cloud ear (wood ear) mushrooms, soaked in warm water for 30 minutes
350g/12oz minced (ground) pork
30nl/2 tbsp fish sauce
10ml/2 tsp sugar
15ml/1 tbsp vegetable or groundnut (peanut) oil
2 garlic cloves, finely chopped
2 shallots, finely chopped
2 spring onions (scallions), trimmed and finely chopped
24 fresh rice sheets, 7.5cm/3in square
ground black pepper
herb oil, for drizzling
hot chilli sauce, for dipping

Serves 6

1 Drain the mushrooms and squeeze out any excess water. Cut off and discard the hard stems. Finely chop the rest of the mushrooms and put them in a bowl. Add the minced pork, fish sauce, and sugar and mix well.

2 Heat the oil in a wok or heavy pan. Add the garlic, shallots and onions. Stir-fry until golden. Add the pork mixture and stir-fry for 5–6 minutes, until the pork is cooked. Season with pepper.

3 Place the rice sheets on a flat surface. Spoon a tablespoon of the pork mixture onto the middle of each sheet. Fold one side over the filling, tuck in the sides, and roll to enclose the filling, so that it resembles a short spring roll.

4 Place the filled rice rolls on a serving plate, drizzle with herb oil, and serve with chilli sauce.

Cook's Tip

To make life easy, prepared, fresh rice sheets are available in Asian markets and grocery stores.

noodles w. pork Energy 593kcal/2504kJ; Protein 47.8g; Carbohydrate 72.1g, of which sugars 4.7g; Fat 14.6g, of which saturates 2.8g; Cholesterol 106mg; Calcium 53mg; Fibre 3.2g; Sodium 1461mg.
rice rolls stuffed w. pork Energy 160kcal/670kJ; Protein 13.8g; Carbohydrate 16g, of which sugars 2.4g; Fat 4.4g, of which saturates 1.1g; Cholesterol 37mg; Calcium 13mg; Fibre 0.6g; Sodium 43mg.

Crispy Noodles with Beef

Rice vermicelli is deep-fried before being added to this multi-textured dish.

Ingredients

450g/1lb rump (round) steak
teriyaki sauce, for brushing
175g/6oz rice vermicelli
groundnut (peanut) oil, for deep-frying and stir-frying
8 spring onions (scallions), diagonally sliced
2 garlic cloves, crushed
4–5 carrots, cut into julienne strips
1–2 fresh red chillies, seeded and finely sliced
2 small courgettes (zucchini), diagonally sliced
5ml/1 tsp grated fresh root ginger
60ml/4 tbsp rice vinegar
90ml/6 tbsp light soy sauce
about 475ml/16fl oz/2 cups spicy stock

Serves 4

1 Beat the steak to about 2.5cm/1in thick. Place in a shallow dish, brush with teriyaki sauce and marinate for 2–4 hours.

2 Separate the rice vermicelli into manageable loops. Pour oil into a large wok to a depth of about 5cm/2in, and heat until a strand of vermicelli cooks as soon as it is lowered into the oil.

3 Carefully add a loop of vermicelli to the oil. Almost immediately, turn to cook on the other side, then remove and drain on kitchen paper. Repeat with the remaining loops. Transfer the cooked noodles to a bowl and keep them warm.

4 Clean out the wok and heat 15ml/1 tbsp groundnut oil. Fry the steak for about 30 seconds on each side, then remove and cut into thick slices.

5 Add a little extra oil to the wok, and stir-fry the spring onions, garlic and carrots for 5–6 minutes. Add the chillies, courgettes and ginger and stir-fry for 1–2 minutes.

6 Stir in the rice vinegar, soy sauce and stock. Cook for 4 minutes until the sauce has thickened slightly. Return the steak to the wok and cook for a further 1–2 minutes. Spoon the steak, vegetables and sauce over the noodles and toss lightly.

Noodles with Crab & Mushrooms

This is a dish of contrasting flavours, textures and colours, and requires some skill and dexterity from the cook. While one hand gently turns the noodles in the pan, the other takes chunks of fresh crab meat and drops them into the steaming wok. Here the crab meat is cooked separately to make it easier.

Ingredients

25g/1oz dried cloud ear (wood ear) mushrooms, soaked in warm water for 20 minutes
115g/4oz dried cellophane noodles, soaked in warm water for 20 minutes
30ml/2 tbsp vegetable or sesame oil
3 shallots, halved and thinly sliced
2 garlic cloves, crushed
2 fresh green or red chillies, seeded and sliced
1 carrot, peeled and cut into thin diagonal rounds
5ml/1 tsp sugar
45ml/3 tbsp oyster sauce
15ml/1 tbsp soy sauce
225g/8oz fresh, raw crab meat, cut into bitesize chunks
ground black pepper
fresh coriander (cilantro) leaves, to garnish

Serves 4

1 Remove the centres from the soaked cloud ear mushrooms and cut the mushrooms in half. Drain the soaked noodles and cut them into 30cm/12in pieces and put aside.

2 Heat a wok and add 15ml/1 tbsp of the oil. Stir in the shallots, garlic and chillies, and cook until fragrant. Add the carrots and cook for 1 minute, then add the mushrooms and cook for 1 minute more. Stir in the sugar with the oyster and soy sauces, followed by the noodles. Pour in 400ml/14fl oz/1⅔ cups water or chicken stock, cover the wok and cook for about 5 minutes, or until the noodles are soft and have absorbed most of the sauce.

3 Meanwhile, heat the remaining oil in a heavy pan. Add the crab meat and cook until it is nicely pink and tender. Season well with black pepper. Arrange the noodles and crab meat on a serving dish and garnish with coriander.

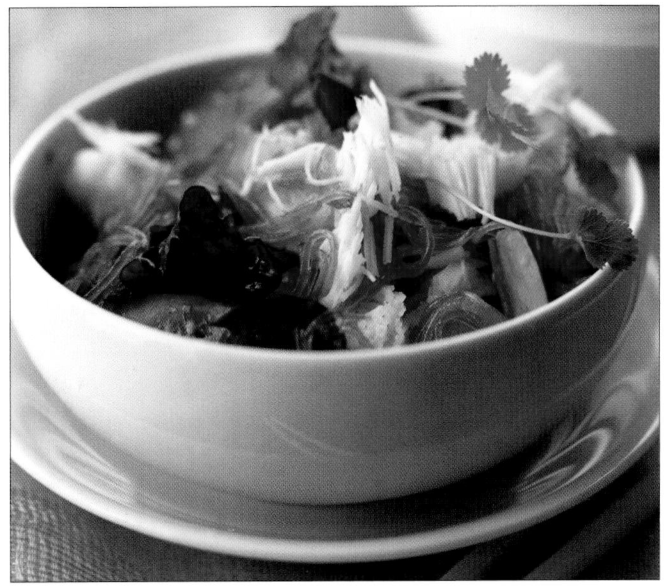

crispy noodles w. beef Energy 410kcal/1712kJ; Protein 30.7g; Carbohydrate 41.4g, of which sugars 6.6g; Fat 13.5g, of which saturates 3g; Cholesterol 66mg; Calcium 49mg; Fibre 1.9g; Sodium 1687mg.
noodles w. crab Energy 252kcal/1051kJ; Protein 12.9g; Carbohydrate 35.7g, of which sugars 10.3g; Fat 6.3g, of which saturates 0.7g; Cholesterol 41mg; Calcium 97mg; Fibre 1.6g; Sodium 770mg.

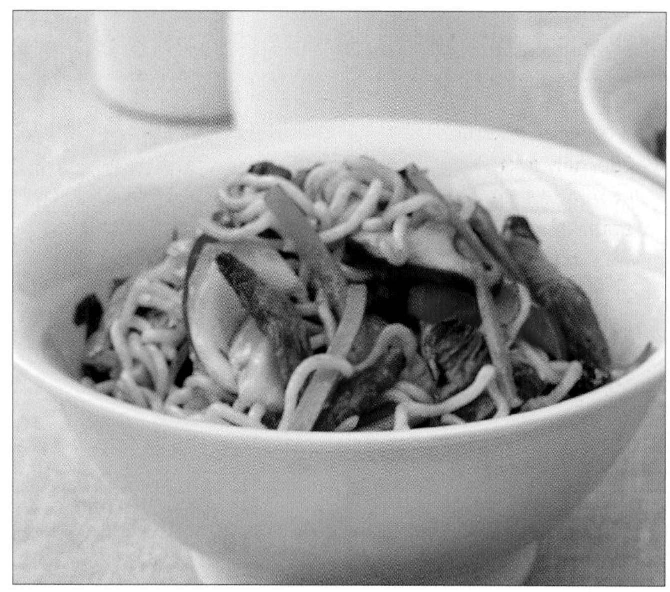

Lamb & Ginger Noodle Stir-fry

Fresh root ginger adds a bright tang to this lamb and noodle dish, giving it a simultaneously hot and yet refreshing taste.

Ingredients

45ml/3 tbsp sesame oil
3 spring onions (scallions), sliced
2 garlic cloves, crushed
2.5cm/1in piece fresh root ginger, peeled and finely sliced
1 fresh red chilli, seeded and finely sliced
1 red (bell) pepper, seeded and sliced
450g/1lb lean boneless lamb, cut into fine strips
115g/4oz/1½ cups fresh shiitake mushrooms, sliced
2 carrots, cut into matchstick strips
300g/11oz fresh Chinese egg noodles
300g/11oz pak choi (bok choy), shredded
soy sauce, to serve

Serves 4

1 Heat half the oil in a wok. Stir-fry the spring onions and garlic for about 5 minutes, or until golden. Add the ginger, chilli and red pepper and fry for 5 minutes more, until the chilli and pepper start to soften. Remove the vegetables and set aside.

2 Add the remaining oil and stir-fry the lamb in batches until golden. Add the mushrooms and carrots and stir-fry for 2–3 minutes.

3 Remove the lamb mixture from the wok and set aside with the red pepper mixture. Add the noodles and pak choi to the wok and stir-fry for 5 minutes.

4 Finally, replace all the cooked ingredients and stir-fry for a couple more minutes. Serve in heated bowls, with soy sauce.

Cook's Tip

If fresh egg noodles are not available, use the dried type. Cook them according to the packet instructions, drain and rinse under cold water, then drain well.

Wheat Noodles with Stir-fried Pork

Dried wheat noodles, sold in straight bundles like sticks, are versatile and robust. They keep well, so are handy items to have in the storecupboard, ready for quick and easy recipes like this one.

Ingredients

225g/8oz pork loin, cut into thin strips
225g/8oz dried wheat noodles, soaked in lukewarm water for 20 minutes
15ml/1 tbsp groundnut (peanut) oil
2 garlic cloves, finely chopped
2–3 spring onions (scallions), trimmed and chopped
45ml/3 tbsp kroeung or magic paste
15ml/1 tbsp fish sauce
30ml/2 tbsp unsalted roasted peanuts, finely chopped
chilli oil, for drizzling

For the marinade

30ml/2 tbsp fish sauce
30ml/2 tbsp soy sauce
15ml/1 tbsp peanut oil
10ml/2 tsp sugar

Serves 4

1 In a bowl, combine the ingredients for the marinade, stirring constantly until the all the sugar dissolves. Toss in the strips of pork, making sure that they are well coated in the marinade. Put aside for 30 minutes.

2 Drain the wheat noodles. Bring a large pan of water to the boil. Drop in the noodles, untangling them with chopsticks, if necessary. Cook for 4–5 minutes, until tender.

3 Drain the noodles thoroughly, then divide them among individual serving bowls. Keep the noodles warm until the dish is ready to serve.

4 Meanwhile, heat a wok. Add the oil and stir-fry the garlic and spring onions, until fragrant. Add the pork, tossing it around the wok for 2 minutes. Stir in the kroeung or magic paste and fish sauce for 2 minutes – add a splash of water if the wok gets too dry – and tip the pork on top of the noodles. Sprinkle the peanuts over the top and drizzle with chilli oil to serve.

lamb & ginger Energy 820kcal/3418kJ; Protein 46g; Carbohydrate 76.4g, of which sugars 9.4g; Fat 36g, of which saturates 11.7g; Cholesterol 143mg; Calcium 55mg; Fibre 4.1g; Sodium 709mg.
noodles w. pork Energy 340kcal/1435kJ; Protein 19.6g; Carbohydrate 46g, of which sugars 4.4g; Fat 9.9g, of which saturates 1.4g; Cholesterol 35mg; Calcium 23mg; Fibre 1.9g; Sodium 41mg.

Fried Noodles with Beef & Saté

If you relish chillies and peanuts, this delicious dish makes the perfect choice, but remember – it's fiery.

Ingredients

15–30ml/1–2 tbsp vegetable oil
300g/11oz beef sirloin, cut against the grain into thin slices
225g/8oz dried rice sticks (vermicelli), soaked in warm water for 20 minutes
225g/8oz/1 cup beansprouts
5–10ml/1–2 tsp fish sauce
1 small bunch each of fresh basil and mint, stalks removed, leaves shredded, to garnish
pickles, to serve

For the saté

4 dried Serrano chillies, seeded
60ml/4 tbsp groundnut (peanut) oil
4–5 garlic cloves, crushed
5–10ml/1–2 tsp curry powder
40g/1½oz/⅓ cup roasted peanuts, finely ground

Serves 4

1 To make the saté, grind the Serrano chillies in a mortar with a pestle. Heat the oil in a heavy pan and stir in the garlic until it begins to colour. Add the chillies, curry powder and the peanuts and stir over a low heat, until the mixture forms a paste. Remove the pan from the heat and leave the mixture to cool.

2 Heat a wok or heavy pan, and pour in 15ml/1 tbsp of the oil. Add the sliced beef and cook for 1–2 minutes, and stir in 7.5ml/1½ tsp of the spicy peanut saté. Tip the beef on to a clean plate and set aside. Drain the rice sticks.

3 Add 7.5ml/1½ tsp oil to the wok and add the rice sticks and 15ml/1 tbsp saté. Toss the noodles until coated and cook for 4–5 minutes. Toss in the beef for 1 minute, then add the beansprouts with the fish sauce. Tip the noodles on to a serving dish and sprinkle with the basil and mint. Serve with pickles.

Variation
Prawns (shrimp), pork or chicken can be used instead of beef, and the fresh herbs can be varied accordingly.

Bamie Goreng

This fried noodle dish is wonderfully accommodating. You can add other vegetables, such as mushrooms, tiny pieces of chayote, broccoli, leeks or beansprouts. Use whatever is to hand, balancing textures, colours and flavours.

Ingredients

450g/1lb dried egg noodles
2 eggs
25g/1oz/2 tbsp butter
90ml/6 tbsp vegetable oil
1 chicken breast fillet, sliced
115g/4oz pork fillet (tenderloin), sliced
115g/4oz calf's liver, sliced (optional)
2 garlic cloves, crushed
115g/4oz peeled cooked prawns (shrimp)
115g/4oz pak choi (bok choy)
2 celery sticks, finely sliced
4 spring onions (scallions), shredded
about 60ml/4 tbsp chicken stock
dark soy sauce and light soy sauce
salt and ground black pepper
deep-fried onions and shredded spring onions (scallions), to garnish

Serves 6–8

1 Cook the noodles in a pan of lightly salted water for about 3–4 minutes. Drain, rinse and drain again. Set aside.

2 Put the eggs in a bowl, beat and season to taste. Heat the butter with 5ml/1 tsp oil in a small pan, add the eggs and stir over a low heat until scrambled but still moist. Set aside.

3 Heat the remaining oil in a wok and fry the chicken, pork and liver, if using, with the garlic for 2–3 minutes, until the meat has changed colour. Add the prawns, pak choi, sliced celery and shredded spring onions and toss to mix.

4 Add the noodles and toss over the heat until the prawns and noodles are heated through and the greens are lightly cooked.

5 Add enough stock to moisten, and season with dark and light soy sauce to taste. Add the scrambled eggs and toss to mix. Spoon on to a serving platter and serve, garnished with onions.

noodles w. beef & saté Energy 566kcal/2353kJ; Protein 24.4g; Carbohydrate 50.5g, of which sugars 2.1g; Fat 28.8g, of which saturates 5.7g; Cholesterol 44mg; Calcium 52mg; Fibre 2.3g; Sodium 253mg.
bamie goreng Energy 478kcal/2010kJ; Protein 16.8g; Carbohydrate 64.2g, of which sugars 5.1g; Fat 18.9g, of which saturates 3.2g; Cholesterol 86mg; Calcium 323mg; Fibre 2.9g; Sodium 466mg.

Chow Mein

This is a hugely popular way of dealing with leftovers.

Ingredients
225g/8oz lean beef steak
225g/8oz can bamboo shoots, drained
1 leek, trimmed
25g/1oz dried shiitake mushrooms, soaked until soft
150g/5oz Chinese leaves (Chinese cabbage)
450g/1lb cooked egg noodles, drained
90ml/6 tbsp vegetable oil
30ml/2 tbsp dark soy sauce
15ml/1 tbsp cornflour (cornstarch)
15ml/1 tbsp dry sherry
5ml/1 tsp sesame oil
5ml/1 tsp caster (superfine) sugar
salt and ground black pepper

Serves 2–3

1 Slice the beef, bamboo shoots and leek into matchsticks. Drain the mushrooms, reserving 90ml/6 tbsp of the soaking water. Cut off and discard the stems, then slice the caps. Chop the Chinese leaves and sprinkle with salt. Pat the noodles dry.

2 Heat a third of the oil in a large frying pan and sauté the noodles. After turning them over once, use a wooden spatula to press against the bottom of the pan until they form a flat, even cake. Cook for about 4 minutes or until crisp at the bottom. Turn over, cook for 3 minutes more, then slide on to a heated plate and keep warm.

3 Heat 30ml/2 tbsp of the remaining oil in a wok. Add the leek and meat strips and stir-fry for 10–15 seconds. Sprinkle over half the soy sauce and then add the bamboo shoots and mushrooms. Toss for 1 minute, then push to one side.

4 Heat the remaining oil in the centre of the wok and sauté the Chinese leaves for 1 minute. Mix with the meat and vegetables and toss together for 30 seconds.

5 Mix the cornflour with the reserved mushroom water. Stir into the wok with the sherry, sesame oil, sugar and remaining soy sauce. Cook for 15 seconds to thicken, then serve with the noodle cake.

Warm Lamb & Noodle Salad

Here, thin slices of wok-fried lamb, fresh vegetables and rice noodles are tossed in an aromatic dressing.

Ingredients
30ml/2 tbsp red curry paste
60ml/4 tbsp sunflower oil
750g/1lb 11oz lamb neck (US shoulder or breast) fillets, thinly sliced
250g/9oz sugar snap peas
500g/1¼lb fresh rice noodles
1 red (bell) pepper, seeded and very thinly sliced
1 cucumber, sliced paper thin
6–7 spring onions (scallions), sliced diagonally
a large handful of fresh mint leaves

For the dressing
15ml/1 tbsp sunflower oil
juice of 2 limes
1 garlic clove, crushed
15ml/1 tbsp sugar
15ml/1 tbsp fish sauce
30ml/2 tbsp soy sauce

Serves 4

1 In a shallow dish, mix together the red curry paste and half the oil. Add the lamb slices and toss to coat. Cover and leave to marinate in the refrigerator for up to 24 hours.

2 Blanch the sugar snap peas in a pan of lightly salted boiling water for 1–2 minutes. Drain, refresh under cold water, drain again thoroughly and transfer to a large bowl.

3 Put the noodles in a separate bowl and pour over boiling water to cover. Leave to soak for 5–10 minutes, until tender, then drain well and separate into strands with your fingers.

4 Add the noodles to the sugar snap peas, then add the sliced red pepper, cucumber and spring onions. Toss lightly to mix.

5 Heat a wok over a high heat and add the remaining sunflower oil. Stir-fry the lamb, in two batches, for 3–4 minutes, or until cooked through, then add to the bowl of salad.

6 Place all the dressing ingredients in a jar, screw on the lid and shake well. Pour the dressing over the warm salad, sprinkle over the mint leaves and toss well to combine. Serve immediately.

chow mein Energy 604kcal/2541kJ; Protein 41.1g; Carbohydrate 71.5g, of which sugars 15.1g; Fat 18.9g, of which saturates 4.5g; Cholesterol 100mg; Calcium 115mg; Fibre 7.4g; Sodium 1194mg.
lamb & noodle salad Energy 820kcal/3418kJ; Protein 46g; Carbohydrate 76.4g, of which sugars 9.4g; Fat 36g, of which saturates 11.7g; Cholesterol 143mg; Calcium 55mg; Fibre 4.1g; Sodium 709mg.

Sesame Duck & Noodle Salad

This salad is complete in itself and makes a lovely summer lunch.

Ingredients

2 skinless duck breast fillets
1 tbsp oil
150g/5oz sugar snap peas
2 carrots, cut into 7.5cm/3in batons
225g/8oz medium egg noodles
6 spring onions (scallions), sliced
salt
30ml/2 tbsp coriander (cilantro) leaves, to garnish

For the marinade

15ml/1 tbsp sesame oil
5ml/1 tsp ground coriander
5ml/1 tsp five-spice powder

For the dressing

15ml/1 tbsp garlic vinegar or white wine vinegar
5ml/1 tsp soft light brown sugar
5ml/1 tsp soy sauce
15ml/1 tbsp toasted sesame seeds
45ml/3 tbsp sunflower oil
30ml/2 tbsp sesame oil
ground black pepper

Serves 4

1 Slice the duck breast fillets thinly across and put them in a shallow dish. Mix the ingredients for the marinade, pour over the duck and coat thoroughly. Cover and leave to marinate in a cool place for 30 minutes.

2 Heat the oil in a wok, add the slices of duck breast and stir-fry for 3-4 minutes until cooked. Set aside.

3 Bring a pan of lightly salted water to the boil. Place the sugar snap peas and carrots in a steamer that will fit on top of the pan. When the water boils, add the noodles. Place the steamer on top and steam the vegetables, while cooking the noodles for the time suggested on the packet. Set the steamed vegetables aside. Drain the noodles, refresh them under cold running water and drain again. Place them in a serving bowl.

4 Make the dressing by whisking all the ingredients in a bowl. Pour over the noodles and mix well. Add the sugar snap peas, carrots, spring onions and duck slices and toss to mix. Garnish with the coriander leaves and serve.

Shredded Duck & Noodle Salad

This piquant marinated duck salad makes a mouthwatering first course or a delicious light meal. If you like, toss the salad in a quick and easy dressing made by whisking together soy sauce, mirin, sugar, garlic and chilli oil.

Ingredients

4 skinless duck breast fillets, sliced
30ml/2 tbsp Chinese rice wine
10ml/2 tsp finely grated fresh root ginger
60ml/4 tbsp soy sauce
15ml/1 tbsp sesame oil
15ml/1 tbsp clear honey
10ml/2 tsp five-spice powder
toasted sesame seeds, to sprinkle

For the noodles

150g/5oz cellophane noodles, cooked
large handful of fresh mint and coriander (cilantro) leaves
1 red (bell) pepper, seeded and finely sliced
4 spring onions (scallions), finely shredded and sliced
50g/2oz mixed salad leaves

Serves 4

1 Place the duck breast slices in a non-metallic bowl. Mix together the rice wine, ginger, soy sauce, sesame oil, clear honey and five-spice powder. Toss to coat, cover and marinate in the refrigerator for 3–4 hours.

2 Heat the oil in a wok or a frying pan, add the slices of duck breast and stir-fry for 3-4 minutes until cooked. Set aside.

3 Double over a large sheet of heavy foil. Place the foil on a heatproof plate. Place the duck breast portions on it and spoon the marinade over. Fold the foil to enclose the duck and juices and scrunch the edges to seal. Steam on a rack over simmering water for 50–60 minutes, then leave to rest for 15 minutes.

4 Mix the noodles, herbs, red pepper, spring onions and salad leaves in a bowl. Remove the skin from the duck and shred the flesh. Divide the noodle salad among four plates and top with the duck. Sprinkle with the sesame seeds and serve immediately.

duck & noodle salad Energy 550kcal/2301kJ; Protein 25.3g; Carbohydrate 47g, of which sugars 4.2g; Fat 31.6g, of which saturates 5.2g; Cholesterol 99mg; Calcium 70mg; Fibre 4.5g; Sodium 192mg.
duck & noodle salad Energy 398kcal/1671kJ; Protein 32.8g; Carbohydrate 41.7g, of which sugars 10.8g; Fat 11.6g, of which saturates 2.2g; Cholesterol 165mg; Calcium 40mg; Fibre 1g; Sodium 1688mg.

Index

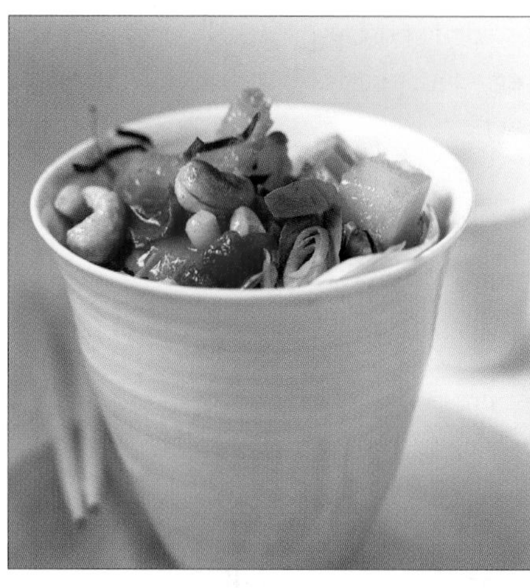